Declaring Rights

A Brief History with Documents

Related Titles in
THE BEDFORD SERIES IN HISTORY AND CULTURE
Advisory Editors: Lynn Hunt, *University of California, Los Angeles*
David W. Blight, *Yale University*
Bonnie G. Smith, *Rutgers University*
Natalie Zemon Davis, *Princeton University*
Ernest R. May, *Harvard University*

THE BEDFORD SERIES IN HISTORY AND CULTURE

Declaring Rights
A Brief History with Documents

Jack N. Rakove
Stanford University

BEDFORD BOOKS   Boston 〰 New York

To the memory of my first Stanford student, Sandra Lynn Rose, and of our young Hamilton neighbor, John Samuel Stephenson, III

For Bedford/St. Martin's
President and Publisher: Charles H. Christensen
General Manager and Associate Publisher: Joan E. Feinberg
History Editor: Katherine E. Kurzman
Developmental Editor: Charisse Kiino
Managing Editor: Elizabeth M. Schaaf
Production Editor: Bridget Leahy
Copyeditor: Carolyn Ingalls
Text Design: Claire Seng-Niemoeller
Indexer: Sherri Dietrich
Cover Design: Richard Emery Design
Cover Art (clockwise from upper left): Engraved portrait of Patrick Henry (detail), copyright Archive Photos. Portrait of Thomas Jefferson by Charles Willson Peale, ca. 1791 (detail), courtesy of Independence National Historical Park. Portrait of James Madison by Charles Wilson Peale, ca. 1792 (detail), courtesy of Thomas Gilcrease Institute of American History and Art, Tulsa, Oklahoma. Portrait of George Mason, after portrait by Toole (detail), courtesy of The Library of Virginia.
Composition: ComCom
Printing and Binding: Haddon Craftsmen, Inc.

Library of Congress Catalog Card Number: 97-72375

Manufactured in the United States of America.

4 3 2 1 0
n m l k j

For information, write: Bedford/St. Martin's, 75 Arlington Street, Boston, MA 02116 (617-399-4000)

ISBN-10: 0-312-13734-6 (paperback); 0-312-17768-2 (hardcover)
ISBN-13: 978-0-312-13734-2 (paperback); 978-0-312-17768-3 (hardcover)

Acknowledgments

The Virginia Statute for Religious Freedom. Courtesy, Cambridge University Press.
Jefferson's Third Draft of Virginia's Constitution, 1776. Courtesy, Princeton University Press.
Richard Henry Lee's Proposed Amendments to the New Constitution, Sept. 27, 1787. National Society Daughters of the American Revolution, Americana Collection.

Acknowledgments and copyrights are continued at the back of this book on page 209, which constitutes an extension of the copyright page. It is a violation of the law to reproduce these selections by any means whatsoever without the written permission of the copyright holder.

Foreword

The Bedford Series in History and Culture is designed so that readers can study the past as historians do.

The historian's first task is finding the evidence. Documents, letters, memoirs, interviews, pictures, movies, novels, or poems can provide facts and clues. Then the historian questions and compares the sources. There is more to do than in a courtroom, for hearsay evidence is welcome, and the historian is usually looking for answers beyond act and motive. Different views of an event may be as important as a single verdict. How a story is told may yield as much information as what it says.

Along the way the historian seeks help from other historians and perhaps from specialists in other disciplines. Finally, it is time to write, to decide on an interpretation and how to arrange the evidence for readers.

Each book in this series contains an important historical document or group of documents, each document a witness from the past and open to interpretation in different ways. The documents are combined with some element of historical narrative—an introduction or a biographical essay, for example—that provides students with an analysis of the primary source material and important background information about the world in which it was produced.

Each book in the series focuses on a specific topic within a specific historical period. Each provides a basis for lively thought and discussion about several aspects of the topic and the historian's role. Each is short enough (and inexpensive enough) to be a reasonable one-week assignment in a college course. Whether as classroom or personal reading, each book in the series provides firsthand experience of the challenge— and fun—of discovering, recreating, and interpreting the past.

Lynn Hunt
David W. Blight
Bonnie G. Smith
Natalie Zemon Davis
Ernest R. May

Preface

In 1789, the First Congress proposed twelve amendments to the Constitution that had been framed in Philadelphia in 1787 and ratified by eleven of the thirteen original states. Ten of these amendments were in turn approved by the legislatures of the states, and these amendments have come to be known as the Bill of Rights. The American revolutionaries had written other bills of rights a decade earlier, when the states had adopted new constitutions of government to replace the royal charters under which the colonists had previously been governed. Americans knew, too, that their English countrymen had been the beneficiaries of similar statements, including the parliamentary Bill of Rights of 1689 and the Magna Carta of 1215. The idea that rights should be declared thus appears to have been a familiar theme in the Anglo-American tradition from which the Federal Constitution and its first amendments emerged.

Today our discussions of rights range far beyond the spare and antique language of these early statements. What scholars call "rights-talk" provides the currency with which we conduct a host of legal, political, and academic controversies. Many of our ideas of rights are, of course, distinctly modern, and could not be easily translated into the political language of past centuries. Yet questions about the original meaning of the Bill of Rights of 1789–91 remain a source of active concern and controversy. So does the larger issue that this book addresses and hopes to inform. What did the English revolutionaries of 1689 or the American revolutionaries of 1776 and 1789 think they were doing when they adopted constitutional declarations of rights? What did it mean to declare rights, and what functions would such declarations serve?

Today we tend to think of all such statements as legally enforceable claims subject to ultimate vindication by an independent judiciary. We tend to assume, too, that the framers of the Bill of Rights anticipated that this is how later generations would read their work. Yet they may well have had other concerns and expectations; their assumptions about what it meant to declare rights may not have completely dovetailed with our notions of what it means to interpret a bill of rights.

This book should help readers understand the relation between the Bill of Rights of 1789 and our contemporary debates. But it will do so primarily by tracing the tradition and describing the considerations from which the Bill of Rights emerged. For the study of history is not always about connecting the present with the past; sometimes it is also about explaining why the past was different.

ACKNOWLEDGMENTS

Chuck Christensen, Joan Feinberg, and Ernest May knew this book might have a rocky history after we first discussed it over an anomalous brunch in Chicago some years ago. I remain grateful for their confidence in the project and their willingness to wait until I'd cleared my deck a few times to get to work on it. Several members of the staff at Bedford Books helped nurse the work along: Sabra Scribner at its inception, Neils Aaboe during early gestation, and especially Charisse Kiino and Bridget Leahy in delivery. Katherine Kurzman, my fellow Haverfordian, has played a part in this production as well.

I am extraordinarily appreciative of the careful, thoughtful reading given to the first complete draft by four reviewers. Rick Beeman and Edward Countryman will see that I have not quite answered all their criticisms about its omissions, but I hope this book comes close to the high standards they set for it. Marilyn Baseler helped me to appreciate the need to clarify the English background of American thinking.

So, too, did Pauline Maier, an old friend to whom I owe special thanks. When I first started out as an early Americanist, we haunted the same aerie in Widener Library, where intrepid scholars were granted the liberty of typing in their carrels. Now we regularly communicate by e-mail, still swapping tidbits about our favorite revolutionaries. It was a fortuitous coincidence that I finished this book just as Pauline was completing her own study of the Declaration of Independence (*American Scripture: Making the Declaration of Independence*), which she graciously allowed me to read in manuscript. I benefited from it enormously, as well as from her reading of my own manuscript.

Alastair Bellany, a talented young Stuart historian, took precious time from his preparations to remove to the mysterious East (New Jersey) to read my material on the seventeenth century. I thank him for valiantly attempting to purge its excessive whiggery.

My thinking about the problems addressed in this book owes much to a workshop on rights held at the Woodrow Wilson International Center for Scholars in 1989–90. I would again like to thank Michael Lacey and Knud Haakonssen for the invitation to participate in that project and my friend Gordon Wood for the detailed comments he presented on my paper there. As always, the opportunity to teach this subject to talented undergraduates at Stanford (especially, in this case, Jessica Koran and Colleen Kreuger) has been an inspiration. Elizabeth Borgwardt (née Kopelman) helped me present it as well to the 1995 Coe Workshop in American History, whose enthusiastic participants taught us much in turn.

Finally, I thank Helen, Rob, and Dan for not minding my plunging so quickly into this book after I had just completed another. But then again, I never let it interfere with my duty to cook and drive, or my liberty to swim and bike, for that matter. As one of Rob's classic eighties songs would have it, we have to fight for our right to party.

Jack N. Rakove

Contents

Declaring Rights

A Brief History with Documents

Introduction: Rights across the Centuries

On June 14, 1776, the *Virginia Gazette* of Williamsburg published the sixteen articles of "A Declaration of Rights made by the representatives of the good people of Virginia, assembled in full and free Convention." Today, visitors strolling through Colonial Williamsburg can obtain authentic reproductions of this celebrated document at the print shop on Duke of Gloucester Street. In that setting, with handsomely restored buildings and costumed guides all around, it takes only a little effort to imagine how the free inhabitants of Virginia first glimpsed or heard the Declaration, three weeks before their colony became one of the newly independent states of the American union. This was how Americans of the Revolutionary era learned what rights their state or federal constitutions promised to secure for them: by reading these documents as they were published in local newspapers or by hearing them read aloud on street corners or in taverns or coffeehouses. Tourists who know their history will also recall that the Virginia Declaration of Rights was the first of a chain of similar documents that Americans adopted over the next thirteen years, culminating in the Bill of Rights that the First Federal Congress under the Constitution proposed to the states in 1789 and that was ratified two years later.

When we compare the Virginia Declaration of 1776 with the Bill of Rights of 1789, we find some striking similarities and some equally striking differences. Articles 8–13 and 16 of the Virginia Declaration evoke strong echoes in the First, Second, Fourth, Fifth, Sixth, and Eighth Amendments of 1789. In both documents, we find those essential civil liberties that we regard as our fundamental rights: freedom of conscience, speech, and the press; security against improper searches and seizures; guarantees of trial by jury, bail, and legal counsel; the benefits of "a well-regulated Militia," and so on. But the Virginia Declaration also contains grand statements of the principles of government that have no counter-

1

parts in the federal Bill of Rights—or are at best only faintly echoed in the unenumerated rights and reserved powers of the Ninth and Tenth Amendments. Careful readers will also note a curious difference in the verb forms used in the two texts. Whereas the Virginia Declaration tends to say "ought" or "should," suggesting that a lesson is being taught, the federal amendments prefer the mandatory "shall," implying that a command is being given. Thus if the Virginia Declaration can still be regarded as a forerunner of the Bill of Rights, it is equally true that the Bill of Rights departed from the precedents of 1776. How and why it did so reveals much about the progress of constitutional thinking in the decade after Independence.

This book traces the ways in which American ideas about the nature and function of declarations (or bills) of rights evolved from 1776 to 1789. To tell this story properly, we also have to know something of the constitutional history of England and its American colonies in the seventeenth and eighteenth centuries. The idea that bills of rights were a vital safeguard of liberty had gained a key place in Anglo-American thinking well before the American Revolution. All right-thinking Britons and Americans worshipped the great charter (Magna Carta) of rights that the English barons had wrested from King John at Runnymede in 1215. All admired, too, the Declaration of Rights that the Convention Parliament of 1689 presented to their new monarchs, William of Orange and his wife, Mary Stuart, after her father, James II, abandoned his throne during the Glorious Revolution. Nor did Americans always have to look across the Atlantic for examples of such declarations. At one time or another, many of the colonies had adopted documents affirming the rights and liberties that their free settlers had carried with them from Britain.

These vital precedents formed a crucial part of the political inheritance the colonists carried with them as they struggled to define their position within the British empire. Yet in at least two ways, these documents represented a tradition from which Americans began to move away after 1776, at first tentatively, then decisively. First, these earlier declarations were often regarded as *compacts* negotiated between the king and some other authority (the barons or Parliament or the colonial legislatures) that claimed to speak on behalf of some or all of the king's subjects. But would such documents still be necessary, some Americans asked, now that they had banished monarchy from the republican governments they established with Independence? Why would a free people need to negotiate a compact with itself? Second, and more important, bills of rights were never regarded as the ultimate *sources* of the rights they protected. Rather, they were confirmations of rights whose origins lay elusively elsewhere: in the authority of God or the law of nature, in the social contract men had formed long ago, or in immemorial custom. However, after 1776, Americans increasingly thought that their rights would be secure only when they were explicitly incorporated in the texts of their newly written constitutions. Rights left unmentioned might lose their authority—literally be lost and forgotten, and thus cease to be rights.

Americans could express these concerns because Independence also amounted to a break with the British constitutional tradition. The enlightened thinkers of the eighteenth century regarded the "boasted" British constitution as the great achievement of the modern "science of politics." But when these thinkers spoke of a constitution, they did not use that term as Americans have used it since 1776. The British constitution was not a fixed document, adopted at a particular moment in time, by special procedures that gave it an authority superior to all ordinary acts of government. It was really the entire set of institutional arrangements, parliamentary statutes, judicial precedents, and political understandings that together shaped the exercise of power. The British constitution could not be found in any one document—not even in Magna Carta or in the parliamentary Declaration of Rights of 1689—but rather in many texts or even none. Moreover, none of these documents could prevent a sovereign parliament from adopting any law it chose, even if that law violated some fundamental right or dearly held tradition. In a sense, the idea of parliamentary sovereignty *was* the ruling principle of the eighteenth-century British constitution.

After 1776, however, Americans began to think about constitutions in an entirely different sense. In their new view, a constitution was a document adopted at a known moment of historical time and an expression of supreme law that would henceforth regulate what government could and could not do. How Americans thought about bills of rights was a function of how they thought about constitutionalism more generally. And here lay the source of the dilemma that the delegates to the Philadelphia Convention of 1787 failed to resolve when they proposed a Constitution conspicuously lacking a bill of rights. Are rights secure only if they are explicitly incorporated in a constitutional text, as the Anti-Federalist critics of the Constitution argued? Or are there valid reasons to think that the enumeration of rights may actually undermine their authority, as the Federalist supporters of the Constitution argued in reply?

Important arguments can be made to support both positions—and these arguments are not merely dusty artifacts of the past, for debates about the sources and extent of our rights remain as urgent today as they did then. The documents reprinted in this book thus tell an important story about the emergence of American constitutionalism in the final quarter of the eighteenth century. They also raise questions that trouble us today and repeatedly lead us back to the political ferment of the Revolutionary era.

The subject of this book, then, is the debate that unfolded from 1776 to 1789 over the potential benefits and drawbacks of the inclusion of bills of rights in the new constitutions that the American revolutionaries were writing. Both the Federalists and Anti-Federalists of 1787–88 had powerful arguments to make and their positions identified a fundamental and persisting dilemma of American constitutionalism. Just as there are advantages to be gained by grounding the rights we can identify on the authority of a written constitution, so there may be costs as well if the enumeration or textualization of particular rights has the effect of limiting the scope of what the Constitution protects. Just as Anti-Federalists had reason to fear that a people lacking a bill of rights might forget what their liberties truly were, so James Madison had cause to worry that reliance on these "parchment barriers" might leave fundamental rights vulnerable to infringement.

PART ONE

Rights in Revolution

1

The Seventeenth-Century Background

ENGLISH PRECEDENTS

When we speak about rights, we often imagine that we are striving to define certain fundamental aspects of our existence. Freedom of religious conscience, the capacity to criticize public officials, security against arbitrary arrest or physical torture: these are all rights that most Americans think we should always enjoy and that we would like to see extended around the world—because fundamental rights should also be universal rights. But how we think about these rights is a function of our education and upbringing, our history and our experience. Just as our ideas of rights are not universally held, so we know, too, that these ideas have not existed since time out of mind. They have a history of their own, which we have to reconstruct to be able to think critically about what those rights should mean today.

Where does that history begin? Historical research is always a quest for antecedents, origins, and causes, and with a concept as broad and abstract as rights, the possible starting points are numerous. Within the Anglo-American constitutional tradition, however, it is almost universally agreed that the Magna Carta of 1215 marks the most obvious point of departure. "In it one sees for the first time in English history," Bernard Schwartz has observed in a representative statement, "a written instrument extracted from a sovereign ruler by the bulk of the politically articulate community that purports to lay down binding rules of law that the ruler himself may not violate."[1] Nearly all of the sixty-three items (or "chapters") of this Great Charter relate to aspects of feudal law that seem utterly foreign to modern readers; nor did the rebellious barons imagine that they were striking a decisive blow for the cause of freedom or universal human rights when they insisted that King John accept these pro-

---

[1]Bernard Schwartz, *The Great Rights of Mankind: A History of the American Bill of Rights,* expanded ed. (Madison, Wis.: Madison House, 1992), 3. This is an excellent introduction to the subject as a whole.

visions to regain their allegiance. But at least one article of Magna Carta has acquired these attributes: Chapter 39, which states (in translation from the original Latin) that "no free man shall be taken, imprisoned, disseised, outlawed, banished, or in any way destroyed, nor will We proceed against or prosecute him, except by the lawful judgment of his peers and by the law of the land." Though "judgment of his peers" did not yet mean trial by jury, that phrase is often interpreted as a cornerstone for the development of this essential institution; and Chapter 39 as a whole seems to express the same idea that we now ascribe to the concept of "due process of law." Other articles, too, can be read as antecedents of familiar civil liberties, such as Chapters 30 and 31, which prohibit royal sheriffs and bailiffs from expropriating horses, carts, or wood "without the owner's consent."[2]

For Magna Carta to attain its exalted status, however, it had to acquire meanings it did not originally possess. It was not written as a beacon of liberty to shine across the ages, but as a negotiated settlement to the bitter controversy between the king and the nobility. As J. C. Holt, the Magna Carta's most recent historian, notes,

> In 1215 Magna Carta was a failure. It was intended as a peace and it provoked war. It pretended to state customary law and it promoted disagreement and contention. It was legally valid for no more than three months, and even within that period its terms were never properly executed.

But, Holt continues, Magna Carta was also reissued three times in the next decade, and the revised version of 1225 did become part of English statutory law, enacted by Parliament as it was also repeatedly confirmed by successive kings. Soon, too, Magna Carta did begin to acquire a mythic status, making it capable of reinterpretation as a statement of fundamental English rights and liberties.[3]

Reinterpretation occurs in response to the events of an ongoing present, however, not the dictates of a receding past. As large as Magna Carta looms in the genealogy of Anglo-American rights, its influence depended on the later course of English history—and that history, in turn, has to be placed within a broader European setting. In the most general sense, the context within which recognizably modern ideas of rights emerged was the post-Reformation world of late sixteenth- and seventeenth-century

---

[2]A. E. Dick Howard, *Magna Carta: Text and Commentary* (Charlottesville: University Press of Virginia, 1964), 42–43.

[3]J. C. Holt, *Magna Carta,* 2nd ed. (Cambridge, Eng.: Cambridge University Press, 1992), 1–22 (quotation at 1), 396–405.

Europe. In the wake of the Protestant Reformation that Martin Luther launched in 1517, a new and disturbing political universe appeared in Europe, marked by three fundamental developments:

1. The course of the Reformation, and the vigorous response it drew from the Church of Rome, generated intense religious conflicts among the peoples of Europe. The ensuing persecutions raised questions about the capacity and right of individual men and women to follow the dictates of conscience in matters of religious belief and behavior—or, conversely, about the power of the state or established churches to compel conformity and suppress dissent.

2. The Reformation irreparably shattered the unity of Latin Christendom, producing a near-century of religious war in Western and Central Europe, including civil wars (as in France), a war of independence (when the Protestants of the Netherlands revolted against the imperial rule of Catholic Spain), and a general war of Protestant and Catholic states (the Thirty Years' War of 1618–48). When the Treaty of Westphalia ended this last conflict, Europe was now a region of sovereign nation-states, with no common authority, like the papacy, capable of acting as a mediator among them.

3. In this brave new world of competitive nation-states, success promised to go to those countries that could organize their resources most efficiently and project their power most effectively. The efforts of Europe's monarchs to meet these demands generated internal political conflicts, as different classes or communities or religious confessions resisted the policies that kings favored or (especially) the taxes that they needed.

In this newly divided Europe, questions about rights could arise in multiple ways. Some questions had to do with the respective powers of different institutions of government (monarchs and parliaments and the local jurisdictions that had often enjoyed substantial autonomy from central control). Others concerned the rights of citizens and subjects to enjoy protection against the naked coercive power of the state (especially, again, when it was trying to collect unpopular taxes or when it was repressing its political critics). And still others concerned the relentless desire of devout Protestants and Catholics to worship as they wished and to live their lives in a way consistent with the dictates of conscience, free of persecution from the state or its legally established church.

England in the sixteenth century was largely spared the conflicts wracking Europe. True, after Henry VIII carried England out of the orbit of the Church of Rome in the 1530s, his eldest daughter, Mary, tried to reverse his course, allowing numerous Protestants to be persecuted and some even martyred during her brief rule as queen (1553–1558). But the much longer reign of her younger half-sister, Elizabeth (1558–1603), left the majority of the populace firmly Protestant, though large numbers of Catholics were still to be found in England, across the border in the independent kingdom of Scotland, and in Ireland (partly ruled by England, but the site of recurring, horrific warfare). As English Protestants observed the Catholic repression of dissent in France and Holland, they remained fearful of the danger of allowing their own country to fall again under the influence of Rome or its allies.

When Elizabeth died unmarried and childless in 1603, the throne passed to James Stuart, who was known north of the Tweed River as James VI of Scotland but remembered elsewhere as James I of England. The accession of the Stuart dynasty marked the crucial moment in the expansion of the meaning of the concept of rights in English constitutionalism. In the eyes of their critics, the four Stuart kings (James I, 1603–1625; Charles I, 1625–1649; Charles II, 1660–1685; and James II, 1685–1688) seemed bent on converting England into an island replica of the absolutist monarchies of France and Spain, where older representative institutions had lost their power and where centralizing royal authority seemed to hold the upper hand. Strapped for resources and revenues, James I and Charles I periodically tried to raise money without securing the consent of Parliament by imposing fees and "forced loans" on their reluctant subjects and by using the royal courts, whose judges held office at the pleasure of the crown, to enforce these policies. When they met opposition from Parliament, the Stuart kings tried to govern as often and as long as possible without calling Parliament into session, until their financial needs or mounting civil unrest forced them to summon the Commons and Lords. Moreover, while only James II was an avowed Catholic, militant Protestants in the Puritan movement, who favored carrying the work of the Reformation further, feared that the Stuarts were plotting a restoration of the old faith.

These struggles over constitutional issues waxed and waned over the seventeenth century, but in its middle two decades they erupted into open conflicts that brought the experience of England closer to that of continental Europe. Deteriorating relations between Charles I and his opponents in Parliament and the Puritans led to the outbreak of civil war in 1642. That struggle ended with the capture of the king and his eventual execution in 1649. The victorious revolutionaries soon abolished both the monarchy and the House of Lords. Allowed to govern on their own, the members of the Long Parliament (so called because it was elected in 1640) soon lost popularity; eventually they were disbanded by Oliver Cromwell, the great general of the revolutionary New Model Army, who governed after 1653 as a surrogate king (of sorts) under the title of Lord Protector. His death in 1658 left his less qualified son, Richard, in a precarious position, clearing the way for the restoration of the Stuart monarchy and the House of Lords in 1660.

The next two decades were a period of prolonged reaction. The newly elected Parliament enacted laws (such as the Test Acts) restricting the civil rights of religious dissenters, and these laws were vigorously enforced against the radical Protestant sects, such as the Quakers, which had flourished after 1640. Relations between Charles II and Parliament deteriorated sharply after 1678, when Parliament sought to exclude the king's younger brother, James, Duke of York, who was a Catholic, from the succession. This Exclusion Crisis produced a rich polemical literature, including the famous *Two Treatises of Government* of John Locke, which provided a powerful theoretical justification for the right to resist misrule and to revolt against tyrannical government. It did little, however, to reconcile James to the opponents he would face after he succeeded to the throne in 1685.

After a briefly successful start to his reign, James soon undermined his position. Both his reliance on Catholic advisers and his appointment of Catholic officers to the army that he used as a domestic police force were especially alarming. James faced increasing opposition not only from the aristocracy and gentry but also from the Church of England. In effect, he was unifying the country against his rule. The birth of a male heir, Prince James Edward, in 1688, raised the prospect of a Catholic succession to the throne, and this further encouraged his opponents to plot the end of his rule. Opening negotiations with Prince William of Orange—the king's nephew and son-in-law, and Stadtholder (elective monarch) of the Netherlands—they cleared the path for William to descend on England with an invading army, which landed at Torbay on November 5, 1688. Aware of his loss of support, James abandoned the ship of state, cast the Great Seal into the Thames River, and fled into exile.

To establish the legitimacy of this coup d'état, a Convention Parliament met to set the conditions under which the monarchy would be jointly vested in William and Mary (James's daughter). It was a "Convention" in the sense that it was legally defective: Parliament lawfully met only when summoned by the king, and it could lawfully act only by securing the royal assent to its measures. A legal Parliament thus had three constituent parts: the House of Commons, the House of Lords, and the king. In early February 1689,[4] the Convention Parliament drafted a Declaration of Rights that in effect set the terms under which William and Mary—and later monarchs—would rule. On February 13, a delegation from the two houses presented this Declaration to the royal couple. William did not sign the document but instead gave a speech indicating his acceptance of its terms. To confirm its somewhat problematic legal status, the Declaration was subsequently enacted (with some amendments) by Parliament as the Bill and ultimately the Act of Rights once it received the royal seal.[5]

The Declaration/Bill/Act of Rights was the most influential forerunner of the documents that the American revolutionaries adopted a century later, including the Declaration of Independence, which also deposed a king on the basis of his infringements of the rights and liberties of his subjects. It was the capstone to the event that the English recalled as their Glorious Revolution—glorious, in no small part, because it had been far less revolutionary than the mid-century upheavals. Though it took another quarter century to work out the implications of the Glorious Revolution, the events of 1688–89 and the Declaration of Rights did confirm that Britain would henceforth be a limited constitutional monarchy. That meant that the crown could not pretend to make law and govern on its own authority. It could act lawfully only with the consent of Parliament, which could now claim "supremacy" because it was no longer regarded as a body that was merely advising or assenting to whatever measures the king put before it. At least in theory, Parliament was now the source of law to which the king (as one of its members) would have to assent. And the glory of this understanding was that the major elements of the polity—Commons, Lords, and Crown—existed in a balanced constitutional arrangement.

This near century of political turmoil and constitutional controversy made possible a dramatic expansion and inflation in the language of rights. When in 1628 Parliament protested against the means the crown

---

[4]In the seventeenth century, England and its colonies still followed the Julian (old style, or o.s.) calendar, under which the new year began on March 25. Thus while the Declaration of Rights would have been adopted in February 1689 under our calendar, it was February 1688 to the members of the Convention Parliament. Not until 1752 did Britain and America move to the Gregorian (new style) calendar, which restored the ancient Roman practice of marking January 1 as the beginning of the new year.

[5]The definitive work is Lois G. Schwoerer, *The Declaration of Rights, 1689* (Baltimore: The Johns Hopkins University Press, 1981).

was employing to collect revenues, prosecute individuals not complying with its dictates, and quarter soldiers among the civilian population, it did so by presenting Charles I with a Petition of Right, reminding him how Magna Carta and other medieval statutes had secured the rights in question.[6] Two decades later, when the so-called Levellers in the revolutionary New Model Army proposed to give England a written, nonmonarchical constitution, they included in their "Agreement of the People" a number of articles limiting the power of Parliament in the name of securing the rights and liberties of the people at large.[7] A concern that Parliament as well as the king might violate essential rights also drove the poet-revolutionary John Milton to write his famous tract *Areopagitica*, a stirring attack on the capacity of the state to censor opinion and an impassioned defense of the right of individuals to judge religious truth. And these celebrated examples of the prevalence of rights-talk in Stuart England represent only the tip of an iceberg of concern and agitation that penetrated deeply into the population.

This dramatic expansion in the language of rights left a powerful if ambiguous legacy for the more stable politics of the next century. The conviction that the British constitution was the one regime in Europe that prized liberty as the end of good government became a staple theme in the political science of the Enlightenment.[8] The English were a people born in freedom, the envy of Europe. They knew what their rights were — and knew, too, that the Declaration of 1689, like Magna Carta, had helped place those rights beyond the reach of arbitrary government. Yet Britain remained a deeply conservative society, ruled by an elite whose wealth and power exorbitantly exceeded the slender resources on which much of the population scraped out their existence. In the new century so many crimes against property were made subject to capital punishment that one legal authority mused whether "the chief object of legislation in England"

[6]The text is in J. P. Kenyon, ed., *The Stuart Constitution, 1603–1688: Documents and Commentary*, 2nd ed. (Cambridge, Eng.: Cambridge University Press, 1986), 68–71; for a political account of its drafting, see Conrad Russell, *Parliaments and English Politics, 1621–1629* (Oxford: Oxford University Press, 1979), 340–89.

[7]For the text of *An Agreement of the Free People of England, Tendered as a Peace-Offering to this Distressed Nation* (1649), see William Haller and Godfrey Davies, eds., *The Leveller Tracts, 1647–1653*, reprint ed. (Gloucester, Mass.: Peter Smith, 1964), 318–28 (provisions protecting rights begin with Article IX).

[8]The classic statement can be found in the famous chapter on the English constitution in Book XI, Chapter 6, of Charles Louis de Secondat [Baron de Montesquieu], *L'esprit des Lois*, first published in 1748 and almost immediately translated into English as *The Spirit of the Laws*.

might be "the extirpation of mankind."[9] In many ways, the legacy of this inflation of rights-thinking was destined to be felt more strongly in Britain's colonies in America.

AMERICAN PRECEDENTS

Across the Atlantic, in the mainland settlements still huddled close to the seashore, the colonists too regarded themselves as beneficiaries and heirs of the Glorious Revolution. Their legislative assemblies were entitled to the same rights and privileges as the great Parliament in London; their inhabitants were expected to enjoy the same civil liberties as their countrymen "at home," as many Americans still called the mother country.

But American claims to rights were not simply derivative or imitative of British precedent and practice. Nearly all the colonies had conducted their own versions of the constitutional conflicts occurring at home, as representative assemblies struggled to gain a significant voice in public affairs. True, many early colonists were little concerned with matters of politics. The indentured servants who dominated the early English migration to the Chesapeake colonies of Virginia and Maryland were drawn mostly from the ranks of young, unskilled, propertyless males; few of them had any innate interest in politics—though as an exploited proletariat they soon acquired a stake in the operations of local court systems. But the planters who emerged as the ruling gentry in the Chesapeake were familiar with the great issues of politics, and so were the Puritan families of middling property who came to New England during the Great Migration of 1630–42. And in the middle colony of Pennsylvania, settled in the 1680s, the dominant group of immigrants came from the Quaker dissenters who had borne much of the brunt of the religious persecution of the 1660s and 1670s.

Moreover, the very process of settlement probably encouraged the colonists to seek formal declarations of their rights, in part to clarify their legal status as settlers, and in part to encourage further immigration. In 1641, for example, the General Court of Massachusetts Bay adopted a seventeen-article statement of rights under the title of "The Body of Liberties of the Massachusetts Colonie in New England." A generation later, the Quaker proprietors of New Jersey included eleven "chapters" of rights in their new settlement's first charter of fundamental laws (1677).

---

[9]William Eden, quoted in David Lieberman, *The Province of Legislation Determined: Legal Theory in Eighteenth-Century Britain* (Cambridge, Eng.: Cambridge University Press, 1989), 14.

William Penn did the same when he founded his colony of Pennsylvania in 1682 and then refined this statement of rights in the Frame of Government of 1701. Penn was already something of an expert on the subject. Not only had he written tracts in defense of his fellow Quakers, but he was also a defendant in the proceedings that led to a landmark ruling in Bushell's Case of 1670, which established that the government could not jail and starve jurors whose decisions ran counter to its wishes.[10]

At one point, Penn worried that his colonists, beset by the heavy work of settlement, might forget and therefore forfeit their precious "birthright" of English liberty. Experience soon taught him, however, that the immigrants still had time enough to recall their rights —and to act on them.[11] Time and again, eighteenth-century American politics sounded an encore to the disputes of seventeenth-century England. In colony after colony, conflicts between representative assemblies and royal or proprietary governors reprised the struggles that had culminated in 1689. In this context, the language of rights continued to flourish.[12] And in many ways, the once-primitive settlements huddled along the eastern seaboard of North America were becoming more refined societies; their cultural elites were increasingly eager to think of themselves not as rude, rustic, colonial pioneers, but instead as the refined (if provincial) citizens of a great empire, entitled to the same rights and privileges as their compatriots "at home."[13] Had the American colonists not already learned to think of themselves as the bearers of the essential rights of Englishmen, they could not have reacted as sharply as they did to the new measures that the imperial government began to impose after 1763.[14]

[10]For this case, see Thomas Green, *Verdict According to Conscience: Perspectives on the English Criminal Jury Trial, 1200–1800* (Chicago: University of Chicago Press, 1985), 200–64.

[11]William Penn, *The Excellent Priviledge of Liberty and Property Being the Birth-Right of the Free-Born Subjects of England* (1687); excerpt reprinted in Philip Kurland and Ralph Lerner, eds., *The Founders' Constitution* (Chicago: University of Chicago Press, 1987), I, 432. Gary Nash, *Quakers and Politics: Pennsylvania, 1681–1726* (Princeton: Princeton University Press, 1968), is an excellent account of Penn's difficulties in governing his colony.

[12]The best short statement of the sources of contention in colonial politics is Bernard Bailyn, *The Origins of American Politics* (New York: Alfred Knopf, 1968). For a valuable study of the role of rights-talk in one colony's politics, see Richard L. Bushman, *King and People in Provincial Massachusetts* (Chapel Hill: University of North Carolina Press, 1985), 88–134.

[13]The new gentility of colonial culture is examined in fine detail in Richard L. Bushman, *The Refinement of America: Persons, Houses, Cities* (New York: Alfred Knopf, 1992).

[14]For the pre-Revolutionary absorption of this conviction of an equality of rights within the empire, see John Phillip Reid, *Constitutional History of the American Revolution*, vol. 1, *The Authority of Rights* (Madison: University of Wisconsin Press, 1986), 60–64; and Jack P. Greene, *Peripheries and Center: Constitutional Development in the Extended Polities of the*

These events and developments set the context within which a new language of rights appeared in England and America. That language remained primarily antimonarchical, for in both countries constitutional controversy and historical memory operated largely to identify the executive power of the crown as the chief danger to the rights of the people. Yet to say that appeals to rights now became an essential feature of Anglo-American political discourse does not by itself explain what this language meant or why it became so attractive. Nor does it identify the conceptual difficulties into which this new language soon led even those who had learned its vocabulary and syntax reasonably well. The precise way in which we talk about rights always reflects historical circumstances; but it is also a function of certain recurring puzzles in the very concept of rights.

British Empire and the United States, 1607–1788 (Athens: University of Georgia Press, 1986), 19–42.

2
Puzzles about Rights

Historians face an easier task in talking about rights than their colleagues in philosophy, political theory, or law. Often all that historians need to do is to describe some incident or episode or legal case in which claims about a particular right were asserted, resisted, and finally resolved. But scholars in other disciplines such as philosophy or political theory or law face more vexing questions of principle and theory. Here there is general agreement that the subject of rights is both enormously important and highly perplexing. Even as "the language of human rights plays an increasingly important part in normal political debate," Richard Tuck, a historian of political thought, has observed, "academic philosophers find it on the whole an elusive and unnecessary mode of discourse." A long line of thought, dating to the seventeenth century, has held that the claims of rights we make on our own behalf are better understood as the duties owed to us by someone else. "If this is true," Tuck continues, "then the language of rights is irrelevant, and to talk of 'human rights' is simply to raise the question of what kinds of duty we are under to other human beings, rather than to provide us with any independent moral insights."[1]

If philosophers find it difficult to define just what they mean by rights, legal scholars face a similar dilemma in sorting out the multiple claims of rights that swirl through our politics and legal culture. The modern American legal system operates amid a breathless Babel of voices all claiming or asserting rights, often in direct conflict with each other. The right of a mother not to carry an unwanted pregnancy to term is met by the counterargument that the fetus has a right to life from the moment of conception. The rights of accused and convicted criminals are met by

[1] Richard Tuck, *Natural Rights Theories: Their Origin and Development* (Cambridge, Eng.: Cambridge University Press, 1979), 1; and see Knud Haakonssen, "From Natural Law to the Rights of Man: A European Perspective on American Debates," in Michael Lacey and Knud Haakonssen, eds., *A Culture of Rights: The Bill of Rights in Philosophy, Politics, and Law: 1791 and 1991* (New York: Cambridge University Press, 1991), 19–61.

17

countervailing claims of the rights of victims and their families. The right of religious minorities or atheists not to be subjected to public expressions of faith (school prayer or invocations at graduation ceremonies) is met by the claim that majority groups have a right to see their religious values acknowledged in a public setting. The right of racial minorities to enjoy preferential programs of affirmative action to remedy past discrimination encounters the contrary claim that all individuals have an equal right to be judged solely on the merit of their talents and abilities, regardless of race, gender, or history of discrimination. And so it goes.

This tendency to translate claims of interest into the language of rights has produced a backlash against the popularity of "rights-talk" itself. Because claims of rights are often presented as' absolutes, critics like Mary Ann Glendon argue that rights-talk impoverishes "our political discourse" through "its starkness and simplicity, its prodigality in bestowing the rights label, its legalistic character, its exaggerated absoluteness, its hyperindividualism, its insularity, and its silence with respect to personal, civic, and collective responsibilities."[2] Too great an emphasis on rights, Glendon concludes, discourages the political deliberation and compromise that democracy requires. And because the judiciary has played a leading role in extending and enforcing constitutional rights, the ensuing controversies have raised questions both about the proper role of courts in a democracy and about their capacity to enforce the new rights they have recognized.[3] On the other side of the question, a legal philosopher like Ronald Dworkin can plausibly argue that the law and politics of an egalitarian constitutional democracy ought to be concerned with *Taking Rights Seriously* (the title of Dworkin's best-known work) or that judicial decision-making in "hard cases" inevitably involves morally grounded claims of rights.[4]

At first glance, these contemporary questions may seem irrelevant to the task of considering how rights were regarded in the eighteenth cen-

[2]Mary Ann Glendon, *Rights Talk: The Impoverishment of Political Discourse* (New York: The Free Press, 1991), x.

[3]For two examples, see Donald L. Horowitz, *The Courts and Social Policy* (Washington, D.C.: The Brookings Institution, 1977), and Gerald Rosenberg, *The Hollow Hope: Can Courts Bring About Social Change?* (Chicago: University of Chicago Press, 1991). For a principled defense of judicial discretion in enlarging rights, see Michael J. Perry, *The Constitution, the Courts, and Human Rights* (New Haven and London: Yale University Press, 1982). This is only the tip of an iceberg of literature by legal scholars, political scientists, and historians.

[4]Ronald Dworkin, *Taking Rights Seriously* (Cambridge: Harvard University Press, 1977); for the most recent statement of his ideas, see Dworkin, *The Moral Reading of the Constitution* (Cambridge: Harvard University Press, 1996).

tury. But if the concerns of people living two hundred years ago obviously differed from ours, confusion about the definition, sources, nature, and protection of rights was as much a part of their discussions as it is of ours. And to make sense of the American debates of the 1770s and 1780s, we have to explore what their sources of uncertainty were. For then as now, the ease and frequency with which Americans and Britons invoked rights did not answer a host of questions about the nature, extent, and sources of those rights.

Consider, then, the variety of problems they faced in trying to appeal to the authority of rights.

DEFINING A RIGHT

Perhaps the most basic problem involves the deceptively simple matter of defining a right. What does the word *right* literally mean? Before the seventeenth century, this now-potent word had a surprisingly limited meaning in English usage. In the legal sense, a right was nothing more than a valid title of ownership, especially as it related to real property (land). All the other activities that later generations came to associate with the concept of rights were more frequently and familiarly described as "liberties and privileges." These words embraced not only the legal guarantees that protected individuals against the arbitrary power of government but also the benefits that the state conferred on particular groups within the larger society: members of guilds, stockholders in trading companies, the voting citizens of chartered communities.[5] Nor was the difference between the traditional idea of liberties and privileges and the modern idea of rights merely a matter of usage. Many liberties and privileges were regarded not as inherent qualities or attributes of individuals but rather as legal powers granted by the crown. The liberty or privilege of doing something did not belong to individuals as a matter of course; it was a specific power allowed or permitted by the state—and as easily revocable by the same authority.

But amid the great political and religious disputes of the seventeenth century, the word *right* shed its original limited meaning and began to acquire its bewildering modern associations. When the Stuarts attempted to raise public revenues without parliamentary consent, their opponents insisted that the crown must act lawfully through Parliament, because the

---

[5] James H. Hutson, "The Emergence of the Modern Concept of a Right in America: The Contribution of Michel Villey," *American Journal of Jurisprudence*, 39 (1994), 197–201.

citizens it represented had the right to be governed only through laws enacted with Parliament's consent. When the Stuarts prosecuted and imprisoned their critics, in Parliament and out, their opponents responded with new arguments asserting the political privileges of legislators and the civil rights of ordinary subjects. And when both the crown and, on occasion, Parliament persecuted members of the radical religious sects, the defenders of these dissenters asserted that a fundamental right of conscience empowered individuals to form their own religious opinions, uncoerced either by established churches or by the state.

The seventeenth-century debates thus transformed the concept and usage of *right* in at least two major ways. First, the concept of right now expanded in meaning to embrace and even subsume the variety of claims and activities formerly classified as "liberties and privileges." Second, the notion of ownership that lay at the core of the original meaning of right now described just what it was that the holders of rights enjoyed. A right was something more than a liberty or privilege that the state could offer or revoke. It was literally something that individuals owned. And this ownership was not merely a matter of casual purchase; it was a *birthright* to which the English people were entitled by virtue of living in a realm where monarchy was limited, not absolute; where Parliament and trial by jury provided effective checks on royal power; and where Protestant traditions of dissent and toleration had supplanted Roman Catholic demands for orthodoxy and uniformity of religious belief.[6]

When the great philosopher John Locke (1632–1704) published his *Two Treatises of Government* in 1689, he revealed how radically the concept of right had grown since the previous century. Locke grounded his entire theory of government on the right of property. Just as men left the state of nature and formed civil societies and governments to protect the property they created through their labor, so too they enjoyed a property, an ownership, of their rights and faculties—including the right to a free exercise of religious conscience. But society as a whole also had a right to protect its property and its rights against tyrannical government. It had, that is, a right of resistance. And that right was something more than a mere matter of private choice; it was, at bottom, a collective duty that a society owed to itself and its posterity.[7]

---

[6]For a brief but illuminating discussion of this aspect of the idea of rights as property and birthright, see John Phillip Reid, *The Authority of Rights* (Madison: University of Wisconsin Press, 1986), 96–113.

[7]The scholarly literature on Locke is enormous. For an introduction to his thinking about rights, see A. John Simmons, *The Lockean Theory of Rights* (Princeton: Princeton University Press, 1992); James Tully, *An Approach to Political Philosophy: Locke in Contexts* (Cambridge, Eng.: Cambridge University Press, 1993); the introduction to John Locke, *Two*

The crucial statement of the theory of revolution under which James II was deposed and William and Mary crowned in his place, however, was the Declaration of Rights that Parliament presented to William and Mary as a condition of their accession to the throne. In this document, *rights* and *liberties* appear as interchangeable terms. From this time forward, we can trace the steady expansion of the use of *right* to the point where it would eclipse *liberty*. By the eighteenth century, liberty itself was regarded as a right, joining life and property in the trinity of great natural rights that the British constitution was widely hailed as protecting.[8] When Britons and Americans spoke of rights in the eighteenth century, they could apply this flexible term to embrace a staggering variety of activities and claims, ranging from such prosaic matters as *estover*, the customary right of gathering wood, to the great civil and political rights of representation, trial by jury, and free exercise of religious conscience.[9]

THE HOLDERS OF RIGHTS

A second fundamental problem involves identifying the holders or possessors of the rights that constitutional government should protect. In our time we answer this question with little hesitation. Our dominant conception of rights is liberal, subjective, and potentially universal. That is, we regard the free individual as the true rights-bearer, and we aspire to extend the protection of rights to all of humankind, regardless of race, gender, nationality, class, or even age. In the modern understanding, rights belong to autonomous individuals who are presumed to be capable of choosing how they will exercise their liberty and entitled to protection against the coercive powers of government and society alike.

There were certainly important antecedents for this point of view in the new conception of rights that flourished in the seventeenth century. For example, in making the individual's natural right of self-preservation the groundwork for his entire political theory—a right that one could exercise even against the lawful sovereign—Thomas Hobbes advanced

---

Treatises of Government, Peter Laslett, ed. (Cambridge, Eng.: Cambridge University Press, 1988); and the major work of the late Richard Ashcraft, *Revolutionary Politics and Locke's Two Treatises of Government* (Princeton: Princeton University Press, 1986).

[8]On the valence of the word *liberty,* see especially John Phillip Reid, *The Concept of Liberty in the Age of the American Revolution* (Chicago: University of Chicago Press, 1988); and Bernard Bailyn, *The Ideological Origins of the American Revolution,* enlarged ed. (Cambridge: Harvard University Press, 1992), 55–93.

[9]For examples, see the survey of "The Rights of Englishmen" in Forrest McDonald, *Novus Ordo Seclorum: The Intellectual Origins of the Constitution* (Lawrence: University Press of Kansas, 1985), 9–55.

an essentially subjectivist concept of rights in his great political treatise, *Leviathan* (1651).[10] Locke was concerned with individual rights of a very different kind when he wrote his *Second Treatise* in good measure to enable religious dissenters to hold their own beliefs, free from the coercion of church and state, and when he further argued that parents could hold only a limited trust to shape the religious convictions of their children.[11] Indeed, the prominent place that freedom of conscience gained in seventeenth-century thinking strongly suggests that religious concerns were a crucial foundation for the modern view of rights as the possession of autonomous individuals.

A good case can nevertheless be made that this liberal conception of rights was more a product of the nineteenth century than a mark of the ideas that flourished between the Glorious Revolution of 1688 and the American Revolution of 1776. The classic statements of a liberal theory of rights were works like Alexis de Tocqueville's *Democracy in America* (1840) or John Stuart Mill's extended essay *On Liberty* (1859), both of which were concerned with enabling free-thinking individuals to withstand the conformist pressures of a mass democratic society.

In the eighteenth century, however, many authorities would still have held that the primary holders of rights were not individuals but rather the collective body of the people. The real issue was not to enable individuals to enjoy a maximum degree of choice in their private lives—to choose their lifestyles, we might say—but to protect the people at large from tyranny. A people had a right not to be subjected to the capricious decrees or ukases of unchecked rulers; to be bound to obey only those laws and taxes enacted with their consent, through some process of representation; and to be secured against the arbitrary acts of courts and sheriffs by the "inestimable" right to trial by jury and other restraints. Of course, individuals would be the beneficiaries of the protection that these rights would secure. But the great imperative remained to prevent the revival of the forms of tyranny that Britons and Americans associated with the absolutist monarchies of the seventeenth century.

For Anglo-American whigs, absolutism was simply a synonym for tyranny, and tyranny endangered not merely the rights of individuals but also the security of the entire population. A people ruled by tyranny lived in a condition of slavery—a word that was often used as an antonym for

---

[10]The scholarly literature is, again, staggering. For a beginning, see Tuck, *Natural Rights Theories,* 119–42, and his introduction to his scholarly edition of *Leviathan* (Cambridge, Eng.: Cambridge University Press, 1991).

[11]See Tully, *Locke in Contexts,* 47–62, for a short statement of Locke's evolving position.

liberty, rather than to describe the exploited labor of the plantation colonies of the Americas.[12] And before the law, slaves lacked any individuality; they were an undifferentiated mass lacking rights of any kind— individual or collective, social or political, civil or natural. The idea that rights might one day be extended to the true slaves of the eighteenth century—the human chattels who worked the plantations of the New World—was a prospect that gradually began to emerge in the era of the American Revolution. As Americans became all too aware, they could hardly proclaim that their own rights were sacred while they were busily depriving African Americans of every claim to humanity.[13] Yet because chattel slavery was an entrenched and vital element of plantation society, its hold could be shaken only after free Americans grasped the meaning of their commitment to equal rights for themselves.

THE THREAT TO RIGHTS

There was one question about rights that eighteenth-century commentators could resolve fairly readily. If the problem of rights was to protect the people from the government, the ruled from their rulers, one had only to ask which part of government was most likely to act tyrannically. The answer, again, was the crown—or rather a crown left free to act arbitrarily, unchecked by other institutions that could moderate its tyrannical impulses. That was the great lesson that the struggles of the Stuart era kept alive in the minds and hearts of eighteenth-century Britons and Americans. The Stuarts had tried to rule without Parliament, levying fees that looked much like taxes without Parliament's consent, to support a standing army that was sometimes used as a domestic police force, quelling opposition in the same way that pliant judges and sheriffs (both of whom served at the pleasure of the crown) browbeat those conscientious jurors who might otherwise acquit the opponents of Stuart rule.

---

[12]Reid, *Concept of Liberty*, 47–59.

[13]The question of how slavery became objectionable and the even more difficult problem of understanding how the American revolutionaries resolved their commitment to equality with the existence of chattel slavery have been a source of ongoing controversy among historians. For major statements, see William W. Freehling, "The Founding Fathers and Slavery," *American Historical Review*, 77 (1972), 81–93; Bailyn, *Ideological Origins*, 232–46; Paul Finkelman, "Slavery at the Constitutional Convention: Making a Covenant with Death," in Richard Beeman, Stephen Botein, and Edward C. Carter II, eds., *Beyond Confederation: Origins of the Constitution and American National Identity* (Chapel Hill: University of North Carolina Press, 1987), 188–225; and Winthrop D. Jordan, *White Over Black: American Attitudes Toward the Negro, 1550–1812* (Chapel Hill: University of North Carolina Press, 1968), 269–426.

The Glorious Revolution had presumably remedied this danger for all time. In Britain, unlike France, monarchy itself was constitutionalized and thus limited. Henceforth it would act only with the consent of Parliament. Though judges were still appointed by the crown, they now held their commissions during good behavior, which meant that they could not be removed simply because they had displeased the crown. On this independent tenure, they would no longer be the tools of the crown; and the English people still enjoyed the invaluable right to trial by jury. At the margins of British politics, a few dissenters worried that the political influence used by the crown and its ministers to control both houses of Parliament was sapping the principles of 1689. But amid the general complacency and prosperity of the eighteenth century, their views were largely ignored at home—though not in America.[14]

In this self-satisfied atmosphere, the Declaration of Rights of 1689 was increasingly seen as a conservative act. It had not been a clarion call to revolution, nor had it created new rights to which Parliament and its constituents had not already been entitled. The Declaration simply confirmed that the rights and liberties that the Stuarts had infringed and usurped were again secure.[15] They were rights to which Englishmen had always held clear title and which only a marauding band of royal Scottish ruffians, intoxicated by the example of the absolutist monarchy of France, could have dared to steal.

THE SOURCES OF RIGHTS

If the Declaration of 1689 had only affirmed but not created rights, where, then, did rights originate? On what authority did rights finally rest—especially if they were conceived as something more than liberties or privileges granted by the crown? Some of the most powerful political thinking of the seventeenth century was devoted to this fundamental problem. The famous descriptions of life in the state of nature that generations of American students have encountered in Hobbes's *Leviathan* and Locke's *Second Treatise* were only two of the answers this question evoked. In trying to imagine why men left the state of nature to form ordered societies, both Hobbes and Locke sought to rest their divergent conceptions of gov-

[14] Bailyn, *Ideological Origins,* 34–54.
[15] Schwoerer challenges this view in her recent book. For her summary of this conservative interpretation, see Lois G. Schwoerer, *The Declaration of Rights, 1689* (Baltimore: The Johns Hopkins University Press, 1981), 5–6.

ernment on the idea that men voluntarily formed compacts to provide greater security for their rights.

One reason we still read Hobbes and Locke so closely is that their emphasis on the state of nature gave their writings a universalist appeal that many of their contemporaries failed to attain. The dominant form of argument in the great disputes of the seventeenth century was not philosophical but historical. Royalists and their parliamentary adversaries told two different stories about the origins of English rights, liberties, and privileges. For the opponents of the Stuarts, the history of England was essentially a tale of liberty lost. Prior to the Norman conquest of 1066, there had existed an "ancient constitution" of elective monarchy, legislative assemblies, and popular rights. The arrival of William the Conqueror ("a French bastard landing with an armed banditti," as Thomas Paine observed in *Common Sense*[16]) had changed all that, imposing the "yoke" of Norman feudalism on a once-free, Anglo-Saxon people. During the centuries since, some of their rights had been partly recovered through Magna Carta, in the common-law courts where trial by jury flourished, and in the efforts of the House of Commons to secure its legislative privileges.[17]

The idea of this "ancient constitution" was a shade less mythical than the primordial state of nature that Hobbes, Locke, and other writers imagined. It *was* a history of sorts, but a history that depended on belief in certain customs and rights that dated to time immemorial—time beyond memory—and which was not easily confirmed through hard documentary evidence. In many ways, the royalist critics of this story proved the better historians. The ancient constitution was, they thought, a figment of their adversaries' imagination. Their own research suggested that the rights claimed for Parliament were indeed historical in a more immediate sense: Their origins could all be traced to particular acts of royal authority for which documentary evidence survived. And this in turn suggested that what had been granted once could be revoked later.

Both the philosophical and the historical modes of tracing the origins of rights continued to flourish in the eighteenth century. Many writers invoked the idea of a Lockean social compact to explain the origins of government. It became a great cliché to hold that government originated in a compact in which the rights that individuals exercised in the state of

[16] [Thomas Paine], *Common Sense* (Philadelphia, 1776), in Michael Foot and Isaac Kramnick, eds., *The Thomas Paine Reader* (Harmondsworth, Eng.: Penguin, 1987), 76.

[17] The classic and seminal account of this debate is J. G. A. Pocock, *The Ancient Constitution and the Feudal Law* (Cambridge, Eng.: Cambridge University Press, 1957).

nature were surrendered first to society and then to government. Rejecting Hobbes's naked emphasis on man's fear of death, eighteenth-century writers argued that men reasonably yielded the absolute liberty they enjoyed in nature to gain greater security in the exercise of the rights they retained. But alongside this essentially philosophical position, a belief in the distinctive historical experience of the English-speaking peoples remained an essential part of the Anglo-American understanding of rights.[18]

In one sense, the ability to invoke both philosophical and historical arguments for the origins of rights testifies to the richness of the sources on which eighteenth-century writers could draw. But a diversity of accounts can also be a source of uncertainty—especially when they rely upon the fictive notion of a state of nature, or upon customs dating from time immemorial, or upon the contested documentary evidence of the past. And the extension of these rights from the mother country of England to its American colonies complicated the issue further, for the question of whether the American colonists were entitled to all the rights and liberties of Englishmen was the great issue that disrupted the British empire in North America after 1765.

THE FORM AND FUNCTION
OF A DECLARATION OF RIGHTS

Our modern understanding of the nature and function of the Bill of Rights has been shaped primarily by its judicial interpretation in the twentieth century. For us, the federal Bill of Rights and its great descendant, the Fourteenth Amendment, appear as a set of legally enforceable commands. Although these clauses are addressed to all branches and levels of government, the ultimate responsibility for their enforcement is often ascribed to the judiciary. Just how broadly or narrowly these provisions should be read is, of course, the principal source of much of the controversy that has surrounded the Supreme Court since at least 1954, when its decision in *Brown v. Topeka Board of Education* signaled the end of legal segregation. But the idea that the Bill of Rights and the Fourteenth Amendment comprise a set of legally binding and judicially enforceable commands captures the modern understanding of the essential nature of constitutionally declared rights.

[18] Reid, *Authority of Rights,* 9–15.

That understanding, however, was not immediately or fully available to the constitutionalists of the seventeenth and eighteenth centuries. When they contemplated adopting public statements of rights, they were acting within a different legal context and responding to particular political circumstances. They had no single model of the form that a declaration of rights might take or the function it would serve, but rather a set of possibilities that illuminates the complexity and ambiguity of the concept itself.[19]

In 1628, for example, the parliamentary opponents of arbitrary taxation could have proposed a statute affirming the liberties of the subject against the arbitrary acts of the crown, but such a measure would never have received the assent of Charles I. Instead, the Commons "seized on a suggestion of the more antiquated parliamentary form of a petition to the king," in the hope that Charles might approve this moderate Petition of Right in exchange for the new revenues he sought. In fact, Charles did approve the Petition; but once Parliament was prorogued, he issued his own edited version of the text, one that left him free to collect the duties of "tonnage" and "poundage" against which Parliament had protested. And when Charles went on to govern without Parliament during the next decade, the crown and its royal judges largely ignored the Petition, which survived more as a beacon to an impotent opposition than as a legal text.[20]

The Agreement of the People of 1647 took a different and potentially far more modern form. Drafted at a point when radical revolutionaries could imagine England as a commonwealth without a king, the Agreement was a prototype for the written constitutions the Americans would begin to implement a century and a quarter later. Its protections for rights were incorporated in the body of the Agreement, not set apart as an introductory statement of principle. Equally important, these articles would have operated as restrictions on Parliament itself, the institution normally regarded as the bulwark of popular rights.[21]

---

[19]Here I follow Bailyn, *Ideological Origins*, 184–98; and Gordon S. Wood, *The Creation of the American Republic, 1776–1787* (Chapel Hill: University of North Carolina Press, 1969), 259–305.

[20]Derek Hirst, *Authority and Conflict: England, 1603–1658* (Cambridge: Harvard University Press, 1986), 152–59.

[21]There are several versions of the Agreement dating from the fall of 1647 to 1649; for a 1649 printing, see *An Agreement of the Free People of England*, in William Haller and Godfrey Davies, eds., *The Leveller Tracts, 1647–1653*, reprint ed. (Gloucester, Mass.: Peter Smith, 1964), 318–28. On the potential influence of the Levellers on the American revolutionaries, see Michael Kent Curtis, "In Pursuit of Liberty: The Levellers and the American Bill of Rights," *Constitutional Commentary*, 8 (1991), 359–93.

The Declaration of Rights of 1689 took still another form. It had three distinct parts:

1. a list of thirteen offenses committed by James II "contrary to the knowne Laws and Statutes, and Freedom of this Realm," which justified the rejection of his rule;
2. a second list of thirteen "undoubted Rights and Liberties" of the English people, now being "declare[d]" by the two houses of Parliament; and
3. a resolution to extend the throne to Prince William of Orange and Princess Mary, in the expectation that the new rulers "will still preserve them from the violation of their Rights, which they have here asserted, and from all other Attempts upon their Religion, Rights, and Liberties."

In effect, the Declaration of Rights had a threefold character. Its first section formally ended the reign of James II; the second provided a formal statement of fundamental rights, all of which had been endangered by the excesses of royal power; and the third marked a tentative if incomplete step toward the idea of a written constitution, at least insofar as it specified terms under which the new monarchs would rule.[22]

The American revolutionaries drew on the multifaceted nature of these documents, but again in diverse ways. Their protests against Parliament and the king followed the classic form of petitions seeking the redress of grievances and invoking legal precedents and customary understandings as evidence for their validity. Once petitioning gave way to armed rebellion in 1775, statements of rights were put to more radical ends. Just as the first section of the parliamentary Declaration of Rights of 1689 renounced the authority of James II, so the Declaration of Independence of July 4, 1776, enumerated the traditional English rights and liberties that his successor, George III, was accused of infringing. But most of those charges had already appeared in the preamble to the Virginia constitution, by way of justifying the renunciation of royal authority that accompanied the establishment of a new government. More important, the preamble to the Declaration of Independence affirmed natural rights of a still more fundamental kind when it reminded "a candid world" that Americans were now entitled to exercise their "right" and "duty" to "throw off" the old regime "and to provide new Guards for their future security." The Declaration of Independence was thus not merely an act of state, announcing that a new people were about to "assume among the powers of the

[22]I am grateful to Professor Pauline Maier for stressing this point to me.

earth, the separate and equal station to which the Laws of Nature and of Nature's God entitle them." It was also a retrospective declaration of the English rights whose repeated violation entitled them to exercise the natural right of the people "to institute new Government."[23]

Statements of rights, then, could take any of several forms. They might be protests couched as conciliatory petitions, appealing to legal precedents both well known (Magna Carta, the Petition of Right) and obscure. They could be emboldening declarations of resistance and revolution, justifying a shift of loyalty from one monarch to another—or to none. They might either be incorporated in written constitutions or left to hang as affirmations of great principles, possessing great rhetorical power but of uncertain legal effect. Or they could be cast in statutory form, which would give them legal authority but at the cost of leaving them subject to later revision or revocation. The idea that declarations or bills of rights could evolve into judicially enforceable, legal commands may well have been implicit in these possibilities—especially the last—but that was by no means the sole understanding of these documents that the disputes of the seventeenth and eighteenth centuries supported.

THE POPULARITY OF RIGHTS-TALK

There is a final aspect of rights-talk that the politicians, philosophers, and lawyers of the early modern era perhaps did not grasp as well as we might—but which still links the progress in their thinking with our concerns. That connection might be simply stated in this way: Why is rights-talk such an attractive idiom?

The beginnings of an answer to this question lie in the distinction between the traditional notion of "liberties and privileges" and the modern concept of rights. A theory of liberties and privileges is perfectly consistent with a belief in inequality, for it presumes that the state often has good reasons to grant particular legal powers or exemptions to different classes of citizens or subjects. The language of rights, by contrast, is less tolerant of distinctions, and it is therefore at least implicitly egalitarian. It presupposes that the capacity to exercise liberty is an innate quality (or property) of a free people and that when the state seeks to limit the exercise of that right to some class of persons, it must have a compelling rationale for doing so. And it follows from this supposition that those who feel

---

[23]For a broader reading of the cultural import of the Declaration, see Jay Fliegelman, *Declaring Independence: Jefferson, Natural Language, and the Culture of Performance* (Stanford: Stanford University Press, 1993).

that their innate capacity to act has been denied will find the language of rights the most attractive political dialect they can speak, because it will ground their claims on the broadest foundation.

In the seventeenth and eighteenth centuries, the principal holders of rights were the free, adult, property-holding (and white) males who alone were eligible to become citizens in the full meaning of the term, including gaining the right to vote. Wives whose legal identities were subsumed by their husbands; urban artisans who worked only for wages in a master craftsman's shop; tenant farmers in the countryside; younger sons who still did their father's bidding; daughters waiting to choose a groom—all were dependent on someone else for their living, and all could therefore be said to be incompetent to enjoy a full measure of rights. Yet in both seventeenth-century England and eighteenth-century America, the resort to rights-talk worked to subvert that principle, for at least two fundamental reasons.

First, the arguments developed by leading thinkers and politicians were framed in expansive terms. Though John Locke's emphasis on the right of property has been treated as a response to the emergence of a market economy, and therefore to be interpreted in terms of certain economic interests,[24] his *Second Treatise* also defends the rights of mothers to have an equal say with the father in the rearing of children and the rights of children to choose their own religious faith, regardless of the preferences of their parents.[25] Similarly, to maintain their own claims to authority, the political elites who generated the English civil war of the 1640s, the Glorious Revolution of 1688, and the American Revolution of 1776 all spoke as if they were representing their entire society. The broader the mandate they could claim, the greater legitimacy their positions would seem to enjoy. Thus defenders of the legislative privileges of Parliament argued that the whole English people were somehow represented in the House of Commons, while colonial leaders made similar claims for their own representative assemblies. They were acting, that is, not in their own behalf, but as agents for whole peoples whose rights

---

[24]The classic statement of this argument is by the late Canadian political theorist, C. B. Macpherson, *The Political Theory of Possessive Individualism* (Oxford: Oxford University Press, 1962); and see James Tully, "After the Macpherson Thesis," in *Locke in Contexts,* 71–95.

[25]See Chap. VI, "Of Paternal Power," in Locke, *Two Treatises,* ed. Laslett, 303–18. For a gendered reading of the same passage that emphasizes the priority of matters of inheritance over the rights of conscience, see Mary Beth Norton, *Founding Mothers and Fathers: Gendered Power and the Forming of American Society* (New York: Alfred Knopf, 1996), 97–101.

they were merely defending.[26] But once they made that claim, what was to stop ordinary people from thinking that their social superiors really meant what they said or from appropriating elite rhetoric to advance their own claims for recognition and justice?

The language of rights, then, is inherently expansive and potentially egalitarian. Once it enters into common speech, it will no longer be heard only in the salons of the gentry; it will pass into wider usage, come to be spoken in new venues, and be put to new uses. If the whole of the English or American peoples were somehow represented in their assemblies, why should the suffrage (the right to vote) be limited only to male property-holders? Why should the legal identity of women disappear beneath the authority of their fathers or husbands? Why should apprentices and journeymen not enjoy the same rights as their artisan-employers? More troubling still, how can societies whose members enjoy the birthright of liberty systematically deny not only the liberty but also the humanity of the Africans and African Americans they held as chattel slaves?

To say that the elite classes of England and America were reluctant to recognize all the claims of rights that their revolutionary politics inspired is thus only half of the story. By describing their claims as fundamental rights, the elite classes made it possible for groups outside the mainstream to appropriate the universal and egalitarian idiom of rights-talk for their own ends—which were often incidental to the original grievances that political leaders were pressing, but no less important or deserving. Much of the history of American rights since 1776 can be written as a story of the way in which new claimants of rights have appropriated an older language to their own ends.

---

[26]For an extensive development of this theme, see Edmund S. Morgan, *Inventing the People: The Rise of Popular Sovereignty in England and America* (New York: W. W. Norton, 1988).

3

The Colonists' Appeal to Rights

Claims of rights were, of course, at the heart of the dispute that carried the American colonists from resistance to revolution in the decade separating the Stamp Act controversy of 1765 from the outbreak of civil war in Massachusetts in April 1775.[1] The initial American opposition to parliamentary taxation drew deeply from hallowed English traditions. If taxes were the free gift of the people, conveyed through their elected legislators, Americans could not be bound to pay a tax imposed by a Parliament in which they were unrepresented. The potential scope of this debate was broadened when Parliament accompanied its repeal of the Stamp Act in March 1766 with the passage of a Declaratory Act affirming its legal power to bind the colonies "in all cases whatsoever." Should Parliament ever assert this claim in practice, the colonists would have to ask whether they were bound to obey any form of legislation, and not merely the special category of taxation. When the British ministry and Parliament responded to the Boston Tea Party of December 1773 with a set of Coercive Acts punishing Massachusetts for its defiance, it converted the threat of the Declaratory Act into a functioning policy of repression. The result was civil war and, eventually, independence.

Rights other than representation were also invoked during the controversies leading to independence. For example, one provision of the Revenue (or Sugar) Act of 1764 allowed imperial officials to prosecute violations of the navigation system regulating colonial commerce in

---

[1]Early twentieth-century historians would have questioned this statement, but ever since the publication of a seminal article by Edmund S. Morgan, "Colonial Ideas of Parliamentary History, 1764–1766," *William and Mary Quarterly,* 3d ser., 5 (1948), 311–41, the dominant view of the origins of the conflict has stressed both the sincerity and the merits of the colonists' arguments. For the further development of this interpretation, see Edmund S. Morgan and Helen M. Morgan, *The Stamp Act Crisis: Prologue to Revolution,* rev. ed. (New York: Macmillan, 1963); Bernard Bailyn, *The Ideological Origins of the American Revolution,* enlarged ed. (Cambridge: Harvard University Press, 1992), 160–229; and in a somewhat different key, all four volumes of John Phillip Reid, *The Constitutional History of the American Revolution* (Madison: University of Wisconsin Press, 1986–93).

vice-admiralty courts, where defendants did not enjoy trial by jury. The belief that trial by jury was as essential to liberty as representation had become an axiom of Anglo-American thinking.[2] Indeed, these two rights were nearly equivalent in importance and parallel in purpose. Both raised barriers against the abuse of royal power: representation by requiring the crown to govern with the express consent of the governed; and jury trial by preventing royal judges and sheriffs from willfully using the law to punish opponents of the crown.

The colonists were never hard pressed to identify the rights that Parliament and other imperial agencies were endangering. As the legal historian John Phillip Reid has observed, the real problem was to locate the sources of authority for these rights. "The rights were British rights and well known," Reid notes. "Why Americans were entitled to them was more controversial and more complicated." Like their political ancestors, the colonists could tap a potent brew of philosophical, legal, and historical arguments. Reid identifies no fewer than ten distinct sources of authority that Americans invoked as they sought to prove why they did not have to bend their knees to Parliament, ranging from "their rights as Englishmen" to the idea that the first English colonists in the New World had carried their rights with them or had repurchased their rights by the sweat and toil of making settlements. Many of these arguments were formidable, drawing as they did on essential strands of the Anglo-American constitutional tradition.[3]

Yet the arguments used to justify parliamentary sovereignty over America were just as strong, for they drew upon the single most profound consequence of the Glorious Revolution: the recognition that Parliament was the supreme source of law within the extended empire of which the colonies were undeniably a part. The American claim to equal rights might have merit—but only up to a point. When this claim confronted the doctrine of parliamentary sovereignty, something had to give—or so the defenders of British policy insisted. In a sense, their arguments placed American rights in the same tenuous position in which seventeenth-century royalists would have left the liberties and privileges of the English people. If those rights existed, their authority rested on the sovereign consent not of the governed but of the government.

By 1773, some American leaders began to hint that the colonies should

---

[2]Carl Ubbelohde, *The Vice-Admiralty Courts and the American Revolution* (Chapel Hill: University of North Carolina Press, 1960); John Phillip Reid, *The Authority of Rights* (Madison: University of Wisconsin Press, 1986), 47–59.
[3]Reid, *Authority of Rights*, 65–66.

seek to negotiate a "bill of rights" with the government. Such a document would specify exactly what rights and liberties Americans would enjoy within the larger framework of the British empire.[4] Even after Parliament answered the Boston Tea Party with the Coercive Acts, many colonists hoped that the government of Lord North would resolve the crisis by granting an American bill of rights. When the First Continental Congress met in Philadelphia in September 1774, it accordingly adopted a formal Declaration of Rights to publicize the essential principles of the diplomatic settlement it would accept. Nothing came of this initiative, however. The notions of colonial rights advanced by Congress exceeded anything that the British government was prepared to grant. In the view of King George III, his ministers, and most members of Parliament, the first right that the colonists had to exercise was the duty of obedience.

After 1774, however, royal authority over America all but ended. In nearly every colony, legal institutions of government were in a state of collapse. Royal governors could not allow legislatures to meet, because their members would then conspire to promote the cause of resistance. At the local level of government, justices of the county courts held crown commissions, which rendered their authority suspect. In this interregnum, the colonies created an "extralegal" network of committees, conventions, and congresses to coordinate resistance and act as a surrogate government. Moreover, once civil war broke out in Massachusetts in April 1775, Americans could plausibly argue that they no longer owed the crown any obedience. In the familiar version of the social compact theory of government, obedience was something the subject owed the crown in exchange for its protection. Since a king who made war on his subjects was hardly protecting them, Americans need no longer regard George III as their lawful sovereign.[5]

From these circumstances, Americans drew a stunning conclusion: The dissolution of legal government had placed them in a condition akin to the state of nature that they had read about in Locke and Hobbes. Clearly they had not returned to the pure state of nature that preceded both society and government. Wives could not leave their husbands or

[4] Jack N. Rakove, *The Beginnings of National Politics: An Interpretive History of the Continental Congress* (New York: Alfred Knopf, 1979), 12–14.

[5] For accounts of this interregnum, see Pauline Maier, *From Resistance to Revolution: Colonial Radicals and the Development of American Opposition to Britain, 1765–1776* (New York: Alfred Knopf, 1972), 228–96; Jerrilyn Greene Marston, *King and Congress: The Transfer of Political Legitimacy, 1774–1776* (Princeton: Princeton University Press, 1987); Rakove, *Beginnings of National Politics*, 21–86.

husbands their wives or children their parents; servants and slaves could not proclaim a jubilee and bid their masters adieu (though in the Chesapeake Bay, hundreds of slaves rallied to the promise of freedom extended by Lord Dunmore, the last royal governor of Virginia, in November 1775). But Americans believed that they were living in a society that no longer enjoyed legal government—and to restore it, some positive act was required. Some procedure had to be devised to leave this unprecedented condition and to establish new institutions of government. The old colonial charters could not simply be reinstated. One essential limb of government—the executive, representing the crown—had been lopped off. Many of the colonial councils that doubled as upper houses of the assemblies were appointed by the crown; so were the judges. These could not simply be replaced; the entire framework of government had to be designed anew.[6]

This was the occasion that set American constitutionalism on its innovative course, in the process raising new questions about the meaning and import of bills of rights. Americans could no longer regard a constitution as the mixture of law, custom, conventions of governance, and institutions existing at any one moment in time. As the provincial conventions individually began to form new governments in late 1775 and 1776, they naturally thought of the documents they were drafting as *constitutions* in a new sense—as charters drafted at a particular moment of time, creating the institutions that would henceforth act under the authority they bestowed.[7] And such constitutions could acquire deeper aspirations still: to determine what these governments could and could not do. In this sense, a constitution would become supreme fundamental law, superior

---

[6]Gordon S. Wood, *The Creation of the American Republic, 1776–1787* (Chapel Hill: University of North Carolina Press, 1969), 127–61, is the basic account; the book as a whole has shaped the interpretation of this transformation for an entire generation of scholars. Also valuable on the process of constitution making is Willi Paul Adams, *The First American Constitutions: Republican Ideology and the Making of the State Constitutions in the Revolutionary Era*, trans. Rita and Robert Kimber (Chapel Hill: University of North Carolina Press, 1980); and Donald S. Lutz, *Popular Consent and Popular Control: Whig Political Theory in the Early State Constitutions* (Baton Rouge and London: Louisiana State University Press, 1980).

[7]On this fundamental development, see Bernard Bailyn, *The Ideological Origins of the American Revolution*, enlarged ed. (Cambridge: Harvard University Press, 1992), 175–84; Gerald Stourzh, "*Constitution:* Changing Meaning of the Term from the Early Seventeenth to the Late Eighteenth Century," in Terence Ball and J. G. A. Pocock, eds., *Conceptual Change and the Constitution* (Lawrence: University Press of Kansas, 1988), 35–54; and Horst Dippel, "The Changing Idea of Popular Sovereignty in Early American Constitutionalism: Breaking Away from European Patterns," *Journal of the Early Republic*, 16 (1996), 21–45.

to every act that government henceforth undertook in its name. Moreover, if acts of government violated the constitution, they could be judged unconstitutional and thus invalid.[8]

How to make these charters fully constitutional was the great challenge that Americans faced after 1776. To achieve this end, Americans gradually concluded that these documents had to be adopted under exceptional procedures: framed by conventions specially elected for the sole purpose of drafting the constitution and then approved through some act of popular ratification. But these were not the rules under which Americans acted in 1775 and 1776. Few Americans could yet grasp these questions in their full detail, and even if they could, the urgent need to mobilize the country for war and independence left little time for the fine points of constitutional theory.[9]

During the course of the Revolution, eleven of the thirteen states drafted new constitutions of government.[10] Eight of these eleven attached declarations or bills of rights to their completed constitutions. Determining the exact relation of these statements of rights to the main texts of the new constitutions was just one of the questions that could barely be perceived, much less resolved, in 1776. In Virginia, for example, the Provincial Convention approved the Declaration of Rights more than a fortnight before it adopted the constitution; neither document referred to the other; nor was it even clear that contemporaries regarded the Declaration as part of the constitution.[11] In 1787 no less an authority than

---

[8]This was the opposite of the prevailing British understanding of a constitution. There an act of Parliament might be regarded as unconstitutional if it departed from some existing norm or practice; but if it was legally enacted by Parliament and signed by the king, that was all that mattered. One crucial demonstration of this difference revolved around the Septennial Act of 1716. As part of the general constitutional understanding worked out in the wake of the Glorious Revolution, Parliament had adopted a Triennial Act limiting the tenure of an elected Parliament to three years. The idea that a new parliament should be elected every three years was thus part of the British constitution when the throne passed from Queen Anne to King George I, the first of the Hanoverian dynasty. Amid the intense conflict and political uncertainty surrounding this transition, however, the new Parliament adopted an act extending its own tenure to seven years. In a sense, that act was unconstitutional; but it was legal nonetheless, and thus became part of the post-1716 British constitution. See Reid, *Authority of Rights*, 75–78.

[9]For a discussion of the theoretical issues, see Wood, *Creation of the American Republic*, 306–43.

[10]Connecticut and Rhode Island did not, because under their seventeenth-century charters, all officers of government were appointed within the colony; hence there was no royal branch of government to replace.

[11]There are many accounts of the drafting of the Virginia Declaration and Constitution, but two of the best are to be found in the headnotes accompanying relevant documents in Robert A. Rutland, ed., *The Papers of George Mason, 1725–1792* (Chapel Hill: University of North Carolina Press, 1970), I, 274–310; and Julian P. Boyd, ed., *The Papers of Thomas Jefferson* (Princeton: Princeton University Press, 1950–), I, 329–86.

James Wilson, one of the nation's most eminent lawyers and a leading framer of the Federal Constitution, seemed unaware that Virginia had a bill of rights.[12]

To think of these bills of rights as organic parts of a constitution may miss a more important point. Their function was less to establish rules regulating the workings of government than to remind both the people and public officials of the basic principles by which government should conduct its affairs. Rights had to be declared not because the constitutions would be defective without them but rather because that was what Americans believed a people were supposed to do when they left the state of nature to establish a civil government. This was the great lesson they had learned from their reading; they would be remiss not to apply it when they suddenly found themselves reenacting the mythic drama of forming a government.

At first glance, this belief seems so abstract and academic as to have mattered only to a small circle of well-read leaders. But in fact there is evidence that this concern did penetrate into the ranks of the citizenry. In Massachusetts, the one state where the process of constitution writing proved most arduous, a number of towns insisted that a properly designed constitution had to meet three crucial requirements. First, it had to be drafted by a body appointed for that purpose alone, because a constitution drafted by the ordinary legislature could in theory be amended, altered, or even violated by any later meeting of the same body. Second, a constitution had to gain the positive assent of the people at large; it had to be *ratified* in a way that indicated that the people truly had agreed to the compact of government. Third, in forming this compact, the rights it was meant to secure should be formally declared. Without such a declaration, the prevailing theory of legislative supremacy left a troubling implication. Would there be any limit on the reach of legislative power or the methods the legislature could use to enforce its will, if fundamental rights were left undeclared? By combining statements of the broad principles of government with such specific protection as the right to trial by jury, bills of rights could somehow erect a fence around the sovereign powers of government once it was reconstituted.[13]

By insisting that all three of these points be honored, the citizens of

---

[12]John Kaminski and Gaspare Saladino, eds., *The Documentary History of the Ratification of the Constitution* (Madison: State Historical Society of Wisconsin, 1976–), II, 390.

[13]On the drafting of the Massachusetts constitution, see Oscar Handlin and Mary F. Handlin, eds., *The Popular Sources of Political Authority: Documents on the Massachusetts Constitution of 1780* (Cambridge: Harvard University Press, 1966).

Massachusetts effectively delayed the adoption of a constitution in their state for fully four years. With the adoption of the Massachusetts constitution in 1780, American constitutionalism took a major step forward by establishing a clear precedent for procedures for drafting and ratifying constitutions. Yet the question of how bills of rights fitted into this new model of constitutionalism remained poorly formulated and unresolved. Were such declarations something more than statements of principle? Were they legally enforceable guarantees that individuals could apply against improper acts of government? If so, how were they to be enforced? Or were they better regarded as moral injunctions to citizens and officials alike (as their preference for the verb "ought" implied)? And suppose that such a declaration failed to list all the rights, liberties, and principles worth affirming. Did that omission mean that these other rights had somehow been diminished in importance? Or suppose a state failed to add a declaration of rights to its constitution (as had New Jersey, New York, and South Carolina). Would the rights of its citizens then be less secure? Why would Americans need a bill of rights at all, if they were governed by laws passed by their own freely elected representatives?[14]

These questions came to the fore during the debate over the Federal Constitution of 1787. But to explain why they did so, we must understand why the framers of the Constitution could have grown so skeptical about the value and utility of bills of rights, which James Madison dismissed as so many "parchment barriers" to be admired, perhaps, in principle, but not relied upon in practice. Before that perception became possible, the American revolutionaries first had to win a long and arduous war.

[14]Wood, Creation of American Republic, 271–73; Jack N. Rakove, Original Meanings: Politics and Ideas in the Making of the Constitution (New York: Alfred Knopf, 1996), 302–10. The contents of the state bills of rights are surveyed in Bernard Schwartz, The Great Rights of Mankind: A History of the American Bill of Rights, expanded ed. (Madison, Wis.: Madison House, 1992), 53–91. For state-by-state analyses of the history of declarations of rights in the colonial charters and revolutionary constitutions, see the essays collected in Patrick T. Conley and John P. Kaminski, eds., The Bill of Rights and the States: The Colonial and Revolutionary Origins of American Liberties (Madison, Wis.: Madison House, 1992), which includes a valuable bibliographic essay by Gaspare Saladino. The most closely studied state declaration has been Virginia's; see the essays collected in Jon Kukla, ed., The Bill of Rights: A Lively Heritage (Richmond: Virginia State Library, 1987).

4

The Legacy of 1689

When the Convention Parliament of 1689 made acceptance of the Declaration of Rights the condition on which William and Mary would accede to the throne, they seemingly brought the great constitutional disputes of the seventeenth century to a decisive conclusion. In fact, for another quarter century British politics remained almost as tumultuous as it had been since the reign of Charles I.[1] In 1714, with the death of Queen Anne (younger daughter of James II and sister of Queen Mary, who had died in 1694), the English throne passed to a family of German Protestant princes who ruled the Electorate of Hanover. Under the reign of the first two Georges (1714–1760), intense ideological conflict finally receded. An increasingly prosperous society and well-financed state attained a remarkable measure of political stability. Britain's "balanced" constitution became the toast of Enlightened political science. Much of this stability depended on the capacity of the crown—the king and his ministers and councilors—to use patronage and other forms of influence to manage both Parliament and the relatively small electorate that elected the House of Commons. Parliament enjoyed supremacy in principle, but in practice the crown almost always commanded decisive majorities in both houses.

Nevertheless, memories of the previous century retained a powerful hold over the imaginations of eighteenth-century Englishmen and their American compatriots. Homage to 1689 was a defining element of Anglo-American political culture, and within its mythology, the Declaration of Rights was a reminder of how close Britain had steered to the shoals of tyranny and how prudently its people had acted in stating the terms on which they would henceforth be governed. Yet amid the complacency of eighteenth-century politics, an undercurrent of dissent fretted that resistance to unjust rule might again be necessary. Critics of the crown's dom-

---

[1] The classic study is J. H. Plumb, *The Growth of Political Stability in England, 1675–1725* (London: Macmillan, 1967).

ination of Parliament worried that the true principles of 1689 were being subverted and alleged that the danger of a return to arbitrary rule was not a fantasy. Amid these claims, reminders that a people always possessed a fundamental right to resist unlawful acts of government enjoyed a striking vitality.

CONSTRAINING THE KING

Because it was so deeply rooted in feudal law, the Magna Carta of 1215 was far more a precedent for the seventeenth- and eighteenth-century statements of rights than a model of what such a document might look like. But Magna Carta did share one crucial feature with later declarations: It targeted the king and his subordinate officials as the greatest danger to the liberties and privileges that deserved recognition and protection. The idea that Parliament might also abuse power was harder to entertain. True, the excesses of the Long and Rump Parliament of the 1640s and 1650s and the Cavalier Parliament (1661–79) disabused the English people of the idea that the king was the sole threat to their rights. Nevertheless, the politics of the 1680s confirmed the old belief that grasping monarchs were the preeminent danger and that the best means of protecting rights was to confirm the authority of Parliament.

The Declaration of Rights of 1689 was consistent with that view. All the rights it identified in its central section were to be maintained against the crown, on behalf of either Parliament or the people. When William and Mary agreed to govern according to its provisions, they therefore confirmed that Britain would henceforth be a limited, constitutional monarchy, in contrast to the absolutist kingdom across the English Channel. But if the thrust of the Declaration of Rights was clear, its composition revealed other ambiguities about its authority. The Convention Parliament could not cast its statement of rights in the traditional form of a petition, as had the Parliament of 1628, for the simple reason that there was no longer any king whose favor could be solicited—James II having abandoned the throne. Instead, the Convention exploited the multiple meanings of the word "declaration." In ordinary usage, the historian Lois G. Schwoerer observes, *declaration* connoted a clear, strong, emphatic statement; at law, it referred to a statement of charges against a defendant (which is what the first section of the Declaration presented against James); and in political usage, the term had also been used by kings and parliaments to describe public statements of positions on contested issues. In this last sense, Schwoerer adds, a declaration was meant more to state a policy than to explain or justify it.[2]

But no declaration of rights, however emphatic, could entirely resolve the fundamental ambiguity of the origins of rights. For as much as the Declaration of Rights, which was later reenacted in statutory form, sought to lay a firm foundation for the future character of the British constitution, it presumed that the rights it was confirming already existed.

1

CONVENTION PARLIAMENT

Declaration of Rights

February 12, 1688 o.s.

The Declaration of the Lords Spiritual and Temporal, and Commons Assembled at Westminster

Whereas the late King *James* the Second, by the Assistance of divers Evil Counsellors, Judges, and Ministers Employ'd by Him, did endeavour to Subvert and Extirpate the Protestant Religion, and the Laws and Liberties of this Kingdom;

By Assuming and Exercising a Power of Dispensing[3] with, and Suspending[4] of Laws, and the Execution of Laws, without Consent of Parliament.

By Committing and Prosecuting divers Worthy Prelates, for humbly Petitioning to be Excused from concurring to the said assumed Power.

By issuing, and causing to be Executed, a Commission under the Great Seal, for erecting a Court called, *The Court of Commissioners for Ecclesiastical Causes.*[5]

---

[2]Lois G. Schwoerer, *The Declaration of Rights, 1689* (Baltimore: The Johns Hopkins University Press, 1981), 11–29.

[3]A royal power to authorize individuals to disobey a law.

[4]A royal power to set aside the operation of a statute for a limited period.

[5]A royal commission created in July 1686 to discipline clergy of the Church of England who opposed new royal policies favoring Catholics.

Convention Parliament, *The Declaration of the Lords Spiritual and Temporal, and Commons, Assembled at Westminster* (Ann Arbor, Mich.: University Microfilms International, 1983), microfilm, reel 1440:89.

By Levying Money for and to the Use of the Crown, by pretence of Prerogative,[6] for other time, and in other manner, than the same was granted by Parliament.

By raising and keeping a standing Army within this Kingdom in time of Peace, without Consent of Parliament; and Quartering Soldiers contrary to Law.

By causing several Good Subjects, being Protestants, to be Disarmed at the same time, when Papists were both Armed and Imployed contrary to Law.

By violating the Freedom of Election of Members to serve in Parliament.

By Prosecutions in the Court of *Kings-Bench* for Matters and Causes cognizable only in *Parliament;* and by divers other Arbitrary and Illegal Courses.

And whereas of late years, Partial, Corrupt, and Unqualified Persons, have been returned and served on Juries in Trials, and particularly divers Jurors in Trials for High Treason, which were not Freeholders;

And Excessive Bail hath been required of persons committed in Criminal Cases, to elude the benefit of the Laws made for the Liberty of the Subjects.

And Excessive Fines have been imposed.

And Illegal and Cruel Punishments inflicted.

And several Grants and Promises made of Fines and Forfeitures before any Conviction or Judgment against the persons upon whom the same were to be levied.

All which are utterly and directly contrary to the known Laws and Statutes, and Freedom of this Realm.

And whereas the said late King *James* the Second, having Abdicated the Government, and the Throne being thereby vacant,

His Highness the Prince of *Orange* (whom it hath pleased Almighty God to make the Glorious Instrument of Delivering this Kingdom from Popery and Arbitrary Power) did (by the Advice of the Lords Spiritual and Temporal, and divers principal Persons of the Commons) cause Letters to be written to the Lords Spiritual and Temporal, being Protestants, and other Letters to the several Counties, Cities, Universities, Burroughs, and Cinque-Ports,[7] for the Chusing of such Persons to represent them, as were of Right to be sent to Parliament, to Meet and Sit at *Westminster* upon

---

[6]Powers whose exercise was held to be inherent in the Crown and beyond the control of Parliament.

[7]The five English ports of Hastings, Romney, Hythe, Dover, and Sandwich.

the 22d day of *January* in this year 1688, in order to such an Establishment, as that their Religion, Laws and Liberties, might not again be in danger of being Subverted: Upon which Letters Elections having been accordingly made;

And thereupon the said Lords Spiritual and Temporal, and Commons, pursuant to their respective Letters and Elections, being now Assembled in a Full and Free Representative of this Nation, taking into their most serious Consideration the best Means for attaining the Ends aforesaid, do in the first place (as their Ancestors in like Case have usually done) for the Vindicating and Asserting their Ancient Rights and Liberties, Declare,

That the pretended Power of Suspending of Laws, or the Execution of Laws, by Regal Authority, without Consent of Parliament, is Illegal.

That the pretended Power of Dispensing with Laws, or the Execution of Laws, by Regal Authority, as it hath been assumed and exercised of late, is Illegal.

That the Commission for erecting the late *Court of Commissioners for Ecclesiastical Causes,* and all other Commissions and Courts of the like nature, are illegal and Pernicious.

That levying of Money for or to the Use of the Crown, by pretence of Prerogative, without Grant of Parliament, for longer time, or in other manner, than the same is or shall be granted, is Illegal.

That it is the Right of the Subjects to Petition the King, and all Commitments and Prosecutions for such Petitioning, are Illegal.

That the raising or keeping a standing Army within the Kingdom in time of Peace, unless it be with Consent of Parliament, is against Law.

That the Subjects which are Protestants may have Arms for their Defence suitable to their Condition, and as allowed by Law.

That Election of Members of Parliament ought to be free.

That the Freedom of Speech, and Debates or Proceedings in Parliament, ought not to be impeached or questioned in any Court or place out of Parliament.

That Excessive Bail ought not to be required, nor Excessive Fines imposed, nor cruel and unusual Punishments inflicted.

That Jurors ought to be duly empannell'd and return'd, and Jurors which pass upon Men in Trials for High-Treason ought to be Freeholders.

That all Grants and Promises of Fines and forfeitures of particular persons before Conviction, are Illegal and Void.

And that for redress of all Grievances, and for the amending, strengthening and preserving of the Laws, Parliaments ought to be held frequently.

And they do claim, demand, and insist upon all and singular the

Premises, as their undoubted Rights and Liberties; and that no Declarations, Judgments, Doings, or Proceedings, to the prejudice of the People in any of the said Premises, ought in any wise to be drawn hereafter into Consequence or Example.

To which Demand of their Rights they are particularly encouraged by the Declaration of His Highness the Prince of *Orange,* as being the only means for obtaining a full redress and remedy therein.

Having therefore an intire Confidence, that his said Highness the Prince of *Orange* will perfect the Deliverance so far advanced by Him, and will still preserve them from the violation of their Rights, which they have here asserted, and from all other Attempts upon their Religion, Rights, and Liberties;

The said Lords Spiritual and Temporal, and Commons assembled at *Westminster* do resolve,

That *William* and *Mary* Prince and Princess of *Orange* be, and be declared, King and Queen of *England, France,* and *Ireland,* and the Dominions thereunto belonging, to hold the Crown and Royal Dignity of the said Kingdoms and Dominions, to Them the said Prince and Princess, during their Lives, and the Life of the Survivor of them; And that the sole and full Exercise of the Regal Power be only in, and executed by, the said Prince of *Orange,* in the Names of the said Prince and Princess during their joint Lives; and after their Deceases, the said Crown and Royal Dignity of the said Kingdoms and Dominions to be to the Heirs of the Body of the said Princess; and for default of such Issue, to the Princess *Ann* of *Denmark,* and the Heirs of Her Body; and for default of such Issue, to the Heirs of the Body of the said Prince of *Orange.*

And the said Lords Spiritual and Temporal, and Commons, do pray the said Prince and Princess of *Orange* to accept the same accordingly.

And that the Oaths hereafter mentioned be taken by all persons of whom the Oaths of Allegiance and Supremacy might be required by Law, instead of them; and that the said Oaths of Allegiance and Supremacy be Abrogated.

I A. B. do sincerely promise and swear, That I will be faithful, and bear true Allegiance to Their Majesties King WILLIAM and Queen MARY.

So help me God.

I A. B. do swear, That I do from my heart Abhor, Detest, and Abjure, as Impious and Heretical, this Damnable Doctrine and Position, That Princes Excommunicated or Deprived by the Pope, or any Authority of the See of Rome, may be Deposed or Murthered by their Subjects, or any other whatsoever. And I do declare, That no Foreign Prince, Person, Prelate, State, or Potentate, hath, or ought to have, any Jurisdiction, Power, Superiority, Preeminence, or Authority Ecclesiastical or Spiritual, within this Realm.

So help me God.

Jo. Browne, Cleric' Parl.

DIE VENERIS 15 FEB. 1688

His Majesties Gracious Answer,
to the Declaration of Both Houses

My Lords and Gentlemen,

This is certainly the greatest proof of the Trust you have in Us, that can be given, which is the thing that maketh Us value it the more; and We thankfully Accept what you have Offered. And as I had no other Intention in coming hither, than to preserve your Religion, Laws and Liberties; so you may be sure, That I shall endeavour to support them, and shall be willing to concur in any thing that shall be for the Good of the Kingdom, and to do all that is in My power to Advance the Welfare and Glory of the Nation.

DIE VENERIS 15° FEBRUARII 1688.

Ordered by the Lords Spiritual and Temporal, Assembled at *Westminster,* That His Majesties Gracious Answer to the Declaration of Both Houses, and the Declaration, be forthwith Printed and Published; And that His Majesties Gracious Answer this Day be added to the Engrossed Declaration in Parchment, to be Enrolled in Parliament and Chancery.

Jo. Browne, Cleric'
Parliamentorum

5

Rights in Resistance

When Parliament passed the Stamp Act in 1765, the colonists were initially uncertain what form their protest should take. The colonial assemblies had known of the pending bill since the previous year, and their petitions against it had been ignored. Nevertheless, by the early fall of 1765, an effective strategy of resistance had been fashioned. Angry crowds mobbed the homes of the hapless individuals appointed to distribute the stamps, intimidating them into resigning their posts, and thus stopping the Act from taking effect. An intercolonial congress of twenty-seven deputies met in New York to fashion a common platform of resistance. The colonial assemblies also separately adopted their own petitions, asking the British government to repeal the Stamp Act as a violation of the fundamental right of British citizens to be taxed only with their own consent, freely given by their duly elected representatives.[1]

Thus began the constitutional debate that ended a decade later in civil war. The initial American argument about the link between taxation and representation was answered with the claim that the colonists were "virtually" represented in Parliament. That is, even though they sent no deputies to the House of Commons, its members were somehow capable of legislating in good faith for every section of the extended British empire. But this argument was subject to derision in America and serious criticism even in Britain. There it was well known that entire communities and whole classes of the population had no real voice in a Commons chosen by a minuscule electorate. Rather than rely on arguments about representation, the defenders of Parliament's power to legislate for America retreated to the high ground of sovereignty. They argued that

---

[1]The best account of this opening phase of controversy is Edmund S. Morgan and Helen M. Morgan, *The Stamp Act Crisis: Prologue to Revolution,* rev. ed. (New York: Macmillan, 1963); and see P. D. G. Thomas, *British Politics and the Stamp Act Crisis: The First Phase of the American Revolution, 1763–1767* (Oxford, Eng.: Clarendon Press, 1975); and Pauline Maier, *From Resistance to Revolution: Colonial Radicals and the Development of American Opposition to Britain, 1765–1776* (New York: Alfred Knopf, 1972), 51–76.

Parliament was the supreme legislature of the larger polity of which the colonies were undeniably a part, and that sovereignty—the ultimate power to give law—was by its nature complete and indivisible.[2] The impasse over these competing claims was the rock on which the British empire in North America sundered. Over the next ten years the rival positions grew more strident and more refined, as writers on both sides probed weak points in their adversaries' arguments and smoothed out rough spots in their own. But the basic dispute remained straightforward. For Americans, the principal problem was to explain why they were not subject to the jurisdiction of Parliament in matters of taxation or internal legislation. However, to affirm this position, the Americans had to identify the sources of authority for the rights they were asserting. How could Americans be sure that they actually possessed the rights they needed to defy the legitimate power of Parliament—the body they revered as the fountain of English liberty?

CHALLENGING THE STAMP ACT

The most important colonial protest against the Stamp Act was the set of fourteen resolutions that the Stamp Act Congress adopted on October 19, 1775. But perhaps because the deputies in New York were anxious to appear conciliatory, they couched their protest in language that softened the radical implications of the agitation that was taking place in the streets and the press. A more revealing statement of the American position can be found in another set of fourteen resolutions adopted only ten days later by the lower house of the Massachusetts legislature. In that colony, resistance was dominated by a group of radical ideologues who were deeply suspicious of the character of British politics, deeply mistrustful of the crown's appointed officials in their own colony, and deeply committed to the principles of British constitutionalism—at least as they understood them.[3]

The Massachusetts resolutions illustrate the striking variety of authorities that the colonists could invoke to deny the jurisdiction of Parliament. In different permutations and combinations, these resolutions appealed to the principles of the British constitution and the laws of nature (resolutions 1–3, 10, 12, and 13); to the authority of Magna Carta and their own

---

[2] The escalation of this debate is traced in Bernard Bailyn, *The Ideological Origins of the American Revolution,* enlarged ed. (Cambridge: Harvard University Press, 1992), 160–229.

[3] Perhaps the best account of these events, as viewed through the eyes of their chief victim, Lieutenant Governor Thomas Hutchinson, is in Bernard Bailyn, *The Ordeal of Thomas Hutchinson* (Cambridge: Harvard University Press, 1974), 35–155.

charter of government, granted by the crown (resolutions 4, 6, and 11); to a general principle of equality giving citizens of the colonies the same political rights as those of Britain (resolution 5); to the authority of a parliamentary statute of 1740 providing for the naturalization of foreign-born Protestants settling in America (resolution 7); and to the title the people of Massachusetts had acquired to their rights by virtue of the expense of settlement and their prior support for the empire (resolutions 8 and 9).

2

Resolutions of the House of Representatives of Massachusetts

October 29, 1765

Whereas the just Rights of His Majesty's Subjects of this Province, derived to them from the *British Constitution,* as well as the *Royal Charter,* have been lately drawn into Question: In order to ascertain the same, this House do UNANIMOUSLY come into the following resolves.

1. *Resolved,* That there are certain essential Rights of the *British* Constitution of government which are founded in the Law of God and Nature, and are the common Rights of Mankind—Therefore

2. *Resolved,* That the Inhabitants of this Province are *unalienably* entitled to those essential rights in common with all Men: and that no Law of Society can, consistent with the Law of God and Nature, divest them of those Rights.

3. *Resolved,* That no Man can justly take the Property of another without his Consent: and that upon this original Principle the Right of Representation in the same Body, which exercises the Power of making Laws for levying Taxes, which is one of the main Pillars of the British Constitution, is evidently founded.

4. *Resolved,* That this *inherent* Right, together with all other essential Rights, Liberties, Privileges and Immunities, of the People of *Great Britain,* have been fully confirmed to them by *Magna Charta,* and by former and by later Acts of Parliament.

Resolutions of the House of Representatives of Massachusetts, October 29, 1765; Boston Gazette and Country Journal, November 4, 1765, from Lamont Library, Harvard University, microfilm NB442.

5. *Resolved,* That His Majesty's Subjects in *America,* are in Reason and common Sense, entitled to the same Extent of Liberty with His Majesty's Subjects in *Britain.*

6. *Resolved,* That by the Declaration of the Royal Charter of this Province, the Inhabitants are entitled to all the Rights, Liberties, and Immunities of free and natural Subjects of *Great Britain,* to all Intents, Purposes, and Constructions whatever.

7. *Resolved,* That the Inhabitants of this Province appear to be intitled to all the Rights aforementioned, by an Act of Parliament 13th of Geo. 2d.

8. *Resolved,* That those Rights do belong to the Inhabitants of this Province, upon Principles of *common Justice;* their Ancestors, having settled this *Country* at their *sole Expense,* and *their* Posterity, having constantly approved themselves most loyal and faithful Subjects of *Great Britain.*

9. *Resolved,* That every Individual in the Colonies, is as advantageous to *Great Britain,* as if he were in *Great Britain,* and held to pay his full Proportion of Taxes there: And as the Inhabitants of this Province pay their full Proportion of Taxes for the Support of His Majesty's Government *here,* it is unreasonable for them to be called upon, to pay any Part of the Charges of the Government *there.*

10. *Resolved,* That the Inhabitants of this Province are not, and never have been, represented in the Parliament of *Great Britain:* and that such a Representation *there,* as the Subjects in *Britain* do actually and rightfully enjoy, is *impracticable* for the Subjects in *America:* — And further, That in the Opinion of this House, the several subordinate Powers of Legislation in *America,* were constituted, upon the Apprehensions of this *Impracticability.*

11. *Resolved,* That the *only* Method, whereby the constitutional Rights of the Subjects of this Province can be secure, consistent with a Subordination to the supreme Power of *Great Britain,* is by the continued Exercise of such Powers of Government as are granted in the Royal Charter, and a firm Adherence to the Privileges of the same.

12. *Resolved,* as a just Conclusion from some of the foregoing Resolves, That all Acts made, by any Power whatever, other than the General Assembly of this Province, imposing Taxes on the Inhabitants, are Infringements of our *inherent* and *unalienable* Rights as *Men* and *British subjects:* and render void the most valuable Declarations of our *Charter.*

13. *Resolved,* That the Extension of the Powers of the Court of Admiralty within this Province, is a most violent Infraction of the Right of Trials by Juries, — A Right, which this House upon the Principles of their *British Ancestors,* hold most dear and sacred; it being the only Security of the Lives, Liberties and Properties of his Majesty's Subjects here.

14. *Resolved,* That this House owe the strictest Allegiance to His Most Sacred Majesty King GEORGE the Third: That they have the greatest Veneration for the Parliament: And that they will, after the Example of *all* their Predecessors, from the Settlement of this Country, exert themselves to their utmost in supporting his Majesty's Authority in the Province—in promoting the true Happiness of his Subjects: and in enlarging the Extent of his Dominion.

Ordered, That all the foregoing Resolves be kept in the Records of this House, that a just Sense of Liberty, and the firm Sentiments of Loyalty be transmitted to Posterity.

DISPUTING THE AMERICAN CLAIM

The formal resolutions adopted by congresses and assemblies were only one element of the wide-ranging debate that the Stamp Act launched. Positions were stated and attacked, defended and debunked, in numerous forums: in newspaper essays, pamphlets, broadsides, and sermons; and in the coffeehouses, taverns, and churches where colonists gathered to discuss events. It was widely believed that the existence of an open press was a "palladium of liberty" that enabled Britons and Americans to enjoy more political freedom than any other people. And while the existing state of legal doctrine left printers and writers vulnerable to prosecution for libel when they attacked government officials, in practice the political debate conducted in the press was robust, direct, and salty.[4]

Not all Americans agreed that the colonists were entitled to the same rights as Britons, or conceded that such claims could trump the authority of king and Parliament. One of the first statements of this position came from the pen of Martin Howard, Jr., a Rhode Island lawyer who was sympathetic with the needs of empire and disdainful of the highly fractious politics of his own colony. In 1765 Howard published a pamphlet to rebut the arguments that Governor Samuel Hopkins had made in his own pamphlet,

---

[4]The classic work on eighteenth-century notions of freedom of the press is Leonard Levy, *The Emergence of a Free Press* (New York: Oxford University Press, 1985), a significantly revised version of his earlier work, *Legacy of Suppression: Freedom of Speech and Press in Early American History* (Cambridge: Harvard University Press, 1963). Levy's work has attracted a substantial number of critics; for the work of one of the most important, see David Rabban, "The Ahistorical Historian: Leonard Levy on Freedom of Expression in Early American History," *Stanford Law Review,* 37 (1985), 795–856. For further discussion of the role of the press in colonial politics, see the essays collected in Bernard Bailyn and John B. Hench, eds., *The Press and the American Revolution* (Worcester, Mass.: American Antiquarian Society, 1980); and the important article by the late Stephen Botein, " 'Meer Mechanics' and an Open Press: The Business and Political Strategies of Colonial American Printers," *Perspectives in American History,* 9 (1975), 127–225.

The Rights of Colonies Examined. In the following excerpt, Howard distinguished the "personal" rights of individual *colonists,* which he conceded should rest on a condition of equality with those of Britons, from the "political" rights of *colonies,* which could be ascertained only in terms of the specific liberties granted in the colonial charters. If an exemption from parliamentary jurisdiction was not explicitly provided when those charters were granted, Howard implied, the Americans could hardly claim it now.

Part of Howard's argument relies on a distinction between *common law,* on the one hand, and what is sometimes called the *black letter law* of legislative statute and royal charters. There is no simple definition of common law, but as eighteenth-century Britons and Americans used the term, it described a set of legal principles, precedents, and doctrines developed in centuries of litigation in the courts of England. As judges and juries resolved cases, it was believed, they did not so much create new law as discover and apply the true principles of justice that had existed since time out of mind and that owed their ultimate authority to natural and divine law and the accrued wisdom embodied in custom. Statutes and charters, by contrast, were forms of positive law, adopted by particular acts of legislative or royal will. Americans believed that the benefits of common law were also an essential part of their rights. When Howard claimed that parliamentary supremacy was itself part of the common law, then, he was trying to undermine the colonists' position on its own terms.

3

MARTIN HOWARD, JR.

A Letter from a Gentleman at Halifax

(1765)

I have endeavored to investigate the true natural relation, if I may so speak, between colonies and their mother state, abstracted from compact or positive institution, but here I can find nothing satisfactory; till this relation is clearly defined upon a rational and natural principle, our reason-

Martin Howard, Jr., *A Letter from a Gentleman at Halifax, to His Friend in Rhode Island, Containing Remarks upon a Pamphlet, Entitled, The Rights of Colonies Examined* (Newport, 1765) from Houghton Library, Harvard University, AAS copy, microfiche W2571, Readex Early American Imprints 10012, 7–11.

ing upon the measure of the colonies obedience will be desultory and inconclusive. Every connection in life has its reciprocal duties; we know the relation between a parent and child, husband and wife, master and servant, and from thence are able to deduce their respective obligations; but we have no notices of any such precise natural relation between a mother state and its colonies, and therefore cannot reason with so much certainty upon the power of the one, or the duty of the others. The ancients have transmitted to us nothing that is applicable to the state of modern colonies, because the relation between these is formed by political compact; and the condition of each variant in their original, and from each other. The honorable author[5] has not freed this subject from any of its embarrassments: Vague and diffuse talk of rights and privileges, and ringing the changes upon the words liberty and slavery, only serve to convince us, that words may affect without raising images, or affording any repose to a mind philosophically inquisitive. For my own part, I will shun the walk of metaphysicks in my enquiry, and be content to consider the colonies rights upon the footing of their charters, which are the only plain avenues, that lead to the truth of this matter.

The several *New-England* charters ascertain, define and limit the respective rights and privileges of each colony, and I cannot conceive how it has come to pass that the colonies now claim any other or greater rights than are therein expressly granted to them. I fancy when we speak, or think of the rights of freeborn *Englishmen,* we confound those rights which are personal, with those which are political: There is a distinction between these, which ought always to be kept in view.

Our personal rights, comprehending those of life, liberty and estate, are secured to us by the common law, which is every subject's birthright, whether born in *Great-Britain,* on the ocean, or in the colonies; and it is in this sense we are said to enjoy all the rights and privileges of *Englishmen.* The political rights of the colonies, or the powers of government communicated to them, are more limited, and their nature, quality and extent depend altogether upon the patent or charter which first created and instituted them. As individuals, the colonists participate of every blessing the *English* constitution can give them: As corporations created by the crown, they are confined within the primitive views of their institution. Whether therefore their indulgence is scanty or liberal, can be no cause of complaint; for when they accepted of their charters, they tacitly submitted to the terms and conditions of them.

[5]Governor Samuel Hopkins, whose pamphlet Howard was answering.

The colonies have no rights independent of their charters, they can claim no greater than those give them, by those the Parliamentary jurisdiction over them is not taken away, neither could any grant of the king abridge that jurisdiction, because it is founded upon common law, as I shall presently show, and was prior to any charter or grant to the colonies: Every *Englishman,* therefore, is subject to this jurisdiction, and it follows him wherever he goes. It is of the essence of government, that there should be a supreme head, and it would be a solecism[6] in politics to talk of members independent of it.

With regard to the jurisdiction of Parliament, I shall endeavor to show, that it is attached to every *English* subject wherever he be: and I am led to do this from a clause in page nine of his honor's pamphlet, where he says, "That the colonies do not hold their rights as a privilege granted them, nor enjoy them as a grace and favor bestowed; but possess them, as an inherent, indefeasible right." This postulatum cannot be true with regard to political rights, for I have already shown, that these are derived from your charters, and are held by force of the king's grant; therefore these inherent, indefeasible rights, as his honor calls them, must be personal ones, according to the distinction already made. Permit me to say, that inherent and indefeasible as these rights may be, the jurisdiction of parliament, over every *English* subject, is equally as inherent and indefeasible: That both have grown out of the same stock, and that if we avail ourselves of the one, we must submit to and acknowledge the other.

It might here be properly enough asked, Are these personal rights self-existent? Have they no original source? I answer, They are derived from the constitution of *England,* which is the common law; and from the same fountain is also derived the jurisdiction of Parliament over us.

But to bring this argument down to the most vulgar apprehension: The common law has established it as a rule or maxim, that the plantations are bound by *British* acts of parliament, if particularly named: and surely no *Englishman,* in his senses, will deny the force of a common law maxim. One cannot but smile at the inconsistency of these inherent, indefeasible men:[7] If one of them has a suit at law, in any part of *New-England,* upon a question of land, property, or merchandize, he appeals to the common law, to support his claim, or defeat his adversary; and yet is so profoundly stupid as to say, that an act of parliament does not bind him: when, perhaps, the same page in a law book, which points him out a remedy for a

---

[6]Inconsistency.
[7]That is, those who argue that the colonies have an inherent, unrelinquishable right to invoke the common law against Parliament.

libel, or a slap in the face, would inform him that it does. — In a word, The force of an act of parliament, over the colonies, is predicated upon the common law, the origin and basis of all those inherent rights and privileges which constitute the boast and felicity of a *Briton*.

Can we claim the common law as an inheritance, and at the same time be at liberty to adopt one part of it, and reject the other? Indeed we cannot: The common law, pure and indivisible in its nature and essence, cleaves to us during our lives, and follows us from *Nova Zembla* to *Cape Horn:* And therefore, as the jurisdiction of parliament arises out of, and is supported by it, we may as well renounce our allegiance, or change our nature, as to be exempt from the jurisdiction of parliament: Hence, it is plain to me, that in denying this jurisdiction, we at the same time take leave of the common law, and thereby, with equal temerity and folly, strip ourselves of every blessing we enjoy as *Englishmen:* A flagrant proof this, that shallow draughts in politics and legislation confound and distract us, and that an extravagant zeal often defeats its own purposes.

CONSTITUTIONAL RIGHTS IN THE BRITISH TRADITION

If *rights* and *liberties* were potentially ambiguous terms in the eighteenth-century lexicon, so was the word *constitution*. In one of his earliest essays, written before the Stamp Act was repealed, John Adams (1735–1826) provided a revealing account of the multiple meanings that this word possessed. To answer the question, "What is the British constitution?" Adams surveyed the existing definitions from which contemporaries could choose, and he then used two metaphors (one biological, the other mechanical) that nicely reflect the ways in which his contemporaries could also compare political phenomena with natural and artificial ones. Read as a whole, Adams's essay illustrates just how slippery yet potent a term *constitution* can be.

But Adams also concluded his essay with two arguments that Anglo-Americans repeatedly used to cut through this ambiguity. In their thinking, two constitutional rights mattered beyond all others: the right to representation and the right to trial by jury. These two rights secured the people in their liberty in exactly parallel ways. For as Adams went on to explain, representation and trial by jury were the institutional defenses upon which Anglo-American constitutionalism relied to prevent the standing government of the crown and its lackeys from acting in arbitrary or self-aggrandizing ways.

4

JOHN ADAMS

The Earl of Clarendon to William Pym

January 27, 1766

Sir,[8]

You are pleased to charge the Colonists with ignorance of the British constitution—But let me tell you there is not even a *Son of Liberty*[9] among them who has not manifested a deeper knowledge of it, and a warmer attachment to it, than appears in any of your late writings—They know the true constitution and all the resources of liberty in it, as well as in the law of nature which is one principal foundation of it, and in the temper and character of the people, much better than you, if we judge by your late most impudent pieces, or than your patron and master,[10] if we judge by his late conduct.

The people in America have discovered the most accurate judgment about the real constitution, I say, by their whole behaviour, excepting the excesses of a few,[11] who took advantage of the general enthusiasm, to perpetrate their ill designs: tho' there has been great enquiry, and some apparent puzzle among them about a formal, logical, technical definition of it.—Some have defined it to [be] the practice of parliament; others, the judgments and precedents of the King's courts; but either of these definitions would make it a constitution of wind and weather, because, the parliaments have sometimes voted the King absolute and the judges have sometimes adjudg'd him to be so.—Some have call'd it custom, but this is as fluctuating and variable as the other.—Some have call'd it the most perfect combination of human powers in society, which finite wisdom has yet contrived and reduced to practice, for the preservation of liberty and the production of happiness.—This is rather a character of the constitu-

---

[8]Adams addresses his letters to William Pym, an English writer who had defended the legality of the Stamp Act.

[9]"Sons of Liberty" was the name taken by colonists who actively organized to oppose the Stamp Act.

[10]Probably George Grenville, the minister who was the architect of the Stamp Act.

[11]Adams refers to rioting that took place during the earliest phase of resistance to the Stamp Act.

[John Adams], *The Earl of Clarendon to William Pym*, no. III, *Boston Gazette and Country Journal*, January 27, 1766, from Lamont Library, Harvard University, microfilm NB442.

When he posed for this portrait in 1766, John Adams was a rising member of the Boston bar and an active patriot anxious to make his mark in the world. His diary for this period records the passion with which he linked his personal ambitions with the political dilemma the colonies were facing in challenging imperial authority.

tion, and a just observation concerning it, than a regular definition of it; and leaves us still to dispute what it is.—Some have said that the whole body of the laws; others that King, Lords, and Commons, make the constitution. There has also been much inquiry and dispute about the essentials and fundamentals of the constitution, and many definitions and descriptions have been attempted: But there seems to be nothing satisfactory to a rational mind in any of these definitions: Yet I cannot say, that I am at any loss about any man's meaning when he speaks of the British constitution, or of the essentials and fundamentals of it.

What do we mean when we talk of the constitution of the human body? What by a strong and robust, or a weak and feeble constitution? Do we not mean certain contextures of the nerves, fibres and muscles, or certain qualities of the blood and juices, as fizy, or watery, phlegmatic or fiery, acid or alkaline? We can never judge of any constitution without considering the *end* of it; and no judgment can be formed of the human constitution, without considering it as productive of *life* or *health* or *strength*. —The physician shall tell one man that certain kinds of exercise, or diet, or medicine, are not adapted to his constitution, that is, not compatible with his *health*, which he would readily agree are the most productive of *health* in another. The patient's habit abounds with acid, & acrimonious juices: Will the doctor order vinegar, lemmon juice, barberries and cramberries, to work a cure?—These would be unconstitutional remedies; calculated to increase the evil, which arose from the want of a balance, between the acid and alkaline ingredients, in his composition.—If the patient's nerves are overbraced, will the doctor advise to jesuits bark? There is a certain quantity of exercise, diet, and medicine, best adapted to every man's constitution, will keep him in the best health and spirits, and contribute the most to the prolongation of his life. These determinate quantities are not perhaps known to him, or any other person: but here lies the proper province of the physician to study his constitution and give him the best advice what and how much he may eat and drink; when and how long he shall sleep; how far he may walk or ride in a day; what air and weather he may improve for this purpose; when he shall take physick, and of what sort it shall be; in order to preserve and perfect his *health*, and prolong his *life*. But there are certain other parts of the body, which the *physician* can in no case have any *authority* to *destroy* or *deprave;* which may properly be called *stamina vitæ*, or *essentials* and *fundamentals of the constitution*. Parts, without which life itself cannot be preserved a moment. Annihilate the heart, lungs, brain, animal spirits, blood; any one of these, and life will depart at once.— These may be strictly called fundamentals, of the human constitution: Tho' the limbs may be all amputated, the eyes put out, and many other mutilations practiced to impair the strength, activity and other attributes of the man; and yet the essentials to life may remain, unimpaired many years.

Similar observations may be made with equal propriety concerning every kind of machinery. A clock has also a constitution, that is a certain combination of weights, wheels and levers, calculated for a certain use and end, the mensuration of time. Now the constitution of a clock, does not imply such a perfect constructure of movement as shall never go too fast or too slow, as shall never gain nor lose a second of time, in a year or century.—This is the proper business of Quare, Tomlinson, and Graham,[12] to execute the workmanship like artists, and come as near to perfection, i.e. as near to a perfect mensuration of time, as the human eye and finger will allow. But yet there are certain parts of a clock, without which, it will not go at all, and you can have from it no better account of the time of day, than from the ore of gold, silver brass and iron, out of which it was wrought. These parts therefore are the essentials and fundamentals of a clock.

Let us now enquire whether the same reasoning is not applicable in all its parts to government.——For government is a frame, a scheme, a system, a combination of powers, for a certain end, viz the good of the whole community.——The public good, the salus populi[13] is the professed end of all government, the most despotic, as well as the most free. I shall enter into no examination which kind of government, whether either of the forms of the schools, or any mixture of them is the best calculated for this end. This is the proper inquiry of the founders of Empires. I shall take for granted, what I am sure no Briton will controvert, viz. that Liberty is essential to the public good, the salus populi.—And here lies the difference between the British constitution, and other forms of government, viz. that Liberty is its end, its use, its designation, drift and scope, as much as grinding corn is the use of a mill, the transportation of burdens the end of a ship, the mensuration of time the scope of a watch, or life and health the designation of the human body.

Were I to define the British constitution, therefore, I should say, it is a limited monarchy, or a mixture of the three forms of government commonly known in the schools, reserving as much of the monarchial splendor, the aristocratical independency, and the democratical freedom, as are necessary, that each of these powers may have a controul both in legislation and execution, over the other two, for the preservation of the subjects liberty.

[12]Eighteenth-century watchmakers and clockmakers.
[13]Welfare of the people.

According to this definition, the first grand division of constitutional powers is, into those of legislation and those of execution. In the power of legislation, the King, Lords, Commons, and People, are to be considered as essential and fundamental parts of the constitution. I distinguish between the house of commons, and the people who depute them, because there is in nature and fact a real difference; and these last have as important a department in the constitution as the former, I mean the power of election. The constitution is not grounded on "the enormous faith of millions made for one." It stands not on the supposition that kings are the favourites of heaven; that their power is more divine than the power of the people, and unlimited but by their own will and discretion. It is not built on the doctrine that a few nobles or rich commons have a right to inherit the earth, and all the blessings and pleasures of it: and that the multitude, the million, the populace, the vulgar, the mob, the herd and the rabble, as the great always delight to call them, have no rights at all, and were made only for their use, to be robbed and butchered at their pleasure. No, it stands upon this principle, that the meanest and lowest of the people, are, by the unalterable indefeasible laws of God and nature, as well intitled to the benefit of the air to breathe, light to see, food to eat, and clothes to wear, as the nobles or the king. All men are born equal: and the drift of the British constitution is to preserve as much of this equality, as is compatible with the people's security against foreign invasions and domestic usurpation. It is upon these fundamental principles, that popular power was placed as essential in the constitution of the legislature; and the constitution would be as compleat without a kingly as without a popular power.—This popular power however, when the numbers grew large, became impracticable to be exercised by the universal and immediate suffrage of the people: and this impracticability has introduced from the feudal system, an expedient which we call a representation.——This expedient is only an equivalent for the suffrage of the whole people, in the common management of public concerns. It is in reality nothing more than this, the people chuse attornies to vote for them in the great council of the nation, reserving always the fundamentals of the government, reserving also a right to give their attornies instructions how to vote, and a right, at certain stated intervals of choosing a new, discarding an old attorney, and choosing a wiser and a better.—And it is this reservation, of fundamentals, of the right of giving instructions, and of new elections, which creates a popular check, upon the whole government which alone secures the constitution from becoming an aristocracy, or a mixture of monarchy and aristocracy only.

The other grand division of power, is that of execution.—And here the King is by the constitution, supreme executor of the laws, and is always present in person or by his judges, in his courts, distributing justice among the people. — But the executive branch of the constitution, as far as respects the administration of justice, has in it a mixture of popular power too. — The judges answer to questions of law: but no further. Were they to answer to questions of fact as well as law, being few they might be easily corrupted; being commonly rich and great, they might learn to despise the common people, and forget the feelings of humanity: and then the subjects liberty and security would be lost. But by the British constitution, *ad questionem facti respondent juratores,* the jurors answer to the question of fact. In this manner the subject is guarded, in the execution of the laws. The people choose a grand jury to make enquiry and presentment of crimes. Twelve of these must agree in finding the Bill. And the petit jury must try the same fact over again, and find the person guilty before he can be punished. Innocence therefore, is so well protected in this wise constitution, that no man can be punished till twenty four of his Neighbours have said upon oath, that he is guilty. So it is also in the tryal of causes between party and party: No man's property or liberty can be taken from him, till twelve men in his Neighbourhood, have said upon oath, that by laws of his own making it ought to be taken away, i.e. that the facts are such as to fall within such laws.

Thus it seems to appear that two branches of popular power, voting for members of the house of commons, and tryals by juries, the one in the legislative and the other in the executive part of the constitution are as essential and fundamental, to the great end of it, the preservation of the subject's liberty, to preserve the balance and mixture of the government, and to prevent its running into an oligarchy or aristocracy; as the lords and commons are to prevent its becoming an absolute monarchy. — These two popular powers therefore are the heart and lungs, the main spring, and the center wheel, and without them, the body must die; the watch must run down; the government must become arbitrary, and this our law books have settled to be the death of the laws and constitution. In these two powers consist wholly, the liberty and security of the people: They have no other fortification against wanton, cruel power: no other indemnification against being ridden like horses, fleeced like sheep, worked like cattle, and fed and cloathed like swine and hounds: No other defence against fines, imprisonments, whipping posts, gibbets, bastenadoes[14] and racks. This is that constitution which has prevailed in Britain from an immense antiquity: It prevailed, and the House of Commons and tryals by

---

[14]A stick or cudgel used to beat prisoners on the soles of their feet.

juries made a part of it, in Saxon times, as may be abundantly proved by many monuments still remaining in the Saxon language: That constitution which had been for so long a time the envy and admiration of surrounding nations: which has been, no less than five and fifty times, since the Norman conquest, attacked in parliament, and attempted to be altered, but without success; which has been so often defended by the people of England, at the expence of oceans of their blood, and which, co operating with the invincible spirit of liberty, inspired by it into the people, has never yet failed to work the ruin of the authors of all settled attempts to destroy it.

What a fine reflection and consolation is it for a man to reflect that he can be subjected to no laws, which he does not make himself, or constitute some of his friends to make for him: his father, brother, neighbour, friend, a man of his own rank, nearly of his own education, fortune, habits, passions, prejudices, one whose life and fortune and liberty are to be affected like those of his constituents, by the laws he shall consent to for himself and them.—What a satisfaction is it to reflect, that he can lie under the imputation of no guilt, be subjected to no punishment, lose none of his property, or the necessaries, conveniencies or ornaments of life, which indulgent providence has showered around him: but by the judgment of his peers, his equals, his neighbours, men who know him, and to whom he is known; who have no end to serve by punishing him; who wish to find him innocent, if charged with a crime; and are indifferent, on which side the truth lies, if he disputes with his neighbour.——

Your writings, Mr. Pym, have lately furnished abundant Proofs, that the infernal regions, have taken from you, all your shame, sense, conscience and humanity: otherwise I would appeal to them who has discovered the most ignorance of the British constitution; you who are for exploding the whole system of popular power, with regard to the Americans, or they who are determined to stand by it, in both its branches, with their lives and fortunes?——

CLARENDON

DECLARATIONS OF RIGHTS
AS INSTRUMENTS OF NEGOTIATION

Ten years separated the repeal of the Stamp Act in March 1766 from the American decision for independence. In both countries, politically astute leaders—men like Benjamin Franklin and Edmund Burke—thought they knew how to preserve the empire. Let Parliament proclaim its sovereignty over America if it wished, as it had in the Declaratory Act that accompanied the Stamp Act repeal, but also let it not apply that principle in practice. As heirs to a common political tradition, culture, and religion, and as the mutual beneficiaries of a powerful and prosperous empire, let Britain and America rely on commerce, language, and affection to preserve their political links.

Instead, a series of political crises brought the empire to the brink of collapse by the fall of 1774. Between 1767 and 1770 a fresh effort to impose taxes in the form of duties on imported goods brought renewed agitation and political violence. After these Townshend Duties were repealed, politics quieted down in most of the colonies during the early 1770s. But Massachusetts remained as turbulent as ever. There an explosive debate erupted in 1773 between the advocates of American rights, led by Samuel Adams and the newly organized Boston Committee of Correspondence, and the royal governor, Thomas Hutchinson. This debate revived the constitutional disputes of the late 1760s, and it set the stage for the repressive policy that the British government adopted after the Boston "patriots" opposed the enforcement of the Tea Act of 1773 by brewing three shiploads of dutied tea in Boston harbor.[15]

To punish Massachusetts, the ministry of Lord North forced a series of punitive acts through Parliament. Among other things, these measures closed the port of Boston until restitution was made for the sea-brewed tea; altered the colony's structure of government under its existing royal charter; and provided that British officials accused of crimes against colonists could be remanded to England for trial. Together, these Coercive Acts demonstrated that there were no practical limits to the parliamentary sovereignty proclaimed by the Declaratory Act of 1766. The issue was no longer taxation but the power of government in the broadest sense.[16]

In response, twelve colonies sent delegates to the First Continental Congress, which convened in Philadelphia in September 1774. The statement of rights it adopted on October 14 was both an affirmation of American claims and an ultimatum, for it ended by insisting that stability could

---

[15]The debate and its consequences are examined in Bailyn, *Ordeal of Hutchinson*, 201–11; and Richard D. Brown, *Revolutionary Politics in Massachusetts; The Boston Committee of Correspondence and the Towns, 1772–1774* (Cambridge: Harvard University Press, 1970), 85–121.

[16]On the Tea Act resistance and its consequences, see Benjamin W. Labaree, *The Boston Tea Party* (New York: Oxford University Press, 1964), 80–216; and Bernard Donoughue, *British Politics and the American Revolution: The Path to War, 1773–1775* (London, 1964), 36–126.

be restored only when a host of offensive parliamentary measures were repealed. Like other such statements, the Declaration revealed the multiple sources of authority on which Americans drew. But in another sense, the Declaration also corresponded to the traditional notion that bills of rights were acts of negotiation or compacts, as had been the case with Magna Carta in 1215 and the Declaration of Rights in 1689.[17]

In the following resolutions, the abbreviation "N.C.D." stands for the Latin phrase, *nemine contra dicente,* signifying a unanimous vote (literally, "no man speaking against" — though in fact Congress voted by delegations). Resolutions 4 and 6 were not adopted unanimously. The sticking point for resolution 4 was the question of whether Congress should acknowledge that Parliament could still regulate imperial commerce, and if so, on what basis; for resolution 6, it was perhaps the wisdom of conceding that any other statutes of Parliament could apply to America.

[17]For the politics of the First Continental Congress, see David Ammerman, *In the Common Cause: American Response to the Coercive Acts of 1774* (Charlottesville: University Press of Virginia, 1974); Jack N. Rakove, *The Beginnings of National Politics: An Interpretive History of the Continental Congress* (New York: Alfred Knopf, 1979), 42–62; and Jerrilyn Greene Marston, *King and Congress: The Transfer of Political Legitimacy, 1774–1776* (Princeton: Princeton University Press, 1987), 67–130.

5

CONTINENTAL CONGRESS

Declaration and Resolves

October 14, 1774

Whereas, since the close of the last war, the British parliament, claiming a power of right to bind the people of America, by statutes in all cases whatsoever, hath in some acts expressly imposed taxes on them, and in others, under various pretences, but in fact for the purpose of raising a revenue, hath imposed rates and duties payable in these colonies, estab-

Continental Congress, *Declaration and Resolves, October 14, 1774,* from *Journals of the Continental Congress, 1774–1789,* Volume I. 1774, from the Library of Congress, Washington, Government Printing Office, (1904), 63–73.

lished a board of commissioners,[18] with unconstitutional powers, and extended the jurisdiction of courts of Admiralty, not only for collecting the said duties, but for the trial of causes merely arising within the body of a county.

And whereas, in consequence of other statutes, judges, who before held only estates at will[19] in their offices, have been made dependant on the Crown alone for their salaries, and standing armies kept in times of peace:

And it has lately been resolved in Parliament, that by force of a statute, made in the thirty-fifth year of the reign of king Henry the eighth, colonists may be transported to England, and tried there upon accusations for treasons, and misprisions, or concealments of treasons committed in the colonies; and by a late statute, such trials have been directed in cases therein mentioned:

And whereas, in the last session of parliament, three statutes were made; one, intituled "An act to discontinue, in such manner and for such time as are therein mentioned, the landing and discharging, lading, or shipping of goods, wares & merchandise, at the town, and within the harbour of Boston, in the province of Massachusetts-bay, in North-America;" another, intituled "An act for the better regulating the government of the province of Massachusetts-bay, in New England;" and another, intituled "An act for the impartial administration of justice, in the cases of persons questioned for any act done by them in the execution of the law, or for the suppression of riots and tumults, in the province of the Massachusetts-bay, in New England." And another statute was then made, "for making more effectual provision for the government of the province of Quebec, &c."[20] All which statutes are impolitic, unjust, and cruel, as well as unconstitutional, and most dangerous and destructive of American rights.

And whereas, Assemblies have been frequently dissolved,[21] contrary to the rights of the people, when they attempted to deliberate on grievances; and their dutiful, humble, loyal, & reasonable petitions to the crown for redress, have been repeatedly treated with contempt, by his majesty's ministers of state:

The good people of the several Colonies of New-hampshire,

---

[18]In 1767 the crown created an American Board of Customs Commissioners to supervise the collection of import duties, which the colonists had long evaded.

[19]That is, judges served at the pleasure of the crown.

[20]The Quebec Act of 1774, though not explicitly a response to the Boston Tea Party, was widely perceived as a threat to the colonists, not least because it extended the boundaries of Quebec into northwestern territories claimed by various colonies.

[21]Royal governors had the power to adjourn legislative sessions when they proved defiant.

Massachusetts-bay, Rhode-island and Providence plantations, Connecticut, New-York, New-Jersey, Pennsylvania, Newcastle, Kent and Sussex on Delaware, Maryland, Virginia, North Carolina, and South Carolina, justly alarmed at these arbitrary proceedings of parliament and administration, have severally elected, constituted, and appointed deputies to meet and sit in general congress, in the city of Philadelphia, in order to obtain such establishment, as that their religion, laws, and liberties may not be subverted:

Whereupon the deputies so appointed being now assembled, in a full and free representation of these Colonies, taking into their most serious consideration, the best means of attaining the ends aforesaid, do, in the first place, as Englishmen, their ancestors in like cases have usually done, for asserting and vindicating their rights and liberties, declare,

That the inhabitants of the English Colonies in North America, by the immutable laws of nature, the principles of the English constitution, and the several charters or compacts, have the following Rights:

Resolved, N. C. D. 1. That they are entitled to life, liberty, & property, and they have never ceded to any sovereign power whatever, a right to dispose of either without their consent.

Resolved, N. C. D. 2. That our ancestors, who first settled these colonies, were at the time of their emigration from the mother country, entitled to all the rights, liberties, and immunities of free and natural-born subjects, within the realm of England.

Resolved, N. C. D. 3. That by such emigration they by no means forfeited, surrendered, or lost any of those rights, but that they were, and their descendants now are, entitled to the exercise and enjoyment of all such of them, as their local and other circumstances enable them to exercise and enjoy.

Resolved, 4. That the foundation of English liberty, and of all free government, is a right in the people to participate in their legislative council: and as the English colonists are not represented, and from their local and other circumstances, cannot properly be represented in the British parliament, they are entitled to a free and exclusive power of legislation in their several provincial legislatures, where their right of representation can alone be preserved, in all cases of taxation and internal polity, subject only to the negative of their sovereign, in such manner as has been heretofore used and accustomed. But, from the necessity of the case, and a regard to the mutual interest of both countries, we cheerfully consent to the operation of such acts of the British parliament, as are bona fide, restrained to the regulation of our external commerce, for the purpose of securing the commercial advantages of the whole empire to the mother country, and the commercial benefits of its respective members; excluding every idea of taxation, internal or external, for raising a revenue on the subjects in America, without their consent.

Resolved, N. C. D. 5. That the respective colonies are entitled to the common law of England, and more especially to the great and inestimable privilege of being tried by their peers of the vicinage,[22] according to the course of that law.

Resolved, 6. That they are entitled to the benefit of such of the English statutes, as existed at the time of their colonization; and which they have, by experience, respectively found to be applicable to their several local and other circumstances.

Resolved, N. C. D. 7. That these, his majesty's colonies, are likewise entitled to all the immunities and privileges granted & confirmed to them by royal charters, or secured by their several codes of provincial laws.

Resolved, N. C. D. 8. That they have a right peaceably to assemble, consider of their grievances, and petition the King; and that all prosecutions, prohibitory proclamations, and commitments for the same, are illegal.

Resolved, N. C. D. 9. That the keeping a Standing army in these colonies, in times of peace, without the consent of the legislature of that colony, in which such army is kept, is against law.

Resolved, N. C. D. 10. It is indispensably necessary to good government, and rendered essential by the English constitution, that the constituent branches of the legislature be independent of each other; that, therefore, the exercise of legislative power in several colonies, by a council appointed, during pleasure, by the crown, is unconstitutional, dangerous, and destructive to the freedom of American legislation.

All and each of which the aforesaid deputies, in behalf of themselves and their constituents, do claim, demand, and insist on, as their indubitable rights and liberties; which cannot be legally taken from them, altered or abridged by any power whatever, without their own consent, by their representatives in their several provincial legislatures.

In the course of our inquiry, we find many infringements and violations of the foregoing rights, which, from an ardent desire, that harmony and mutual intercourse of affection and interest may be restored, we pass over for the present, and proceed to state such acts and measures as have been

---

[22]Vicinity, neighborhood.

adopted since the last war, which demonstrate a system formed to enslave America.

Resolved, N. C. D. That the following acts of Parliament are infringements and violations of the rights of the colonists; and that the repeal of them is essentially necessary in order to restore harmony between Great-Britain and the American colonies, viz:

The several acts of 4 Geo. 3. ch. 15, and ch. 34.—5 Geo. 3. ch. 25.—6 Geo. 3. ch. 52.—7 Geo. 3. ch. 41, and ch. 46.—8 Geo. 3. ch. 22, which impose duties for the purpose of raising a revenue in America, extend the power of the admiralty courts beyond their ancient limits, deprive the American subject of trial by jury, authorize the judges' certificate to indemnify the prosecutor from damages, that he might otherwise be liable to, requiring oppressive security from a claimant of ships and goods seized, before he shall be allowed to defend his property, and are subversive of American rights.

Also 12 Geo. 3. ch. 24, entituled, "An act for the better securing his majesty's dock-yards, magazines, ships, ammunition, and stores," which declares a new offence in America, and deprives the American subject of a constitutional trial by a jury of the vicinage, by authorizing the trial of any person, charged with the committing any offence described in the said act, out of the realm, to be indicted and tried for the same in any shire or county within the realm.

Also the three acts passed in the last session of parliament, for stopping the port and blocking up the harbour of Boston, for altering the charter & government of Massachusetts-bay, and that which is entituled "An act for the better administration of Justice," &c.

Also the act passed in the same session for establishing the Roman Catholick religion in the province of Quebec, abolishing the equitable system of English laws, and erecting a tyranny there, to the great danger, from so total a dissimilarity of Religion, law, and government of the neighbouring British colonies, by the assistance of whose blood and treasure the said country was conquered from France.

Also the act passed in the same session for the better providing suitable quarters for officers and soldiers in his Majesty's service in North-America.

Also, that the keeping a standing army in several of these colonies, in time of peace, without the consent of the legislature of that colony in which such army is kept, is against law.

To these grievous acts and measures, Americans cannot submit, but in hopes their fellow subjects in Great-Britain will, on a revision of them, restore us to that state in which both countries found happiness and prosperity, we have for the present only resolved to pursue the following peaceable measures:

1st. To enter into a non-importation, non-consumption, and non-exportation agreement or association.

2. To prepare an address to the people of Great-Britain, and a memorial to the inhabitants of British America, &

3. To prepare a loyal address to his Majesty; agreeable to Resolutions already entered into.

6

Rights in the First Constitutions

In the seventeenth century, most of the American colonies had been
organized under charters granted either by the crown or by the proprietors (like William Penn) to whom the crown had delegated the
power of government. Before 1774, the colonists often cited these charters as evidence for their right to be governed only by laws made with
their own consent. But because these documents were legally tanta-
mount to a grant of corporate privilege by the crown, their constitutional
authority was less than perfect. What the crown could offer it could also
revoke, though it would have to do so through well-defined legal procedures.

The collapse of royal rule after 1774 gave the colonists an opportunity
that no other people in the annals of history had been known to enjoy.
Believing that a tyrannical king had placed them in something like a state
of nature, the colonists had to undertake some positive act to reestablish
legal government through a process of collective deliberation and the
adoption of a written constitution. Amid the hectic circumstances of 1776,
it was not entirely clear exactly what conditions had to be met to make a
constitution fully constitutional so that it would attain a paramount
supremacy over all subsequent acts of government. Yet the idea that an
American constitution would have a different character from either the
royal charters of the colonial era or the British constitution marked a crucial innovation in American thinking. And because Americans believed
that all well-founded constitutions existed to secure rights that could be

better enjoyed under conditions of good government than in the anarchy of the state of nature, they tended to assume that declarations of rights should be attached to the new instruments of government they were forming. Yet just as the exact legal status of the new constitutions remained problematic, so too did the authority of the early declarations of rights.

CONSTITUTIONS: A NEW DEFINITION

One of the first to offer a new definition of constitution was the anonymous author (possibly Thomas Paine[1]) of *Four Letters on Interesting Subjects,* a tract published in Philadelphia in the spring of 1776. In his third essay, the author set out to debunk both the royal charter that Charles II had given William Penn in 1681, and the much-admired "frame of government" that Penn in turn gave his colonists in Pennsylvania in 1701. All charters of government, "when granted by individuals, are not only a species of tyranny, but of the worst form of tyranny," the writer argued, "because the grantors of them undertake, by an act of their own, to fix what the constitution of a country shall be. . . ." The true right to form a constitution belonged not to exalted individuals but to the people. "All constitutions should be contained in some written Charter; but *that* Charter should be the act of *all* and not that of *one man*. Magna Carta was not a grant from the Crown, but only agreed or acceded to by the Crown, being first drawn up and framed by the people."[2]

This emphasis on popular participation in framing a constitution would develop into a fundamental element of the new American theory. But before that idea could be perfected, it was first necessary to come to a clear agreement as to just what a constitution was. Was it a fundamental law, superior to all acts of government to be enacted later, or simply a super-statute, necessary to restore legal government, but subject to later revision by any duly assembled legislature? That was the question that the same writer took up in his final essay.

---

[1]The identification, which is far from certain, is suggested by A. Owen Aldridge, *Thomas Paine's American Ideology* (Newark, Del., 1984), 219–39.

[2]*Four Letters on Interesting Subjects* (Philadelphia, 1776), reprinted in Charles S. Hyneman and Donald S. Lutz, eds., *American Political Writing during the Founding Era, 1760–1805* (Indianapolis: Liberty Press, 1983), I, 381–2.

6

Four Letters on Interesting Subjects
1776

AMONG the many publications which have appeared on the subject of political Constitutions, none, that I have seen, have properly defined what is meant by *a Constitution,* that word having been bandied about without any determinate sense being affixed thereto. A Constitution, and a form of government, are frequently confounded together, and spoken of as synonomous things; whereas they are not only different, but are established for different purposes: All countries have some form of government, but few, or perhaps none, have truly a Constitution. The form of government in England is by a king, lords and commons; but if you ask an Englishman what he means when he speaks of the English Constitution, he is unable to give you any answer. The truth is, the English have no fixed Constitution. The prerogative of the crown, it is true, is under several restrictions; but the legislative power, which includes king, lords and commons, is under none; and whatever acts *they* pass are laws, be they ever so oppressive or arbitrary. England is likewise defective in Constitution in three other material points, viz. The crown, by virtue of a patent from itself, can increase the number of the lords (one of the legislative branches) at his pleasure. Queen Ann created six in one day, for the purpose of making a majority for carrying a bill then passing, who were afterwards distinguished by the name of the six occasional lords. Lord Bathurst, the father of the present chancellor, is the only surviving one. The crown can likewise, by a patent, incorporate any town or village, small or great, and empower it to send members to the house of commons, and fix what the precise number of the electors shall be. And an act of the legislative power, that is, an act of king, lords, and commons, can again diminish the house of commons to what number they please, by disfranchising any county, city or town.

IT is easy to perceive that individuals by agreeing to erect forms of government, (for the better security of themselves) must give up some part of their liberty for that purpose; and it is the particular business of a Constitution to make out *how much* they shall give up. In this sense it is easy

Letter IV, from *Four Letters on Interesting Subjects* (Philadelphia: Styner & Cist, 1776), from Lamont Library, Harvard University, microfiche W2571, Readex Early American Imprints 14759, pp. 18–22.

to see that the English have no Constitution because they have given up every thing; their legislative power being unlimited without either condition or controul, except in the single instance of trial by Juries. No country can be called *free* which is governed by an absolute power; and it matters not whether it be an absolute royal power or an absolute legislative power, as the consequences will be the same to the people. That England is governed by the latter, no man can deny, there being, as is said before, no Constitution in that country which says to the legislative powers, "Thus far shalt thou go, and no farther." There is nothing to prevent them passing a law which shall exempt themselves from the payment of taxes, or which shall give the house of commons power to sit for life, or to fill up the vacancies by appointing others, like the Corporation of Philadelphia.[3] In short, an act of parliament, to use a court phrase, can do any thing but make a man a woman.

A Constitution, when completed, resolves the two following questions: First, What shall the form of government be? And secondly, What shall be its power? And the last of these two is far more material than the first. The Constitution ought likewise to make provision in those cases where it does not empower the legislature to act. . . .

GOVERNMENT is generally distinguished into three parts, Executive, Legislative and Judicial; but this is more a distinction of words than things. Every king or governor in giving his assent to laws acts legislatively, and not executively: The house of lords in England is both a legislative and judicial body. In short, the distinction is perplexing, and however we may refine and define, there is no more than two powers in any government, viz. the power to make laws, and the power to execute them; for the judicial power is only a branch of the executive, the CHIEF of every country being the first magistrate.

A CONSTITUTION should lay down some permanent ratio, by which the representation should afterwards encrease or decrease with the number of inhabitants; for the right of representation, which is a natural one, ought not to depend upon the will and pleasure of future legislatures. And for the same reason perfect liberty of conscience, security of person against unjust imprisonments, similar to what is called the Habeas Corpus act; the mode of trial in all law and criminal cases; in short, all the great rights which man never mean, nor ever ought, to lose, should be *guaranteed,* not *granted,* by the Constitution; for at the forming a Con-

---

[3]The chartered government of the city.

stitution we ought to have in mind, that whatever is left to be secured by law only, may be altered by another law. That Juries ought to be judges of law, as well as fact, should be clearly described; for though in rare instances Juries may err, it is generally from tenderness, and on the right side. A man cannot be *guilty* of a *good* action, yet if the fact only is to be proved (which is Lord Mansfield's[4] doctrine) and the Jury not empowered to determine in their own minds, whether the fact proved to be done is a crime or not, a man may hereafter be found guilty of going to church or meeting.

THERE is one circumstance respecting trial by Juries which seems to deserve attention; which is, whether a Jury of Twelve persons, which cannot bring in a verdict unless they are all of one mind, or appear so; or, whether a Jury of not less than Twenty-five, a majority of which shall make a verdict, is the safest to be trusted to? The objections against an Jury of Twelve are, that the necessity of being unanimous prevents the freedom of speech, and causes men sometimes to conceal their own opinions, and follow that of others; that it is a kind of terrifying men into a verdict, and that a strong hearty obstinate man who can bear starving twenty-four or forty-eight hours, will distress the rest into a compliance; that there is no difference, in effect, between hunger and the point of a bayonet, and that under such circumstances a Jury is not, nor can be free. In favour of the latter it is said, that the least majority is thirteen; and the dread of the consequences of disagreeing being removed, men will speak freer, and that justice will thereby have a fairer chance.

POPULIST SUSPICIONS

The emerging idea that constitutions had to be adopted in special ways and framed to include some explicit declaration of rights was not an insight confined to a handful of well-read citizens like the author of the *Four Letters* or Jefferson. That idea was a sentiment that also percolated among the people at large — and perhaps nowhere more vigorously than in Massachusetts. In September 1776, the General Court asked the people of the Bay State to assemble in their town meetings and grant it the authority to "enact" a new constitution for the state. In theory, this prior delegation might provide an adequate expression of popular assent to the

---

[4]William Murray, the Earl of Mansfield and Lord Chief Justice, was widely suspected of attempting to subvert the law-finding power of juries.

process of constitution-making. But the legislature's request met widespread criticism from towns who argued that a sitting legislature could not rightfully draft the fundamental rules under which it would exercise power. One telling statement of opposition to the idea of a legislative promulgation of a constitution came from the farming town of Concord, twenty miles west of Boston, where the war with Britain had erupted in April 1775. Its resolutions of October 22, 1776, offer one of the most succinct and powerful expressions of the new idea of constitutionalism to be generated anywhere.

7

Resolutions of Concord, Massachusetts

October 21, 1776

At a meeting of the Inhabitents of the Town of Concord being free and twenty one years of age and upward, met by adjournment on the twenty first Day of October 1776 to take into Consideration a Resolve of the Honorable House of Representatives of this State on the 17th of September Last, the Town Resolved as followes ——

Resolve 1st. That this State being at Present destitute of a Properly established form of Government, it is absolutly necessary that one should be emmediatly formed and established ——

Resolved 2 That the Supreme Legislative, either in their Proper Capacity, or in Joint Committee, are by no means a Body proper to form & Establish a Constitution, or form of Government; for Reasons following.

first Because we Conceive that a Constitution in its Proper Idea intends a System of Principles Established to Secure the Subject in the Possession & enjoyment of their Rights and Priviliges, against any Encroachments of the Governing Part ——

2d Because the Same Body that forms a Constitution have of Consequence a power to alter it. 3d—Because a Constitution alterable by the Supreme Legislative is no Security at all to the Subject against any Encroachment of the Governing part on any, or on all of their Rights and priviliges.

Resolutions of Concord, Massachusetts, October 21, 1776; Boston Gazette and Country Journal, October 29, 1776, from Massachusetts Archives, microfilm vol. 156, folio 182.

Resolve 3d. That it appears to this Town highly necesary & Expedient that a Convention, or Congress be immediately Chosen, to form & establish a Constitution, by the Inhabitents of the Respective Towns in this State, being free and of twenty one years of age, and upwards, in Proportion as the Representatives of this State formerly ware Chosen; the Convention or Congress not to Consist of a greater number then the house of assembly of this State heretofore might Consist of, Except that each Town & District shall have Liberty to Send one Representative or otherwise as Shall appear meet to the Inhabitents of this State in General

Resolve 4th. that when the Convention, or Congress have formed a Constitution they adjourn for a Short time, and Publish their Proposed Constitution for the Inspection and Remarks of the Inhabitents of this State.

Resolved 5ly. That the Honorable house of assembly of this State be Desired to Recommend it to the Inhabitents of the State to Proceed to Chuse a Convention or Congress for the Purpas abovesaid as soon as Possable.

A True Copy of the Proceedings of the Town of Concord at the General Town meeting above mentioned ———— atts. Ephraim Wood Junr. Town Clerk

Concord October the 22. 1776

DECLARING RIGHTS: THE FIRST MODELS

Eight states drafted new constitutions of government during the year of independence, and two more followed suit in 1777. Perhaps the most important of these early documents were the constitutions of Virginia and Pennsylvania, the two most populous of the newly independent states. In Virginia the planter oligarchy that had ruled the colony for generations remained firmly in control, and it presided over a relatively smooth transition to the new republican regime. But in Pennsylvania a group of political upstarts dominated the convention, which met in the fall of 1776, producing a more radical model of government that remained the object of heated partisan controversy for the next decade and a half. Among other noteworthy provisions, the Pennsylvania constitution provided that no statute could be finally enacted until it had been published for the consideration of the people (an impossible condition to meet in wartime).[5]

The Virginia Provincial Convention began work on its constitution in

[5]Gordon S. Wood, *The Creation of the American Republic, 1776–1787* (Chapel Hill: University of North Carolina Press, 1986), 226–37; and see John N. Shaeffer, "Public Consideration of the 1776 Pennsylvania Constitution," *Pennsylvania Magazine of History and Biography*, 98 (1974), 415–37.

acts of those who, "under color of religion . . . disturb the peace, happiness, or safety of society." At Madison's behest, and with the support of two better-known leaders, Patrick Henry and Edmund Pendleton, the convention accepted broader phrasing affirming that "all men are equally entitled to the free exercise of religion," while it dropped completely the reference to the magistrate's authority to preserve social peace.

These changes indicate that the delegates cared about the precise way in which rights were expressed. Somehow the language mattered, presumably because it would guide both officials and citizens in performing their public duties. Yet neither in Virginia nor elsewhere did the framers of these first written constitutions attempt to determine exactly how these principles would be maintained and enforced. Some of these articles were so abstract as to be difficult to translate into the actual conduct of government. But even those articles that affirmed traditional Anglo-American civil rights were couched in language that seemed merely advisory and that did not make the protection of these rights the duty of any particular branch of government.

The Virginia Declaration — or rather the committee draft of May 27 — exerted significant influence in other states, including Pennsylvania. But there are some noteworthy differences of emphasis between the Virginia and Pennsylvania declarations. For example, Article II of the Pennsylvania bill offers a more robust and precise definition of the rights of conscience. Nor does the Virginia Declaration contain anything like the ringing affirmation of the right of emigration proclaimed in Article XV of Pennsylvania's bill — but then again, the most notable immigrants into eighteenth-century Virginia were tens of thousands of enslaved Africans. Pennsylvania, by contrast, was a magnet for free immigrants from England, Scotland, Ireland, and Germany.

These differences cannot disguise a more fundamental truth. Read together, the Virginia and Pennsylvania declarations reveal a common body of assumptions about the purposes of bills of rights. As Gordon Wood has noted, these documents offered "a jarring but exciting combination of ringing declarations of principles with a motley collection of common law procedures."[12] On the one hand, it was important to remind Americans of the fundamental purposes for which government was constituted; on the other, it was also vital to identify certain rules of conduct and law — civil rights — that Anglo-American history had hallowed.

---

[12]Wood, *Creation of the American Republic,* 271.

8

THOMAS JEFFERSON

Third Draft of a Constitution for Virginia, Part IV

June 1776

IV. Rights Private and Public

Unappropriated or Forfeited lands shall be appropriated by the Lands. Administrator[13] with the consent of the Privy council.

Every person of full age neither owning nor having owned [50] acres of land, shall be entitled to an appropriation of [50] acres or to so much as shall make up what he owns or has owned [50] acres in full and absolute dominion, and no other person shall be capable of taking an appropriation.

Lands heretofore holden of the crown in feesimple,[14] and those hereafter to be appropriated shall be holden in full and absolute dominion, of no superior whatever.

No lands shall be appropriated until purchased of the Indian native proprietors; nor shall any purchases be made of them but on behalf of the public, by authority of acts of the General assembly to be passed for every purchase specially.

The territories contained within the charters erecting the colonies of Maryland Pennsylvania, North and South Carolina are hereby ceded, released, & for ever confirmed to the people of those colonies respectively, with all the rights of property, jurisdiction and government and all other rights whatsoever which might at any time heretofore have been claimed by this colony. the Western and Northern extent of this country shall in all other respects stand as fixed by the charter of

until by act of the Legislature one or more territories shall be laid off Westward of the Alleghaney mountains for new colonies, which

[13]Jefferson's proposed title for a republican governor.
[14]A traditional land tenure in which the disposition of the estate was not limited to a particular class of heirs.

Thomas Jefferson Papers, New York Public Library. From Julian P. Boyd, ed., *The Papers of Thomas Jefferson* (Princeton: Princeton University Press, 1950), I, 362–64.

colonies shall be established on the same fundamental laws contained in this instrument, and shall be free and independant of this colony and of all the world.

Descents shall go according to the laws of Gavelkind,[15] save only that females shall have equal rights with males.

No person hereafter coming into this country shall be held within the same in slavery under any pretext whatever.   *Slaves.*

All persons who by their own oath or affirmation, or by other testimony shall give satisfactory proof to any court of record in this colony that they purpose to reside in the same [7] years at the least and who shall subscribe the fundamental laws, shall be considered as residents and entitled to all the rights of persons natural born.   *Naturalization.*

All persons shall have full and free liberty of religious opinion; nor shall any be compelled to frequent or maintain any religious institution.   *Religion.*

No freeman shall be debarred the use of arms [within his own lands or tenements]   *Arms.*

There shall be no standing army but in time of actual war.   *Standing army.*

Printing presses shall be free, except so far as by commission of private injury cause may be given of private action.   *Free press.*

All Forfeitures heretofore going to the king, shall go to the state; save only such as the legislature may hereafter abolish.   *Forfeitures.*

The royal claim to Wrecks, waifs, strays, treasure-trove, royal mines, royal fish, royal birds, are declared to have been usurpations on common right.   *Wrecks.*

No Salaries or Perquisites shall be given to any officer but by some future act of the legislature. no salaries shall be given to the Administrator, members of the Legislative houses, judges of the court of Appeals, judges of the County courts, or other inferior jurisdictions, Privy counsellors, or Delegates to the American Congress: but the reasonable expences of the Administrator, members of the house of representatives, judges of the court of Appeals, Privy counsellors, & Delegates, for subsistence while acting in the duties of their office, may be borne by the public, if the Legislature shall so direct. . . .   *Salaries.*

No person shall be capable of acting in any office, Civil, Military [or Ecclesiastical] who shall have given any bribe to obtain   *Qualifications.*

[15]A system of tenure in which land was equally divided among the heirs.

such office, or who shall not previously take an oath of fidelity to the state.

None of these fundamental laws and principles of government shall be repealed or altered, but by the personal consent of the people on summons to meet in their respective counties on one and the same day by an act of Legislature to be passed for every special occasion: and if in such county meetings the people of two thirds of the counties shall give their suffrage for any particular alteration or repeal referred to them by the said act, the same shall be accordingly repealed or altered, and such repeal or alteration shall take it's place among these fundamentals & stand on the same footing with them, in lieu of the article repealed or altered.

The laws heretofore in force in this colony shall remain in force, except so far as they are altered by the foregoing fundamental laws, or so far as they may be hereafter altered by acts of the Legislature.

9

VIRGINIA PROVINCIAL CONVENTION

Committee Draft of a Declaration of Rights

May 27, 1776

A DECLARATION of RIGHTS *made by the representatives of the good people of* Virginia, *assembled in full and free Convention; which rights do pertain to us, and our posterity, as the basis and foundation of government.*

1. That all men are born equally free and independent, and have certain inherent natural rights, of which they cannot, by any compact, deprive or divest their posterity; among which are, the enjoyment of life and liberty, with the means of acquiring and possessing property, and pursuing and obtaining happiness and safety.

Virginia Provincial Convention, *Declaration of Rights, committee draft, May 27, 1776, The Virginia Gazette,* no. 1295, June 1, 1776 (Williamsburg: Dixon & Hunter) from Lamont Library, Harvard University, microfilm NB21.

When he drafted the Virginia Declaration of Rights in 1776, George Mason was a neighbor and friend of George Washington and one of the most respected political figures in Virginia. Though reluctant to devote too much time to politics—because he had a large family to provide for—Mason was characterized as the embodiment of a virtuous patriot.

2. That all power is vested in, and consequently derived from, the people; that magistrates are their trustees and servants, and at all times amenable to them.

3. That government is, or ought to be, instituted for the common benefit, protection, and security of the people, nation, or community, of all the various modes and forms of government that is best, which is capable of producing the greatest degree of happiness and safety, and is most effectually secured against the danger of mal-administration; and that whenever any government shall be found inadequate or contrary to these purposes, a majority of the community hath an indubitable, unalienable, indefeasible right, to reform, alter, or abolish it, in such manner as shall be judged most conductive to the public weal.

4. That no man, or set of men, are entitled to exclusive or separate emoluments or privileges from the community, but in consideration of public services; which, not being descendible, or hereditary, the idea of a man born a magistrate, a legislator, or a judge, is unnatural and absurd.

5. That the legislative and executive powers of the state should be separate and distinct from the judicative; and that the members of the two first may be restrained from oppression, by feeling and participating the burthens of the people, they should, at fixed periods, be reduced to a private station, return into that body from which they were originally taken, and the vacancies be supplied by frequent, certain, and regular elections.

6. That elections of members to serve as representatives of the people, in assembly, ought to be free; and that all men, having sufficient evidence of permanent common interest with, and attachment to, the community, have the right of suffrage.

7. That no part of a man's property can be taken from him, or applied to public uses, without his own consent, or that of his legal representatives; nor are the people bound by any laws but such as they have, in like manner, assented to, for their common good.

8. That all power of suspending laws,[16] or the execution of laws, by any authority without consent of the representatives of the people, is injurious to their rights, and ought not to be exercised.

9. That laws having retrospect to crimes, and punishing offences, committed before the existence of such laws, are generally oppressive, and ought to be avoided.

---

[16]The royal prerogative of suspending the enforcement of a statute for a limited period.

10. That in all capital or criminal prosecutions a man hath a right to demand the cause and nature of his accusation, to be confronted with the accusers or witnesses, to call for evidence in his favour, and to a speedy trial by an impartial jury of his vicinage, without whose unanimous consent he cannot be found guilty, nor can he be compelled to give evidence against himself; that no man be deprived of his liberty except by the law of the land, or the judgment of his peers.

11. That excessive bail ought not to be required, nor excessive fines impossed, nor cruel and unusual punishments inflicted.

12. That warrants unsupported by evidence, whereby any officer or messenger may be commanded or required to search suspected places, or to seize any person or persons, his or their property, not particularly described, are grievous and oppressive, and ought not to be granted.

13. That in controversies respecting property, and in suits between man and man, the ancient trial by jury is preferable to any other, and ought to be held sacred.

14. That the freedom of the press is one of the great bulwarks of liberty, and can never be restrained but by despotick governments.

15. That a well regulated militia, composed of the body of the people, trained to arms, is the proper, natural, and safe defence of a free state; that standing armies, in time of peace, should be avoided, as dangerous to liberty; and that, in all cases, the military should be under strict subordination to, and governed by, the civil power.

16. That the people have a right to uniform government; and therefore, that no government separate from, or independent of, the government of *Virginia,* ought, of right, to be erected or established within the limits thereof.

17. That no free government, or the blessing of liberty, can be preserved to any people but by a firm adherence to justice, moderation, temperance, frugality, and virtue, and by frequent recurrence to fundamental principles.

18. That religion, or the duty which we owe to our CREATOR, and the manner of discharging it, can be directed only by reason and conviction, not by force or violence; and therefore, that all men should enjoy the fullest toleration in the exercise of religion, according to the dictates of conscience, unpunished and unrestrained by the Magistrate, unless, under colour of religion, any man disturb the peace, the happiness, or safety of society. And that it is the mutual duty of all to practice Christian forbearance, love, and charity, towards each other.

PENNSYLVANIA CONVENTION

Declaration of Rights

1776

1. That all men are born equally free and independent, and have certain natural inherent and inalienable rights, amongst which are the enjoying and defending life and liberty, acquiring, possessing and protecting property, and pursuing and obtaining happiness and safety.

2. That all men have a natural and unalienable right to worship Almighty God according to the dictates of their own consciences and understandings: And that no man ought, or of right can be compelled to attend any religious worship, or erect or support any place of worship or maintain any ministry, contrary to or against, his own free will and consent. Nor can any man, who acknowledges the being of a God, be justly deprived or abridged of any civil right as a citizen, on account of his religious sentiments or peculiar mode of religious worship. And that no authority can or ought to be vested in, or assumed by, any power whatever, that shall in any case interfere with, or in any manner controul, the right of conscience in the free exercise of religious worship.

3. That the people of this State have the sole, exclusive and inherent right of governing and regulating the internal police[17] of the same.

4. That all power being originally inherent in, and consequently derived from, the people, therefore all officers of government, whether legislative or executive, are their trustees and servants, and at all times accountable to them.

5. That government is, or ought to be, instituted for the common benefit, protection and security of the people, nation or community, and not for the particular emolument or advantage of any single man, family or set of men, who are a part only of that community: And that the community hath an indubitable, unalienable and indefeasible right to reform, alter, or abolish government in such a manner, as shall be by that community judged most conducive to the public weal.

---

[17]All matters of internal government.

Pennsylvania Convention, *Declaration of Rights, August 11, 1776, The Pennsylvania Gazette,* no. 2487, August 21, 1776, from Lamont Library, Harvard University, microfilm NB19.

6. That those who are employed in the legislative and executive business of the State, may be restrained from oppression, the people have a right, at such periods as they may think proper, to reduce their public officers to a private station, and supply the vacancies by certain and regular elections.

7. That all elections ought to be free, and that all free men having a sufficient evident common interest with, and attachment to the community, have a right to elect officers, or to be elected into office.

8. That every member of society hath a right to be protected in the enjoyment of life, liberty and property, and therefore is bound to contribute his proportion towards the expence of that protection, and yield his personal service when necessary, or an equivalent thereto; but no part of a man's property can be justly taken from him or applied to public uses, without his own consent, or that of his legal representatives; nor can any man who is conscientiously scrupulous of bearing arms, be justly compelled thereto, if he will pay such equivalent: Nor are the people bound by any laws, but such as they have in like manner assented to for their common good.

9. That in all prosecutions for criminal offences a man hath a right to be heard by himself and his council, to demand the cause and nature of his accusation, to be confronted with the witnesses, to call for evidence in his favour, and a speedy public trial by an impartial jury of the country, without the unanimous consent of which jury he cannot be found guilty, nor can he be compelled to give evidence against himself, nor can any man be justly deprived of his liberty, except by the laws of the land or the judgment of his peers.

10. That the people have a right to hold themselves, their houses, papers and possessions free from search or seizure, and therefore warrants, without oaths or affirmations first made, affording a sufficient foundation for them, and whereby any officer or messenger may be commanded or required to search suspected places, or to seize any person or persons, his or their property, not particularly described, are contrary to that right, and ought not to be granted.

11. That in controversies respecting property, and in suits between man and man, the parties have a right to trial by jury, which ought to be held sacred.

12. That the people have a right to freedom of speech, and of writing and publishing their sentiments; therefore the freedom of the press ought not to be restrained.

13. That the people have a right to bear arms, for the defence of themselves and the state; and as standing armies in the time of peace are dan-

gerous to liberty, they ought not to be kept up; And that the military should be kept under strict subordination to, and governed by, the civil power.

14. That a frequent recurrence to fundamental principles, and a firm adherence to justice, moderation, temperance, industry, and frugality, are absolutely necessary to preserve the blessings of liberty, and keep a government free: The people ought therefore to pay particular attention to these points in the choice of officers and representatives, and have a right to exact a due and constant regard to them, from their legislatures and magistrates, in the making and executing such laws as are necessary for the good government of the state.

15. That all men have a natural inherent right to emigrate from one state to another that will receive them, or to form a new state in vacant countries, or in such countries as they can purchase, whenever they think that thereby they may promote their own happiness.

16. That the people have a right to assemble together, to consult for their common good, to instruct their representatives, and to apply to the legislature for redress of grievances, by address, petition or remonstrance.

MASSACHUSETTS: A FINAL EXAMPLE

Having delayed adoption of a constitution at least in part to obtain the bill of rights they sought, the citizens of Massachusetts must have been heartened to read the elaborate declaration of rights that formed the first substantive part of the constitution they finally approved in 1780. There was nothing ambiguous about the relation of this declaration to *its* constitution; its thirty articles were explicitly compiled as "Part the First" of the constitution, while "Part the Second[:] The Frame of Government" was devoted to offices and institutions. Moreover, because both parts had been subject to the sovereign voice of the people, as spoken in the towns of Massachusetts, this was the first bill of rights to be fully constitutionalized in the new sense of the term.

Some of the most revealing passages in this final example of a state declaration are found in Articles II and III, which affirm freedom of conscience while simultaneously making clear that the legislature will retain some power to promote the cause of religion, even to the point of requiring "all the subjects" to attend religious services. Beyond revealing how strongly the Puritan pulse still beat in Massachusetts, Article III also illustrates the continuing association in American thinking between rights and duties. A right was not a power an individual could exercise completely at his or her discretion; its exercise remained bounded by norms of morality and obligation.

11

A Declaration of the Rights of the Inhabitants of the Commonwealth of Massachusetts

1780

A CONSTITUTION OR FRAME OF GOVERNMENT,
Agreed upon by the DELEGATES of the People
of the State of MASSACHUSETTS-BAY,
IN CONVENTION, Begun and held at *Cambridge*
on the First of *September,* 1779, AND Continued by
Adjournments to the Second of *March,* 1780.

To be submitted to the Revision of their Constituents, in Order to the compleating of the same, in Conformity to their Amendments, at a Session to be held for that Purpose, on the First Wednesday in *June* next ensuing.

A Constitution or Form of Government
for the Commonwealth of MASSACHUSETTS.

PREAMBLE.

THE end of the institution, maintenance and administration of government, is to secure the existence of the body-politic; to protect it; and to furnish the individuals who compose it, with the power of enjoying, in safety and tranquility, their natural rights, and the blessings of life: And whenever these great objects are not obtained, the people have a right to alter the government, and to take measures necessary for their safety, prosperity and happiness.

A Declaration of the Rights of the Inhabitants of the Commonwealth of Massachusetts, or *A Constitution or Frame of Government Agreed upon by the Delegates of the People of the State of Massachusetts-Bay* (Boston: Benjamin Edes & Sons, 1780), from Lamont Library, Harvard University, microfiche W2571, Readex Early American Imprints 16844, 6–14.

THE body-politic is formed by a voluntary association of individuals: It is a social compact, by which the whole people covenants with each citizen, and each citizen with the whole people, that all shall be governed by certain laws for the common good. It is the duty of the people, therefore, in framing a Constitution of Government, to provide for an equitable mode of making laws, as well as for an impartial interpretation, and a faithful execution of them; that every man may, at all times, find his security in them.

WE, therefore, the people of Massachusetts, acknowledging, with grateful hearts, the goodness of the Great Legislator of the Universe, in affording us, in the course of His providence, an opportunity, deliberately and peaceably, without fraud, violence or surprise, of entering into an original, explicit, and solemn compact with each other; and of forming a new Constitution of Civil Government, for ourselves and posterity; and devoutly imploring His direction in so interesting a design, DO agree upon, ordain and establish, the following *Declaration of Rights, and Frame of Government,* as the CONSTITUTION of the COMMONWEALTH of MASSACHUSETTS.

PART THE FIRST.

A Declaration of the Rights of the Inhabitants of the Commonwealth of Massachusetts.

Art. I. ALL men are born free and equal, and have certain natural, essential, and unalienable rights; among which may be reckoned the right of enjoying and defending their lives and liberties; that of acquiring, possessing, and protecting property; in fine, that of seeking and obtaining their safety and happiness.

II. IT is the right as well as the duty of all men in society, publicly, and at stated seasons, to worship the SUPREME BEING, the great creator and preserver of the universe. And no subject shall be hurt, molested, or restrained, in his person, liberty, or estate, for worshipping GOD in the manner and season most agreeable to the dictates of his own conscience; or for his religious profession or sentiments; provided he doth not disturb the public peace, or obstruct others in their religious worship.

III. As the happiness of a people, and the good order and preservation of civil government, essentially depend upon piety, religion and morality; and as these cannot be generally diffused through a community, but by the institution of the public worship of GOD, and of public instructions in piety, religion and morality: Therefore, to promote their happiness and to secure the good order and preservation of their government, the people of this Commonwealth have a right to invest their legislature with power to authorize and require, and the legislature shall, from time to time, authorize and require, the several towns, parishes, precincts, and other bodies politic, or religious societies, to make suitable provision, at their own expense, for the institution of the public worship of GOD, and for the support and maintenance of public protestant teachers[18] of piety, religion and morality, in all cases where such provision shall not be made voluntarily.

AND the people of this Commonwealth have also a right to, and do, invest their legislature with authority to enjoin upon all the subjects an attendance upon the instructions of the public teachers aforesaid, at stated times and seasons, if there be any on whose instructions they can conscientiously and conveniently attend.

PROVIDED notwithstanding, that the several towns, parishes, precincts, and other bodies-politic, or religious societies, shall, at all times, have the exclusive right of electing their public teachers, and of contracting with them for their support and maintenance.

AND all monies paid by the subject to the support of public worship, and of the public teachers aforesaid, shall, if he require it, be uniformly applied to the support of the public teacher or teachers of his own religious sect or denomination, provided there be any on whose instructions he attends; otherwise it may be paid towards the support of the teacher or teachers of the parish or precinct in which the said monies are raised.

AND every denomination of christians, demeaning themselves peaceably, and as good subjects of the Commonwealth, shall be equally under the protection of the law: And no subordination of any one sect or denomination to another shall ever be established by law.

IV. THE people of this Commonwealth have the sole and exclusive right of governing themselves as a free, sovereign, and independent state; and do, and forever hereafter shall, exercise and enjoy every power, jurisdiction, and right, which is not, or may not hereafter, be by them expressly delegated to the United States of America, in Congress assembled.

V. ALL power residing originally in the people, and being derived from them, the several magistrates and officers of government, vested with authority, whether legislative, executive, or judicial, are their substitutes and agents, and are at all times accountable to them.

VI. No man, nor corporation, or association of men, have any other title to obtain advantages, or particular and exclusive privileges, distinct from those of the community, than what arises from the consideration of

[18]Ministers.

services rendered to the public; and this title being in nature neither hereditary, nor transmissible to children, or descendants, or relations by blood, the idea of a man born a magistrate, lawgiver, or judge, is absurd and unnatural.

VII. GOVERNMENT is instituted for the common good; for the protection, safety, prosperity and happiness of the people; and not for the profit, honor, or private interest of any one man, family, or class of men: Therefore the people alone have an incontestible, unalienable, and indefeasible right to institute government; and to reform, alter, or totally change the same, when their protection, safety, prosperity and happiness require it.

VIII. IN order to prevent those, who are vested with authority, from becoming oppressors, the people have a right, at such periods and in such manner as they shall establish by their frame of government, to cause their public officers to return to private life; and to fill up vacant places by certain and regular elections and appointments.

IX. ALL elections ought to be free; and all the inhabitants of this Commonwealth, having such qualifications as they shall establish by their frame of government, have an equal right to elect officers, and to be elected, for public employments.

X. EACH individual of the society has a right to be protected by it in the enjoyment of his life, liberty and property, according to standing laws. He is obliged, consequently, to contribute his share to the expense of this protection; to give his personal service, or an equivalent, when necessary: But no part of the property of any individual, can, with justice, be taken from him, or applied to public uses, without his own consent, or that of the representative body of the people: In fine, the people of this Commonwealth are not controulable by any other laws, than those to which their constitutional representative body have given their consent. And whenever the public exigencies require, that the property of any individual should be appropriated to public uses, he shall receive a reasonable compensation therefor.

XI. EVERY subject of the Commonwealth ought to find a certain remedy, by having recourse to the laws, for all injuries or wrongs which he may receive in his person, property, or character. He ought to obtain right and justice freely, and without being obliged to purchase it; compleatly, and without any denial; promptly, and without delay; conformably to the laws.

XII. No subject shall be held to answer for any crime or offence, until the same is fully and plainly, substantially and formally, described to him; or be compelled to accuse, or furnish evidence against himself. And every subject shall have a right to produce all proofs, that may be favourable to him; to meet the witnesses against him face to face, and to be fully heard in his defence by himself, or his council, at his election. And no subject shall be arrested, imprisoned, despoiled, or deprived of his property, immunities, or privileges, put out of the protection of the law, exiled, or deprived of his life, liberty, or estate, but by the judgment of his peers, or the law of the land.

AND the legislature shall not make any law, that shall subject any person to a capital or infamous punishment, excepting for the government of the army and navy, without trial by jury.

XIII. IN criminal prosecutions, the verification of facts in the vicinity where they happen, is one of the greatest securities of the life, liberty, and property of the citizen.

XIV. EVERY subject has a right to be secure from all unreasonable searches, and seizures of his person, his houses, his papers, and all his possessions. All warrants, therefore, are contrary to this right, if the cause or foundation of them be not previously supported by oath or affirmation; and if the order in the warrant to a civil officer, to make search in suspected places, or to arrest one or more suspected persons, or to seize their property, be not accompanied with a special designation of the persons or objects of search, arrest, or seizure: and no warrant ought to be issued but in cases, and with the formalities, prescribed by the laws.

XV. IN all controversies concerning property, and in all suits between two or more persons, except in cases in which it has heretofore been otherways used and practised, the parties have a right to a trial by jury; and this method of procedure shall be held sacred, unless, in causes arising on the high-seas, and such as relate to mariners wages, the legislature shall hereafter find it necessary to alter it.

XVI. THE liberty of the press is essential to the security of freedom in a state: it ought not, therefore, to be restrained in this Commonwealth.

XVII. THE people have a right to keep and to bear arms for the common defence. And as in time of peace armies are dangerous to liberty, they ought not to be maintained without the consent of the legislature; and the military power shall always be held in an exact subordination to the civil authority, and be governed by it.

XVIII. A FREQUENT recurrence to the fundamental principles of the constitution, and a constant adherence to those of piety, justice, moderation, temperance, industry, and frugality, are absolutely necessary to preserve the advantages of liberty, and to maintain a free government: The people ought, consequently, to have a particular attention to all those principles, in the choice of their officers and representatives: And they have a right to require of their law-givers and magistrates, an exact and constant observance of them, in the formation and execution of the laws necessary for the good administration of the Commonwealth.

XIX. The people have a right, in an orderly and peaceable manner, to assemble to consult upon the common good; give instructions to their representatives; and to request of the legislative body, by the way of addresses, petitions, or remonstrances, redress of the wrongs done them, and of the grievances they suffer.

XX. The power of suspending the laws, or the execution of the laws, ought never to be exercised but by the legislature, or by authority derived from it, to be exercised in such particular cases only as the legislature shall expressly provide for.

XXI. The freedom of deliberation, speech and debate, in either house of the legislature, is so essential to the rights of the people, that it cannot be the foundation of any accusation or prosecution, action or complaint, in any other court or place whatsoever.

XXII. The legislature ought frequently to assemble for the redress of grievances, for correcting, strengthening, and confirming the laws, and for making new laws, as the common good may require.

XXIII. No subsidy, charge, tax, impost, or duties, ought to be established, fixed, laid, or levied, under any pretext whatsoever, without the consent of the people, or their representatives in the legislature.

XXIV. Laws made to punish for actions done before the existence of such laws, and which have not been declared crimes by preceding laws, are unjust, oppressive, and inconsistent with the fundamental principles of a free government.

XXV. No subject ought, in any case, or in any time, to be declared guilty of treason or felony by the legislature.

XXVI. No magistrate or court of law shall demand excessive bail or sureties, impose excessive fines, or inflict cruel or unusual punishments.

XXVII. In time of peace no soldier ought to be quartered in any house without the consent of the owner; and in time of war such quarters ought not to be made but by the civil magistrate, in a manner ordained by the legislature.

XXVIII. No person can in any case be subjected to law-martial, or to any penalties or pains, by virtue of that law, except those employed in the army or navy, and except the militia in actual service, but by authority of the legislature.

XXIX. It is essential to the preservation of the rights of every individual, his life, liberty, property and character, that there be an impartial interpretation of the laws, and administration of justice. It is the right of every citizen to be tried by judges as free, impartial and independent as the lot of humanity will admit. It is therefore not only the best policy, but for the security of the rights of the people, and of every citizen, that the judges of the supreme judicial court should hold their offices as long as they behave themselves well; and that they should have honorable salaries ascertained and established by standing laws.

XXX. In the government of this Commonwealth, the legislative department shall never exercise the executive and judicial powers, or either of them: The executive shall never exercise the legislative and judicial powers, or either of them: The judicial shall never exercise the legislative and executive powers, or either of them: to the end it may be a government of laws and not of men.

A LEGISLATIVE MILESTONE

Perhaps more important than any of the compilations of rights attached to the state constitutions, however, was a single bill that Thomas Jefferson drafted for Virginia in 1777 and introduced in the assembly in 1779, and that his younger ally James Madison succeeded in enacting in 1786. The Statute for Religious Freedom, effectively disestablishing religion in the largest state in the union, is a true milestone in American constitutionalism and the classic expression of its author's (and his ally's) underlying commitment to the separation of church and state.[19]

It is also a most curious text. Most of the apparent statute is in fact only its preamble: a rhetorically powerful but legally inefficacious statement of all the reasons why the legislature is "well aware" that coercion of religious belief and behavior lies beyond the competence of civil authority. The legally binding element of the text is contained in the single extended sentence of the second paragraph. And from the vantage point of a theory of constitutional rights, the final paragraph is the most curious of all: Here Jefferson conceded that while the rights of conscience "are of the natural rights of mankind," the statute itself could not place them beyond danger of "infringement," because a statute adopted by one assembly could be as easily amended or revoked by another. The right of conscience, in other words, was both natural in its origins and (for now) statu-

---

[19]For scholarly discussion, see the essays collected in Merrill D. Peterson and Robert C. Vaughan, eds., *The Virginia Statute for Religious Freedom: Its Evolution and Consequences in American History* (Cambridge, Eng.: Cambridge University Press, 1988).

tory in its legal authority—but it was not yet constitutional. Moreover, that reservation applied against the comparable article in the state's Declaration of Rights. That document, too, Jefferson and Madison agreed, could not be regarded as supreme law, because it had never been ratified by the people.

12

Virginia Statute for Religious Freedom

1786

Whereas almighty God hath created the mind free; that all attempts to influence it by temporal punishments or burthens, or by civil incapacitations, tend only to beget habits of hypocrisy and meanness, and are a departure from the plan of the Holy author of our religion, who being Lord both of body and mind, yet chose not to propagate it by coercions on either, as was in his Almighty power to do; that the impious presumption of legislators and rulers, civil as well as ecclesiastical, who being themselves but fallible and uninspired men, have assumed dominion over the faith of others, setting up their own opinions and modes of thinking as the only true and infallible, and as such endeavouring to impose them on others, hath established and maintained false religions over the greatest part of the world, and through all time; that to compel a man to furnish contributions of money for the propagation of opinions which he disbelieves, is sinful and tyrannical; that even the forcing him to support this or that teacher of his own religious persuasion, is depriving him of the comfortable liberty of giving his contributions to the particular pastor, whose morals he would make his pattern, and whose powers he feels most persuasive to righteousness, and is withdrawing from the ministry those temporary rewards, which proceeding from an approbation of their personal conduct, are an additional incitement to earnest and unremitting labours for the instruction of mankind; that our civil rights have no dependence on our religious opinions, any more than our opinions in physics or geometry; that therefore the proscribing any citizen as unwor-

From Merrill D. Peterson and Robert C. Vaughan, eds., *The Virginia Statute for Religious Freedom: Its Evolution and Consequences in American History* (Cambridge, Eng.: Cambridge University Press, 1988), xvii–xviii.

thy the public confidence by laying upon him an incapacity of being called to offices of trust and emolument, unless he profess or renounce this or that religious opinion, is depriving him injuriously of those privileges and advantages to which in common with his fellow-citizens he has a natural right; that it tends only to corrupt the principles of that religion it is meant to encourage, by bribing with a monopoly of worldly honours and emoluments, those who will externally profess and conform to it; that though indeed these are criminal who do not withstand such temptation, yet neither are those innocent who lay the bait in their way; that to suffer the civil magistrate to intrude his powers into the field of opinion, and to restrain the profession or propagation of principles on supposition of their ill tendency, is a dangerous fallacy, which at once destroys all religious liberty, because he being of course judge of that tendency will make his opinions the rule of judgment, and approve or condemn the sentiments of others only as they shall square with or differ from his own; that it is time enough for the rightful purposes of civil government, for its officers to interfere when principles break out into overt acts against peace and good order; and finally, that truth is great and will prevail if left to herself, that she is the proper and sufficient antagonist to error, and has nothing to fear from the conflict, unless by human interposition disarmed of her natural weapons, free argument and debate, errors ceasing to be dangerous when it is permitted freely to contradict them:

Be it enacted by the General Assembly, That no man shall be compelled to frequent or support any religious worship, place, or ministry whatsoever, nor shall be enforced, restrained, molested, or burthened in his body or goods, nor shall otherwise suffer on account of his religious opinions or belief; but that all men shall be free to profess, and by argument to maintain, their opinion in matters of religion, and that the same shall in no way diminish, enlarge, or affect their civil capacities.

And though we well know that this assembly elected by the people for the ordinary purposes of legislation only, have no power to restrain the acts of succeeding assemblies, constituted with powers equal to our own, and that therefore to declare this act to be irrevocable would be of no effect in law; yet we are free to declare, and do declare, that the rights hereby asserted are of the natural rights of mankind, and that if any act shall be hereafter passed to repeal the present, or to narrow its operation, such act will be an infringement of natural right.

PART TWO

The Constitution and Rights

7

Madison and the Problem of Rights

A comprehensive history of rights in American society would have to be democratic. It would have to view its subject, in no small measure, "from the bottom up," to ask what the deprivation of rights has meant to the disenfranchised or to explain how and why ordinary men and women were able to stand up for the rights they felt they owned. Such a history of rights in America would have to ask not only why the Supreme Court in 1954 decided to reverse sixty years of precedent to find that the deliberate racial segregation of public schools was unconstitutional but also where Rosa Parks and the freedom riders found the physical and moral courage to challenge the edifice of Jim Crow. It would have to explain not only how the multidenominational character of American Christianity fostered the separation of church and state, but also how Lillian and William Gobitis, ages twelve and ten, could refuse to pledge allegiance to the flag because it violated their religious scruples as Jehovah's Witnesses.[1] The history of rights, in other words, is not merely a matter of moral philosophy and constitutional theory and law; it is also a story of the beliefs, opinions, passions, and interests of ordinary Americans.

At other times, however, we have to pay special attention to the thoughts and acts of those possessing influence and power, or those endowed with exceptional abilities, because they were well situated to shape the course of events or because their ideas seem more profound than those of their contemporaries.[2] In the history of American ideas of constitutional rights, we find that James Madison is one such individual. His ideas about rights and their protection deserve special attention for the following three reasons.

First, Madison was the crucial actor at both the Federal Convention of 1787 and the First Federal Congress of 1789. To understand why the

---

[1] *Minersville School District v. Gobitis,* 310 U.S. 586 (1940).
[2] On this point, see Ralph Lerner, *The Thinking Revolutionary: Principle and Practice in the New Republic* (Ithaca, N.Y.: Cornell University Press, 1987), 1–38.

framers could leave Philadelphia without adding a bill of rights to the Constitution, we have to understand why Madison, who did so much to set their agenda, held bills of rights in such low regard. Yet two years later, it was only his repeated urging that led the reluctant members of Congress to propose the Bill of Rights to the states. Were it not for Madison, a bill of rights might never have been added to the Constitution—and this fact in turn justifies our asking why he reversed course to force his fellow congressmen to swallow what he called "the nauseous project" of amendments.[3]

Second, Madison's ideas about the protection of rights departed in significant ways from the beliefs that Americans held at the outset of the Revolution. Where traditional theory located the principal dangers to rights in the arbitrary acts of the executive, Madison realized that in a republic, the legislature could prove more oppressive. Where traditional theory held that the problem of rights was to protect the people *against* government, Madison realized that in a republic the pressing necessity was to find ways to protect one segment of the community— individuals and minorities—against the self-interested desires of popular majorities acting *through* government. And where traditional theory sought to protect the customary rights of local communities against the centralizing organs of the nation-state, Madison hoped to empower the national government to intervene *within* the states to defend rights against the threats that individuals faced within the very communities where they lived.

Third, because Madison's concerns have resonated throughout our history, it is all the more important to understand their origins. In part this is because his writings—notably his essays in *The Federalist*—exercise profound influence over modern interpretations of the Constitution. But it is true for another reason as well. Much as Madison foresaw, the history of rights in America has been inextricably intertwined with the structure of federalism—that is, with the existence of two distinct yet overlapping levels of government, national and state. The history of constitutional rights in the twentieth century can be written largely as a story of the use of federal power—both judicial and legislative—either to prevent states from acting in rights-denying ways or to require states to recognize new claims of rights. That does not mean that the national government has infallibly acted to enhance individual and minority rights. The Supreme Court long accepted the legitimacy of state statutes and

---

[3]Madison to Richard Peters, August 19, 1789, Robert Rutland et al., eds., *The Papers of James Madison* (Charlottesville: University Press of Virginia, 1979), XII, 346–47.

This portrait of James Madison, painted by the distinguished Philadelphia artist Charles Willson Peale (ca. 1792), captures him at the point where the leading framer of the Constitution was moving into active opposition to the policies of Secretary of the Treasury Alexander Hamilton.

local ordinances enforcing racial segregation,[4] and all three branches of the national government cooperated in legitimating the disgraceful internment of Japanese American citizens during World War II.[5] Nevertheless, most of the great milestones in the dramatic expansion of constitutional rights in twentieth-century America were passed when federal courts struck down state and local acts as violations of the fundamental liberties protected by the Bill of Rights and the Fourteenth Amendment. Yet at the same time, the reaction against the perceived excesses of federal power has also sustained a strong defense of the rights of states to operate as self-governing communities. And this reaction appeals not only to the last of Madison's amendments of 1789 (the Tenth)[6] but also to the states'-rights arguments that Madison and Jefferson incorporated in the Virginia and Kentucky Resolutions, written to protest the violation of the First Amendment by the federal Sedition Act of 1798.

Madison came to his libertarian convictions early. His education at the College of New Jersey (now Princeton University) gave him the deep commitment to the cause of religious liberty that he demonstrated at the Virginia Provincial Convention of 1776. When he returned to the Virginia assembly in 1784, after long service in the Continental Congress, he led the fight to defeat a general assessment (or tax) to support all ministers of Christianity; he then followed this success with another by securing passage of the celebrated Bill for Religious Freedom.[7]

But the crucial developments in Madison's thinking about rights took

---

[4]For the most famous decision legitimating segregation, see Charles A. Lofgren, *The Plessy Case: A Legal-Historical Interpretation* (New York: Oxford University Press, 1987).

[5]The best study is Peter Irons, *Justice at War: The Story of the Japanese American Internment Cases* (New York: Oxford University Press, 1983).

[6]The best short study of the drafting of this clause is Charles A. Lofgren, "The Origins of the Tenth Amendment: History, Sovereignty, and the Problem of Constitutional Intention," in Lofgren, *"Government from Reflection and Choice": Constitutional Essays on War, Foreign Relations, and Federalism* (New York: Oxford University Press, 1986), 70–115.

[7]This chapter draws extensively on a number of my own writings on Madison and rights, including "Mr. Meese, Meet Mr. Madison," *The Atlantic,* Dec. 1986, 77–86; "The Madisonian Theory of Rights," *William and Mary Law Review* 31 (1989–90), 245–66; "Parchment Barriers and the Politics of Rights, 1776–1791," in Michael Lacey and Knud Haakonssen, eds., *A Culture of Rights: The Bill of Rights in Philosophy, Politics, and Law: 1791 and 1991* (New York: Cambridge University Press, 1991), 98–143; and *Original Meanings: Politics and Ideas in the Making of the Constitution* (New York: Alfred Knopf, 1996). For further discussion of Madison's thinking, see Lance Banning, *The Sacred Fire of Liberty: James Madison and the Founding of the American Republic* (Ithaca, N.Y.: Cornell University Press, 1995); and Banning, "James Madison, the Statute for Religious Freedom, and the Crisis of Republican Convictions," in Merrill D. Peterson and Robert C. Vaughan, eds., *The Virginia Statute for Religious Freedom: Its Evolution and Consequences in American History* (Cambridge, Eng.: Cambridge University Press, 1988), 109–38.

place after 1785, as he grew alarmed about legislative and popular politics within the separate states. His concerns had several complementary dimensions. In part he was troubled by the inability of the state legislatures to provide adequate support to the Continental Congress, which, under the Articles of Confederation, generally had to ask the states to execute its decisions. However, Madison was increasingly disturbed by problems of the internal governance of each state. Some of these problems, he now believed, could be attributed to the defects of the state constitutions, which had been drafted amid conditions of haste and inexperience. The authors of these constitutions, he thought, had erred by concentrating power in the legislative branch of government, leaving the weaker executive and judiciary branches unable to resist legislative encroachments.

To this indictment of the formal defects of the state constitutions, however, Madison soon added a powerful *political* account of the reasons republican lawmaking was likely to prove harmful to rights. One part of his explanation emphasized the vices of the lawmakers themselves, too many of whom sought office for the wrong reasons of self-interest and personal ambition. But the deeper thrust of his concern was to suggest that the "injustice" he detected in state legislation arose because legislators were all too often acting to please their constituents. The people themselves were not innocent bystanders in the enactment of unwise or unjust laws—they were the real source of the problem because they saw politics as the means to assert their private interests and passions over and against the true public good of society and the legitimate rights and interests of their countrymen.

How had Madison reached these conclusions? Disillusionment with the character of his fellow lawmakers in the Virginia assembly was one source of his anxiety. Nor did he have reason to think that the other states were better governed. But a more immediate and concrete concern also shaped his thinking. In the months preceding the Philadelphia Convention, Madison became especially alarmed by the economic legislation that many of the state assemblies were contemplating. Efforts in various states to make paper currency a legal tender for the payment of private debts struck him as an assault on rights of property. The potential popularity of such measures offered a grim portent for the future. In a strikingly pessimistic mood, Madison imagined that America might increasingly resemble the societies of the Old World, with their impoverished peasants and propertyless urban workers.[8] Yet one

---

[8]Madison's long-lasting concern with this problem is discussed in Drew McCoy, *The Last of the Fathers: James Madison and the Republican Legacy* (Cambridge, Eng.: Cambridge University Press, 1989), 192–98.

crucial circumstance would still distinguish Europe from America. In Europe the right to participate in politics was narrowly limited, but here the right to vote was already so widespread as to be almost impossible to retrench. Should the balance of political power ever swing to the impoverished and unpropertied, what security would there be for protecting the fundamental right of property against unjust measures of taxation or redistribution?

In the spring of 1787, newly returned to Congress, Madison drew up a memorandum summarizing the conclusions he had reached. He opened this account of the "vices of the political system of the United States" with a list of the principal failings of the Articles of Confederation.[9] When he reached the ninth item in his ledger, however, the focus of his concern shifted to the problem of lawmaking within the states. There, Madison complained, the years since independence had seen "a luxuriancy of legislation," much of it poorly considered and quickly revised or repealed. But that was not the worst conclusion to be drawn.

> If the multiplicity and mutability of laws prove a want of wisdom, their injustice betrays a defect still more alarming: more alarming not merely because it is a greater evil in itself, but because it brings more into question the fundamental principle of republican Government, that the majority who rule in such Governments, are the safest Guardians both of public Good and of private rights.

Here, in this single extended sentence, Madison called into question the basic premise of a republican theory of rights.

In the standard view, the people at large had an inherent interest in protecting their rights against the abuse of power by their rulers. This was the conventional wisdom that Madison now turned on its head. The real source of the "injustice" (real or imagined) of state laws "lies among the people themselves," he noted. "In republican Government the majority however composed, ultimately give the law. Whenever therefore an apparent interest or common passion unites a majority[,] what is to restrain them from unjust violations of the rights and interests of the minority, or of individuals?" In answering this question, Madison developed the argument that received its final, polished form in the Tenth *Federalist*. When popular interests and passions were aroused, Madison concluded, neither "a prudent regard for the public good," nor "respect for character," nor even "religion" could provide the necessary restraint.

[9]Quotations in this and the following paragraph come from this memorandum, which is printed in Rutland et al., eds., *Papers of Madison* (Chicago: University of Chicago Press, 1962–), IX, 353–57.

No solution to the problem of protecting rights could be found in appealing to these different virtues. But if one extended the "sphere" over which republican government operated, it might be possible to provide a check that did not exist within the narrower bounds of local communities and even states. The larger and more diverse the society, the more difficult it would be for the wrong kinds of majorities to form, and thus to pursue their unjust ends at the expense of the rights of individuals and minorities.

The argument that rights and liberties would be more secure in a large national republic than they currently were in the smaller republics of the states was part of "the glad news that James Madison carried to Philadelphia" in May 1787.[10] But this hypothesis by itself does not capture all of the novelty of Madison's position. The separate states would not disappear from the map of American governance. They would continue to regulate most of the daily activities of the American people; and within their smaller compass, the wrong kinds of "factious" popular majorities would still form to pursue their unjust ends. Within the states, in other words, rights would still be in danger.

To deal with this persisting problem, Madison framed his most radical proposal of all: to give the national government an unlimited negative (or veto) over all state laws. With such a power, the national government would be able not only to defend itself against state efforts to obstruct national laws and policies but also to curb "the aggressions of interested majorities on the rights of minorities and of individuals." It would thus be enabled to act as a "disinterested & dispassionate umpire in disputes between different passions & interests in the State"—that is, within the individual states. And rather than specify the cases in which this powerful weapon might be put to use, Madison thought that it should be allowed to operate "in all cases whatsoever." The new bicameral Congress he proposed to create would thus be empowered to review all state laws— much as the king and his privy council had reviewed all colonial legislation before 1776.[11]

---

[10]This phrase is borrowed from the famous essay of Douglass Adair, "'That Politics May Be Reduced to a Science': David Hume, James Madison, and the Tenth Federalist," reprinted in Trevor H. Colbourn, ed., *Fame and the Founding Fathers: Essays by Douglass Adair* (New York: W. W. Norton, 1974), 93–106.

[11]Madison to Washington, April 16, 1787, in Rutland et al., eds., *Papers of Madison*, IX, 383–84. For general discussion, see Charles Hobson, "The Negative on State Laws: James Madison, the Constitution, and the Crisis of Republican Government," *William and Mary Quarterly*, 3d ser., 36 (1979), 215–35.

Nothing in this analysis suggests that Madison believed that a federal bill of rights would have any practical value in making rights more secure. If the national veto reached "all cases whatsoever," there would be no need to enumerate all the rights it was meant to protect. It seems likely, though, that Madison had also concluded that bills of rights were useless in any event. Two years earlier, when asked to offer his advice about the form of government that Kentucky might adopt when it was separated from its parent state of Virginia, Madison had included a list of rights that might be explicitly protected in the text of the constitution.[12] But since then, his assessment of the real political forces at work in the American republics had persuaded him that such rhetorical statements could rarely withstand the wishes of popular majorities or the wiles of ambitious lawmakers. Certainly the bills of rights attached to the existing constitutions had not prevented the injustices that Madison detected in the states. The real problem was to distribute the powers of government more wisely, both between the national government and the states, and within the national government itself. Nor had these bills of rights imposed any useful restraint on the ordinary citizenry whose impulses so alarmed Madison. The principles they proclaimed had seemingly had no more effect on popular passions than the other virtues whose force he doubted ("a prudent regard for the public good," "respect for character," and "religion"). Bills of rights were nothing more than "parchment barriers"; they were nice to read, perhaps, but had already been tried in the balance and found wanting.

None of Madison's colleagues in Philadelphia had thought about the problem of rights so deeply, and only a few of them were willing to accept his radical (or reactionary) proposal to give the national government an unlimited negative over the laws of the states. Their rejection of that proposal left Madison convinced that the Constitution would not, in fact, solve the problem of misrule and injustice in the states that so alarmed him. But on one point the delegates to the Federal Convention were in near agreement. There was no need to attach a declaration of rights, of the kind found in the state constitutions, to their proposed Constitution. The only dissenters from this view were the handful of delegates who refused to sign the Constitution and who then opposed its ratification, notably George Mason of Virginia, Elbridge Gerry of Massachusetts, and Luther

[12]Madison to Caleb Wallace, Aug. 23, 1785, in Rutland et al., eds., *Papers of Madison,* VIII, 351.

Martin of Maryland.[13] Yet almost immediately the absence of a bill of rights from the Constitution became a major rallying point for its opponents. Indeed, it was the one point on which this somewhat disjointed coalition found it easiest to agree.

[13]Martin left the Convention before it adjourned, but he certainly would not have signed it. Edmund Randolph of Virginia, the third of the nonsigning delegates present at the close of the Convention, did not include the omission of a bill of rights among his objections to the Constitution. Nor could he have done so easily, for in the course of his work on the committee of detail that prepared a draft constitution between July 26 and August 6, Randolph had argued that the type of rhetorical statements that were associated with the state bills of rights, "howsoever proper in the first formation of state governments, *is* unfit here; since we are not working on the natural rights of men not yet gathered into society, but upon those rights, modified by society, and *interwoven* with what we call the rights of states." James H. Hutson, ed., *Supplement to Max Farrand's* The Records of the Federal Convention of 1787 (New Haven and London: Yale University Press, 1987), 183.

8

Framing the Constitution

Two broad sets of issues converged to frame the agenda of the Federal Convention that came to order, eleven days late, on May 25, 1787. One was concerned with the problem of *federalism,* that is, the allocation of authority between two levels of government, state and national, each armed with certain sovereign powers both over the American people and in their behalf. Not only did the framers have to consider which powers were appropriate to each level of government, they also had to ask what would happen when the exercise of these powers overlapped or came into conflict. The second set of issues was concerned with the problem of *republicanism,* that is, with creating institutions of government that would operate in a stable equilibrium or balance with each other, but that would also be accountable to the influence and even control of the people at large. In addressing these problems, the framers drew on a rich body of constitutional theory and political practice. But arguably their thinking was most influenced by the lessons they drew from the experience of republican government under the state constitutions written since independence.

In Madison's view, the underlying problems of federalism and republicanism could ultimately be traced to a common cluster of causes: the "vices" of state legislators and the parochial, self-interested popular majorities whom they represented. The radical vice of the Confederation was that it obliged Congress to act *through* the state legislatures, whose voluntary compliance with national acts could never be taken for granted. A proper national government, Madison concluded, would be empowered to act on the people directly, enacting, executing, and adjudicating its own laws. Such a government could no longer retain the form of a unicameral congress. It would have to be reconstituted as a government in the full sense, with a bicameral legislature whose decisions would be supported (but also checked) by a constitutionally independent executive and judiciary. And to some extent, Madison believed, the new Congress would have to be insulated from the populist excesses of the people themselves.

For a legislature that was too responsive to the people was likely to legislate impulsively—and in ways that would violate the rights of different minorities within society.

Most Americans, and even some of the framers, expected the Convention to do little more than propose some obvious amendments to the Articles of Confederation, giving the existing Continental Congress new powers to regulate trade, collect revenues, and pursue legal remedies against delinquent states. But the agenda that Madison prepared in the spring of 1787 set the delegates on a more ambitious course, opening up a host of issues that took nearly four months to resolve. One set of issues—those relating to the election of Congress—was explicitly concerned with the vital right of representation. The Virginia Plan, which Madison and his colleagues drafted while they waited for the other delegations to appear, proposed abandoning the one state–one vote rule of decision that the First Continental Congress had adopted in 1774, and which the Articles of Confederation had preserved. In its place, the Virginia Plan proposed to apply some rule (or rules) of proportional representation to both houses of the new Congress. This demand quickly generated two sets of conflicts that preoccupied the delegates for the next seven weeks.[1]

The first conflict pitted delegations from the "small" states of New Jersey, Delaware, Maryland, and Connecticut against the large-state coalition of Virginia, Pennsylvania, and Massachusetts. The small-state delegates argued that their constituents would be foolish to place themselves entirely at the mercy of the populous states; at the minimum, their need for protection against large-state domination required retaining the rule of equal state voting in at least one house of Congress. Madison and his allies (James Wilson of Pennsylvania, Alexander Hamilton of New York, and Rufus King of Massachusetts) thought they could wear down the small states in the course of debate, in part by appealing to simple justice, and in part by demonstrating that three societies as different from each other as the large states obviously were could never form a coalition stable enough to dominate the others. But the small states had tough champions of their own in William Paterson of New Jersey and Roger Sherman and Oliver Ellsworth of Connecticut. They refused to back down, and in the crucial vote of July 16, the principle of an equal state vote in the Senate prevailed by the narrow margin of five states to four,

---

[1] For fuller discussion of the argument of this and the following two paragraphs, see Jack N. Rakove, *Original Meanings: Politics and Ideas in the Making of the Constitution* (New York: Alfred Knopf, 1996), 58–80.

with the Massachusetts delegation evenly divided when two of its members, Elbridge Gerry and Caleb Strong, sided with the small states.

By that point, the Convention had already decided the second great dispute over representation. From the start, the delegates agreed that elections to the lower house should be made by the people, and that representation there should be apportioned among the states by some rule of population or wealth — or both. But which rule should be followed? Delegates from the northern states, where slavery was either already abolished or on the road to abolition, argued that representation should be proportioned to free population only. Southern delegates, especially the militant slave-owners from South Carolina, insisted that their states deserved some additional representation for their slaves. Even though slaves could never be considered citizens, their labor would contribute to the national prosperity, southern delegates argued, and slave states deserved additional representation precisely to safeguard their interest in this peculiar form of property. Moreover, the fact that the five southern states would hold an initial minority in both houses of Congress gave them a strong incentive to lock a specific rule of reapportionment into the text of the Constitution rather than allow future congresses to determine when or how reapportionment should occur. Though northern delegates were loath to acknowledge that slavery deserved representation in any form, they conceded that the southern states were unlikely to ratify a Constitution that did not provide them with the political recognition they sought. Accordingly, they agreed to a clause apportioning representation among the states on the basis of population, with slaves (here described by the euphemism "other persons") being counted as three-fifths of free persons.

In many ways, these two intertwined debates represented the Convention's most sustained discussions of rights. The right of representation was the fundamental political right, and in two crucial respects, the Convention's decisions profoundly influenced how Americans hereafter thought about its essential meaning. First, the so-called Great Compromise over the Senate recognized that states, as semisovereign entities, had their own equal rights of representation; and it therefore embedded in the structure of American federalism a potentially undemocratic rule that gave very different aggregates of population the same weight in the upper house of Congress (and set an important precedent for the upper houses of the state legislatures).[2] Second, the three-fifths clause, for all

---

[2]That decision became, in a sense, even less democratic when the Seventeenth Amendment (1913) provided for the direct popular election of senators. Formerly, the fiction had been that the Senate represented either the states as corporate entities or their govern-

its odious association with slavery, was also the mechanism by which the Constitution made population, not wealth, the true principle of representation—and in a way that said that shifts in population among or even within states should be matched by shifts in the allocation of seats in the House of Representatives. For the candid alternative considered by the framers was to leave reapportionment to the discretion of Congress, which southern delegates correctly understood was a formula to enable initial majorities to preserve their advantage, regardless of changes in the distribution of population.[3]

Only after the Convention finally resolved these questions about representation did it turn its attention to the other two branches of government and to the task of determining just what the national government was supposed to do. In late July, the framers tried—and largely failed—to come up with a satisfactory solution to the problem of creating an independent executive who would be neither a monarch nor a mere creature of Congress. No one could easily imagine how a national executive could be safely elected, and serious problems arose with each of the three solutions the Convention explored: election by Congress, or by the people at large, or by an electoral college.[4]

In August the Convention turned its attention back to Congress. In place of the open-ended language in the Virginia Plan, which would have given Congress a broad, discretionary power to legislate, the framers gradually developed a list of specific "enumerated" powers that it would exercise. The debates of August also brought a reaction against the Senate, which many framers saw increasingly as a replica of the Continental Congress (because of the equal vote and its election by the state legislatures). This reaction worked to the advantage of the presidency. In early September the Convention accepted a committee report transferring the power to make treaties and appointments from the exclusive control of the Senate to the joint domain of the president acting with the advice and consent of the Senate. To preserve the political independence of the pres-

---

ments; now senators simply represented the people—or, in the case of places like Idaho, Wyoming, and Kansas, the people and their surrounding rocks, trees, trout, and wheat.

[3]That is what increasingly happened in any case as state legislatures remained under the dominance of rural interests after the massive movement of population to the cities had begun, and as these legislatures refused to apportion either their own districts or congressional districts to compensate for these shifts in population. That is why the Supreme Court's one person–one vote decisions of the early 1960s should be regarded as democratic, rights-protecting actions of the first order of magnitude. See Richard Cortner, *The Apportionment Cases* (Knoxville: University of Tennessee Press, 1970).

[4]Rakove, *Original Meanings,* 256–61; and see Shlomo Slonim, "The Electoral College at Philadelphia: The Evolution of an Ad Hoc Congress for the Selection of a President," *Journal of American History* 73 (1986), 35–58.

ident, the framers also created the electoral college—a body that would meet once in the separate states, cast its votes, and then immediately disband. And should these electors fail to produce a majority for any candidate (which most framers wrongly thought would usually be the case), the final choice would devolve on the House, voting equally by states, rather than the Senate.[5]

The third department of government, the judiciary, received the least sustained consideration. The Virginia Plan had offered a radical proposal, modeled on the New York constitution, to combine the executive and the members of the national judiciary in a council of revision, armed with a limited veto over national legislation, including the exercise of the proposed national negative (or veto) over state laws. But a majority of the framers thought that a prior judicial involvement in lawmaking would make it difficult for the judges to assess the constitutionality of national laws when true legal cases later came before them. Moreover, in place of a congressional negative on state laws, the framers eventually endorsed the supremacy clause, which explicitly required state judges (and implicitly federal judges) to enforce the Constitution, national laws, and national treaties, "any thing in the laws or constitutions of any state to the contrary notwithstanding." The job of policing the boundaries of federalism—of resolving conflicts between national and state laws—would thus fall to the weakest, least-political branch of government, the judiciary.[6]

The adoption of this supremacy clause was one of the least discussed or controversial decisions the Convention took; it was also one of its most momentous. The same can be said about another clause that was quietly and unanimously endorsed on August 20, authorizing Congress "to make all laws necessary and proper for carrying into execution" its explicitly enumerated powers. Both clauses proved absolutely fundamental to the entire course of American constitutional history, and both figured prominently in the public debate over the Constitution that gathered force once the Convention adjourned on September 17.

To give the Constitution the authority of supreme law, and to circumvent the obstructive rule of the Confederation requiring that it could be amended only by the unanimous approval of all thirteen state legislatures, the framers also proposed to submit the Constitution to popularly elected conventions, with the approval of nine states required for its ratification. That would make the Constitution a true expression of popular sover-

---

[5] Rakove, *Original Meanings*, 262–68.
[6] Ibid., 171–77.

eignty, converting the abstract notion of an original compact of government into an explicit act of popular consent.[7] But that also meant that the Constitution had to run the gamut of popular debate and criticism. And in that debate, which escalated quickly in the early fall of 1787, the absence of a bill of rights from the Constitution soon loomed as one of the leading objections to its ratification.

The framers did not completely overlook the idea of including a declaration of rights in their proposed constitution. In piecemeal fashion, the framers adopted several clauses granting constitutional status to particular rights. The draft constitution that the committee of detail reported on August 6, 1787, included clauses requiring trial by jury in criminal cases and affirming that "the Citizens of each State shall be entitled to all privileges and immunities of citizens in the several States."[8] Two weeks later, Charles Pinckney of South Carolina proposed a set of resolutions that included the writ of *habeas corpus* and a ban on religious tests for office, both of which the framers eventually endorsed; but four other rights-like statements (one affirming liberty of the press, the other three relating to the military) fell by the way.[9] Later still, the Convention adopted clauses prohibiting the states from emitting bills of credit and from enacting laws impairing the obligation of contracts. Both measures can be seen as efforts to protect rights of property against the sort of "vicious" state legislation that Madison and other framers so detested.[10]

The Convention's sole discussion of the value of a bill of rights, however, took place on September 12, a scant five days before adjournment. After Hugh Williamson of North Carolina noted "that no provision was yet made for juries in Civil cases," George Mason and Elbridge Gerry moved to appoint "a Committee to prepare a Bill of Rights." As Mason explained, such an addition to "the plan . . . would give great quiet to the people; and with the aid of the State declarations, a bill might be prepared

---

[7] Rakove, *Original Meanings,* 102–08. The legality and significance of this decision have been much disputed recently by a number of legal scholars. See Akhil Amar, "Philadelphia Revisited: Amending the Constitution Outside Article V," *University of Chicago Law Review* 55 (1988), 1043–1104; Amar, "The Consent of the Governed: Constitutional Amendment Outside Article V," *Columbia Law Review* 94 (1994), 457–508; Bruce Ackerman and Neal Katyal, "Our Unconventional Founding," *University of Chicago Law Review* 62 (1995), 475–573; Richard McKay, "The Illegality of the Constitution," *Constitutional Commentary* 4 (1987), 57–80.

[8] Max Farrand, ed., *The Records of the Federal Convention of 1787,* rev. ed. (New Haven and London: Yale University Press, 1937 [reprint ed., 1966]), II, 187.

[9] Farrand, ed., *Records,* II, 334–35, 340–42.

[10] Farrand, ed., *Records,* II, 439–40, 597, 619; and see Steven R. Boyd, "The Contract Clause and the Evolution of American Federalism, 1789–1815," *William and Mary Quarterly,* 3d ser., 44 (1987), 531–33.

in a few hours." By this point, it was known that Mason and Gerry were nearly determined not to sign the completed Constitution. Had the other framers wished to be conciliatory, they could have granted Mason and Gerry's request; instead, they rejected the motion out of hand, ten states to none. The whole exchange could not have taken ten minutes.[11]

One clue to the ease with which the framers dismissed the idea of including a bill of rights appears in a document written some weeks earlier by Edmund Randolph, the third delegate who joined Mason and Gerry in refusing to sign the Constitution. As a member of the five-man committee of detail that was appointed in late July to produce a working draft of the Constitution, Randolph had prepared a memorandum outlining the form the document should take. In it, Randolph suggested, in almost derisory terms, that the grand rhetorical statements associated with the state declarations of rights had no place in a national charter. "This display of theory, howsoever proper in the first formation of state governments, is unfit here," Randolph observed, "since we are not working on the natural rights of men not yet gathered into society, but upon those rights, modified by society, and interwoven with what we call the rights of states."[12] Many of his colleagues must have shared this opinion when they turned the Mason-Gerry motion aside on September 12.

Had the framers thought more deeply about the "great quiet" the inclusion of a bill of rights would give the American people, they might well have accepted Mason's advice and made the task of securing ratification of the Constitution much simpler. But the framers gave the matter little thought, only to learn quite soon that many Americans indeed found their oversight alarming.

[11]Farrand, ed., *Records,* II, 587–88.
[12]See Edmund Randolph, "Draft Sketch of Constitution," in James H. Hutson, ed., *Supplement to Max Farrand's The Records of the Federal Convention of 1787* (New Haven and London: Yale University Press, 1987), 183 and n. 1, for an explanation of the difference between the passage quoted here and other phrasing in the manuscript.

9

The Basic Positions Stated

Opposition to the Constitution first formed within the Federal Convention itself, among the handful of delegates who could not support its adoption. In the waning days of the Convention, George Mason drew up a list of the reasons that had convinced him "that he would sooner chop off his right hand than put it to the Constitution as it now stands."[1] Before leaving Philadelphia, he shared his objections with a circle of Pennsylvania politicians who could be expected to oppose the Constitution. He also sent a copy to Richard Henry Lee, an old Virginia ally who had declined election to the Convention on the grounds that, as a member of the Continental Congress, it would be improper for him to sit in judgment in New York on the same document that he had drafted in Philadelphia.

It was in these two cities that the first skirmishes over the proposed Constitution were fought in the early fall of 1787. Both cities had a vigorous press, and it was from there that most news, foreign and domestic, flowed to outlying communities north, south, and west. But there were political reasons, too, why New York and Philadelphia played key roles in the early struggle over ratification. For the framers and their Federalist supporters, it was crucial to gain the early endorsement of the Continental Congress for the ratification procedures that the Convention had proposed, if not for the Constitution itself. That was why no fewer than ten framers—including James Madison—promptly left Philadelphia to resume their seats in Congress (untroubled by the qualms that had kept Richard Henry Lee in New York all along).

They left behind them in Philadelphia, however, a volatile political situation. When the Convention adjourned *sine die* (indefinitely) on September 17, the Pennsylvania assembly was also meeting upstairs in the Statehouse. Quick action by the assembly to call elections for the ratification convention would get the Constitution off to a good start in the sec-

---

[1] Max Farrand, ed., *The Records of the Federal Convention of 1787,* rev. ed. (New Haven and London: Yale University Press, 1937 [reprint ed., 1966]), II, 479.

ond most populous state in the Union. Moreover, Federalist leaders in Pennsylvania hoped that victory for the proposed Constitution would boost their own efforts to replace the radical state constitution that they had opposed since its adoption in 1776. With these dual objectives in mind, Pennsylvania Federalists were in no mood to conciliate their opponents. Their hardball politics made Anti-Federalist warnings about the darker motives of the Constitution's supporters all the more credible, helping to convince other citizens that a bill of rights might indeed act as a useful restraint on the power of the new government.

A FIRST TRY AT AMENDMENTS

Mason began his list of objections to the Constitution with the complaint that "There is no Declaration of Rights," and near the close of this document, he returned to the same theme. "There is no Declaration of any kind, for preserving the Liberty of the Press, or the Tryal by jury in civil Causes; nor against the Danger of standing Armys in time of Peace."[2] With Mason's comments before him, Richard Henry Lee fashioned a strategy to amend the Constitution *before* it could be transmitted by Congress to the states. In his view, Congress had every right of its own to take the Constitution simply as a report or recommendations presented to it by the Convention. And if that were the case, why should Congress not add such amendments or alterations as it deemed necessary? Accordingly, when Congress took up the matter of the Constitution in late September, Lee introduced a set of amendments that took the form both of a declaration of rights and of changes in the structure of government itself.

Madison and the other framers sitting in Congress could not allow that stratagem to succeed. Not only did they oppose Lee's amendments on their merits, they also argued that if the Constitution were modified as Lee proposed, it would go to the states as the joint work of both the Convention and Congress. That in turn might bring the amending procedure of the Confederation back into play, with its futile requirement that all changes to the charter of national government secure the unanimous approval of the thirteen state legislatures.

On September 27, Congress easily turned back Lee's amendments, and instead endorsed the ratification procedure proposed by the Con-

---

[2]Mason, "Objections to the Constitution," in John Kaminski and Gaspare Saladino, eds., *The Documentary History of the Ratification of the Constitution* (Madison: State Historical Society of Wisconsin, 1976–), XIII, 348, 350.

vention. Like Mason, Lee was reduced to circulating his proposed amendments among his Anti-Federalist allies. Here they fell on fertile soil, helping to propel the case for a declaration of rights to the forefront of the Anti-Federalist position.

13

RICHARD HENRY LEE

Amendments Proposed to Congress

September 27, 1787

It having been found from Universal experience that the most express declarations and reservations are necessary to protect the just rights and liberty of mankind from the silent, powerful, and ever active conspiracy of those who govern—And it appearing to be the sense of the good people of America by the various Bills or Declarations of rights whereon the governments of the greater number of the States are founded, that such precautions are proper to restrain and regulate the exercise of the great powers necessarily given to Rulers—In conformity with these principles, and from respect for the public sentiment on this subject it is submitted.

That the new Constitution proposed for the Government of the U. States be bottomed upon a declaration, or Bill of Rights, clearly and precisely stating the principles upon which this Social Compact is founded, to wit;

That the rights of Conscience in matters of Religion shall not be violated—That the freedom of the Press shall be secured—That the trial by Jury in Criminal and Civil cases, and the modes prescribed by the Common Law for safety of Life in Criminal prosecutions shall be held sacred—That standing Armies in times of peace are dangerous to liberty, and ought not to be permitted unless assented to by two thirds of the Members composing each House of the legislature under the new constitution—That Elections of the Members of the Legislature should be free and frequent—That the right administration of justice should be secured

Richard Henry Lee, *Amendments Proposed to Congress* (New York, September 29, 1787), Accession 2000-document 112, NSDAR Americana Collection, National Society Daughters of the American Revolution.

by the freedom and independency of the Judges—That excessive Bail, excessive Fines, or cruel and unusual punishments should not be demanded or inflicted—That the right of the people to assemble peaceably for the purpose of petitioning the Legislature shall not be prevented—That the Citizens shall not be exposed to unreasonable searches, seizures of their papers, houses, persons, or property. And whereas it is necessary for the good of Society that the administration of government be conducted with all possible maturity of judgement; for which reason it hath been the practise of civilized nations, and so determined by every State in this Union, that a Council of State or Privy Council should be appointed to advise and assist in the arduous business assigned to the Executive power—therefore, that the New Constitution be so amended as to admit the appointment of a Privy Council, to consist of Eleven Members chosen by the President, but responsible for the advise they may give—for which purpose the Advice given shall be entered in a Council Book and signed by the Giver in all affairs of great concern. And that the Counsellors act under an Oath of Office—In order to prevent the dangerous blending of the Legislative and Executive powers, and to secure responsibility—The Privy Council and not the Senate shall be joined with the President in the appointment of all Officers Civil and Military under the new Constitution—That it be further amended so as to omit the Creation of a Vice President, whose duties, as assigned by the Constitution, may be discharged by the Privy Council (except in the instance of presiding in the Senate, which may be supplied by a Speaker chosen from the body of Senators by themselves as usual) and thus render unnecessary the establishment of a Great Officer of State who is sometimes to be joined with the Legislature and sometimes to administer the Executive power, rendering responsibility difficult, and adding unnecessarily to the Aristocratic influence; besides giving unjust and needless preeminence to that state from whence this Officer may come. That such parts of the new Constitution be amended as provide imperfectly for the trial of Criminals by a Jury of the Vicinage, and to supply the omission of a Jury trial in Civil causes or disputes about property between Individuals where by the Common law it is directed, and as generally it is secured by the several State Constitutions. That such other parts be amended as permit the vexatious and oppressive calling of Citizens from their own Country in all cases of controversy concerning property between Citizens of different States, and between Citizens and foreigners, to be tried in far distant Courts, and as it may be, without a Jury. Whereby in a multitude of Cases, the circumstances of distance and expence may compel men to submit to the most unjust and ill founded demands. That in order to secure the rights of the people more effectually from oppression, the power and respectability of the House of Representatives be increased, by increasing the number of Delegates to that House where the democratic interest will chiefly reside. That the New Constitution be so altered as to increase the number of Votes necessary to determine questions relative to the creation of new or the amendment of old Laws, as it is directed in the choice of a President where the Votes are equal from the States; it being certainly as necessary to secure the Community from oppressive Laws as it is to guard against the choice of an improper President. The plan now admitting of a bare majority to make Laws, by which it may happen that 5 States may Legislate for 13 States tho 8 of the 13 are absent—

That the new Constitution be so amended as to place the right of representation in the Senate on the same ground that it is placed in the House of Delegates thereby securing equality of representation in the Legislature so essentially necessary for good government.

A CRUCIAL FEDERALIST RESPONSE

When Lee proposed his amendments on September 27, Madison and other framers who had resumed their seats in Congress replied that there was no need to attach a bill of rights to the Constitution. In the states, Nathaniel Gorham observed, bills of rights were "intended to retain certain powers, as [the] Legis[lature] had unlim[ite]d powers." Madison put the point in slightly different terms. There was no need to add a bill of rights to the proposed Constitution, he observed, "because [the] powers are enumerated and only extend to certain cases."[3]

Read together, these two complementary points could be restated as these propositions:

- Bills of rights were appropriate for the states because their legislatures were understood to possess comprehensive (or plenary) legislative power that would extend to all objects of public regulation, unless specific limitations or exemptions were defined in their constitutions.
- The proposed federal Constitution, however, would delegate only a specific set of legislative powers to the Union.

---

[3] Kaminski and Saladino, eds., *Documentary History of Ratification*, XIII, 237.

- Hence, the people retained all rights that had not been explicitly alienated to the government.

The most important statement of this position came from James Wilson in a widely reported public speech of October 6, delivered to a supportive crowd gathered outside the Pennsylvania statehouse where the Federal Convention had met. Of all the framers of the Constitution, Wilson was the one who most clearly grasped the potential meaning of the theory of popular sovereignty. To counter the expected objection that the Constitution would destroy the sovereignty of the separate states, Wilson argued that sovereignty—the ultimate authority to rule—was not a property or attribute of government itself but rather something that always remained in the people, who were free to divide and delegate portions of it to state *and* national governments alike.[4]

But the *manner* in which that authority would be delegated was not the same for these two levels of government, Wilson told his Philadelphia audience. And in that difference lay a powerful reason for concluding that a federal bill of rights would be superfluous—and even dangerous: if the Constitution would not give the new government any authority to regulate certain activities, the addition of articles protecting those rights could be read to imply that some power over these liberties had indeed been granted. The fact that the Constitution did not explicitly protect rights of conscience or freedom of the press did not matter because nothing in its text could be read to suggest that Congress would have any power to meddle with religion or to regulate the press (except by granting authors limited copyrights over their works).

Whatever might be said about this argument on its merits, Wilson's speech proved crucial to the politics of ratification for two reasons. As the first framer to offer a public defense of the Constitution, Wilson in effect unilaterally established his ideas as an authoritative statement of the Federalist position. Second, and equally important, his argument proved vulnerable to one telling objection. After all, the Constitution did protect some rights explicitly—the right to trial by jury in criminal cases, for example, or the benefit of the writ of habeas corpus. But by the logic of Wilson's own argument, Anti-Federalists reasoned, those clauses should have been superfluous, for where had the Constitution granted the

---

[4]For Wilson's speech, its reception, and republication, see Kaminski and Saladino, eds., *Documentary History of Ratification,* XIII, 337–44. The best studies of Wilson's political thought are in Samuel H. Beer, *To Make a Nation: The Rediscovery of American Federalism* (Cambridge: Harvard University Press, 1993), 341–77; and Jennifer Nedelsky, *Private Property and the Limits of American Constitutionalism: The Madisonian Framework and Its Legacy* (Chicago: University of Chicago Press, 1990), 96–140.

national government any power to violate these fundamental securities for the liberty of the subject? If these rights were explicitly protected, did that fact not imply that other rights left unmentioned were now open to violation? If the Constitution already protected some rights, why should it not be amended to protect all the fundamental rights Americans cherished?

14

JAMES WILSON

Statehouse Speech

October 6, 1787

Mr. Wilson then rose, and delivered a long and eloquent speech upon the principles of the Fœderal Constitution proposed by the late convention. The outlines of this speech we shall endeavour to lay before the public, as tending to reflect great light upon the interesting subject now in general discussion.

Mr. Chairman and Fellow Citizens, Having received the honor of an appointment to represent you in the late convention, it is perhaps, my duty to comply with the request of many gentlemen whose characters and judgments I sincerely respect, and who have urged, that this would be a proper occasion to lay before you any information which will serve to explain and elucidate the principles and arrangements of the constitution, that has been submitted to the consideration of the United States. I confess that I am unprepared for so extensive and so important a disquisition; but the insidious attempts which are clandestinely and industriously made to pervert and destroy the new plan, induce me the more readily to engage in its defence; and the impressions of four months constant attention to the subject, have not been so easily effaced as to leave me without an answer to the objections which have been raised.

It will be proper however, before I enter into the refutation of the charges that are alledged, to mark the leading descrimination between the state constitutions, and the constitution of the United States. When the

James Wilson, "Statehouse Speech," October 6, 1787, *Pennsylvania Herald,* October 9, 1787. From Kaminski and Saladino, eds., *Documentary History of Ratification* (Madison: State Historical Society of Wisconsin, 1976–), XIII, 339–40.

people established the powers of legislation under their separate governments, they invested their representatives with every right and authority which they did not in explicit terms reserve; and therefore upon every question, respecting the jurisdiction of the house of assembly, if the frame of government is silent, the jurisdiction is efficient and complete. But in delegating fœderal powers, another criterion was necessarily introduced, and the congressional authority is to be collected, not from tacit implication, but from the positive grant expressed in the instrument of union. Hence it is evident, that in the former case every thing which is not reserved is given, but in the latter the reverse of the proposition prevails, and every thing which is not given, is reserved. This distinction being recognized, will furnish an answer to those who think the omission of a bill of rights, a defect in the proposed constitution: for it would have been superfluous and absurd to have stipulated with a fœderal body of our own creation, that we should enjoy those privileges, of which we are not divested either by the intention or the act, that has brought that body into existence. For instance, the liberty of the press, which has been a copious source of declamation and opposition, what controul can proceed from the fœderal government to shackle or destroy that sacred palladium of national freedom? If indeed, a power similar to that which has been granted for the regulation of commerce, had been granted to regulate literary publications, it would have been as necessary to stipulate that the liberty of the press should be preserved inviolate, as that the impost should be general in its operation. With respect likewise to the particular district of ten miles, which is to be made the seat of fœderal government, it will undoubtedly be proper to observe this salutary precaution, as there the legislative power will be exclusively lodged in the president, senate, and house of representatives of the United States. But this could not be an object with the convention, for it must naturally depend upon a future compact, to which the citizens immediately interested will, and ought to be parties; and there is no reason to suspect that so popular a privilege will in that case be neglected. In truth then, the proposed system possesses no influence whatever upon the press, and it would have been merely nugatory to have introduced a formal declaration upon the subject—nay, that very declaration might have been construed to imply that some degree of power was given, since we undertook to define its extent.

Another objection that has been fabricated against the new constitution, is expressed in this disingenuous form—"the trial by jury is abolished in civil cases." I must be excused, my fellow citizens, if upon this point, I take advantage of my professional experience to detect the futility of the assertion. Let it be remembered then, that the business of the Fœderal Convention was not local, but general; not limited to the views and establishments of a single state, but co-extensive with the continent, and comprehending the views and establishments of thirteen independent sovereignties. When therefore, this subject was in discussion, we were involved in difficulties which pressed on all sides, and no precedent could be discovered to direct our course. The cases open to a trial by jury differed in the different states, it was therefore impracticable on that ground to have made a general rule. The want of uniformity would have rendered any reference to the practice of the states idle and useless; and it could not, with any propriety, be said that "the trial by jury shall be as heretofore," since there has never existed any fœderal system of jurisprudence to which the declaration could relate. Besides, it is not in all cases that the trial by jury is adopted in civil questions, for causes depending in courts of admiralty, such as relate to maritime captures, and such as are agitated in courts of equity, do not require the intervention of that tribunal. How then, was the line of discrimination to be drawn? The convention found the task too difficult for them, and they left the business as it stands, in the fullest confidence that no danger could possibly ensue, since the proceedings of the supreme court, are to be regulated by the congress, which is a faithful representation of the people; and the oppression of government is effectually barred, by declaring that in all criminal cases the trial by jury shall be preserved.

This constitution, it has been further urged, is of a pernicious tendency, because it tolerates a standing army in the time of peace.—This has always been a topic of popular declamation; and yet, I do not know a nation in the world, which has not found it necessary and useful to maintain the appearance of strength in a season of the most profound tranquility. Nor is it a novelty with us; for under the present articles of confederation, congress certainly possesses this reprobated power, and the exercise of that power is proved at this moment by her cantonments along the banks of the Ohio. But what would be our national situation were it otherwise? Every principle of policy must be subverted, and the government must declare war, before they are prepared to carry it on. Whatever may be the provocation, however important the object in view, and however necessary dispatch and secrecy may be, still the declaration must precede the preparation, and the enemy will be informed of your intention, not only before you are equipped for an attack, but even before you are fortified for a defence. The consequence is too obvious to require any further delineation, and no man, who regards the dignity and safety of his country, can deny the necessity of a military force, under the controul and with the restrictions which the new constitution provides.

10

The Anti-Federalist Case

Scholars have not always found it easy to take seriously Anti-Federalist criticisms of the Constitution. In effect, they have shared the Federalist disdain for the small-minded, parochial, and fearful tenor of Anti-Federalist thought. And indeed, some Anti-Federalist writings bordered on fantasy and paranoia in depicting the evils to which the Constitution would lead. Yet many of their concerns had deep roots in the political culture of the eighteenth century, just as many Anti-Federalist predictions about the potential reach of national power have eventually come to pass. Anti-Federalists may have been "men of little faith" when it came to imagining how republican principles could be applied to a national scale of government, as the late Cecilia Kenyon argued in an influential essay.[1] But in another sense, as Bernard Bailyn observed more recently, Anti-Federalists were all too faithful to the political ideology that had carried the Americans into revolution in 1776.[2] For that ideology took as its starting points of analysis the universal propensity of all officeholders to seek additional power and the need to erect every possible fence against their improper ambitions.

If one began with such assumptions, then every step possible should be taken from the outset to limit the possibility that the necessary grants of power could be transformed into an absolute dominion over the states and the people. And the theoretical elegance of Wilson's argument did not seem all that reassuring. Anti-Federalists had three good reasons to dispute his claim that the Constitution had created a government

[1]Cecilia Kenyon, "Men of Little Faith: The Anti-Federalists on the Nature of Representative Government," *William and Mary Quarterly,* 3d ser., 12 (1955), 3–43. For other broad summaries of the Anti-Federalist position, see Jackson T. Main, *The Anti-Federalists: Critics of the Constitution, 1781–1789* (Chapel Hill: University of North Carolina Press, 1961); and Herbert Storing, ed., *The Complete Anti-Federalist,* vol. I, *What the Anti-Federalists Were For* (Chicago: University of Chicago Press, 1987).

[2]Bernard Bailyn, "The Ideological Fulfillment of the American Revolution: A Commentary on the Constitution," in *Faces of Revolution: Personalities and Themes in the Struggle for American Independence* (New York: Alfred Knopf, 1990).

endowed only with limited, enumerated, specifically delegated powers. First, the "necessary and proper" clause seemed to give Congress an open-ended invitation to legislate in any way it wished. Second, the general taxing powers of the national government would give it a powerful engine to increase its authority at the expense of the states. Third, under the supremacy clause, any duly made law that seemed necessary and proper to carry out the powers of national government must be deemed legally binding, regardless of the danger it might pose to the rights of the citizens. Should Congress find a plausible ("necessary and proper") pretext to pass a law affecting rights of conscience or freedom of the press, its act would become the supreme law of the land. Why, for example, could Congress not use its taxing power to impose something like the detested Stamp Act of 1765 on American newspapers, thereby restricting the free flow of information?[3]

Nor did Anti-Federalists doubt that Congress would be tempted to trample on the rights of both the people and their state governments. The members of the House of Representatives would be elected in districts so large that they would have little knowledge of, or sympathy with, the daily needs and concerns of their constituents. Worse, the Senate seemed like a nursery for a true aristocracy. With its six-year terms and extensive powers—the legislative authority it shared with the House, the executive powers over diplomacy and appointments it shared with the president, and its judicial power as the court of impeachment—the Senate seemed the one branch of government most likely to gain a monopolistic hold over the other branches. The Anti-Federalists took no consolation in the idea that an independent judiciary, removable only by impeachment, would act as impartial guardians of the Constitution. For Anti-Federalists believed that juries, not judges, should be the true triers of law and fact alike; they saw any judicial system relying on juryless appellate courts as equivalent to the dreaded civil law courts of continental Europe, where the Anglo-Saxon benefits of trial by jury were unknown. The fact that Article III of the Constitution protected the right to trial by jury in criminal cases alone also implied that Congress was free to abolish trial by jury in civil matters.

For all intents and purposes, Anti-Federalists argued, the powers of the new government would reach every object of legislation, and as such, it was just as much in need of a declaration of the reserved rights of the

---

[3] In fact, Congress early acted to promote the exchange of ideas in the press by granting newspapers liberal privileges to use the postal service to exchange copies at minimal or no cost. See Richard R. John, *Spreading the News: The American Postal System from Franklin to Morse* (Cambridge: Harvard University Press, 1995).

people as the state governments had been in 1776. Without such a declaration, neither the people nor their governors would know the true limits of the power of the new government. Amid this uncertainty, what was to stop ambitious lawmakers and other officials from exceeding their powers, and how were the people to know whether their rights were being violated or not? Only a bill of rights could erect the landmarks necessary for both the rulers and the ruled to see and know whether the national government had overstepped its limits.

THE TRADITIONAL POSITION RESTATED

One of the clearest expressions of the underlying Anti-Federalist attitude can be found in the essays of "Brutus." Though his identity remains uncertain, modern commentators generally agree that the sixteen essays published under this pen name in the *New York Journal* between October 1787 and April 1788 rank high in the canon of Anti-Federalist writings—especially those late essays (XI–XV) that deal with the nature of judicial power.[4] In his second essay, "Brutus" offered a lucid statement of the fundamental Anti-Federalist reasoning in support of a bill of rights.

[4]See, for example, the assessment of the late Herbert Storing in *The Complete Anti-Federalist*, II, 358.

15

BRUTUS

Second Essay Opposing the Constitution
November 1, 1787

To the CITIZENS *of the* STATE *of* NEW-YORK.

I flatter myself that my last address established this position, that to reduce the Thirteen States into one government, would prove the destruction of your liberties.

But lest this truth should be doubted by some, I will now proceed to consider its merits.

Brutus, *No. II, The New York Journal and Weekly Register,* no. 44, vol. XLI, Thursday, November 1, 1787 (New York: Thomas Greenleaf).

Though it should be admitted, that the argument against reducing all the states into one consolidated government, are not sufficient fully to establish this point; yet they will, at least, justify this conclusion, that in forming a constitution for such a country, great care should be taken to limit and define its powers, adjust its parts, and guard against an abuse of authority. How far attention has been paid to these objects, shall be the subject of future enquiry. When a building is to be erected which is intended to stand for ages, the foundation should be firmly laid. The constitution proposed to your acceptance, is designed not for yourselves alone, but for generations yet unborn. The principles, therefore, upon which the social compact is founded, ought to have been clearly and precisely stated, and the most express and full declaration of rights to have been made—But on this subject there is almost an entire silence.

If we may collect the sentiments of the people of America, from their own most solemn declarations, they hold this truth as self evident, that all men are by nature free. No one man, therefore, or any class of men, have a right, by the law of nature, or of God, to assume or exercise authority over their fellows. The origin of society then is to be sought, not in any natural right which one man has to exercise authority over another, but in the united consent of those who associate. The mutual wants of men, at first dictated the propriety of forming societies; and when they were established, protection and defence pointed out the necessity of instituting government. In a state of nature every individual pursues his own interest; in this pursuit it frequently happened, that the possessions or enjoyments of one were sacrificed to the views and designs of another; thus the weak were a prey to the strong, the simple and unwary were subject to impositions from those who were more crafty and designing. In this state of things, every individual was insecure; common interest therefore directed, that government should be established, in which the force of the whole community should be collected, and under such directions, as to protect and defend every one who composed it. The common good, therefore, is the end of civil government, and common consent, the foundation on which it is established. To effect this end, it was necessary that a certain portion of natural liberty should be surrendered, in order, that what remained should be preserved: how great a proportion of natural freedom is necessary to be yielded by individuals, when they submit to government, I shall not now enquire. So much, however, must be given up, as will be sufficient to enable those, to whom the administration of the government is committed, to establish laws for the promoting the happiness of the community, and to carry those laws into effect. But it is not necessary, for this purpose, that individuals should relinquish all their natural rights. Some are of such a nature that they cannot be surrendered.

Of this kind are the rights of conscience, the right of enjoying and defending life, &c. Others are not necessary to be resigned, in order to attain the end for which government is instituted, these therefore ought not to be given up. To surrender them, would counteract the very end of government, to wit, the common good. From these observations it appears, that in forming a government on its true principles, the foundation should be laid in the manner I before stated, by expressly reserving to the people such of their essential natural rights, as are not necessary to be parted with. The same reasons which at first induced mankind to associate and institute government, will operate to influence them to observe this precaution. If they had been disposed to conform themselves to the rule of immutable righteousness, government would not have been requisite. It was because one part exercised fraud, oppression, and violence on the other, that men came together, and agreed that certain rules should be formed, to regulate the conduct of all, and the power of the whole community lodged in the hands of rulers to enforce an obedience to them. But rulers have the same propensities as other men; they are as likely to use the power with which they are vested for private purposes, and to the injury and oppression of those over whom they are placed, as individuals in a state of nature are to injure and oppress one another. It is therefore as proper that bounds should be set to their authority, as that government should have at first been instituted to restrain private injuries.

This principle, which seems so evidently founded in the reason and nature of things, is confirmed by universal experience. Those who have governed, have been found in all ages ever active to enlarge their powers and abridge the public liberty. This has induced the people in all countries, where any sense of freedom remained, to fix barriers against the encroachments of their rulers. The country from which we have derived our origin, is an eminent example of this. Their magna charta and bill of rights have long been the boast, as well as the security, of that nation. I need say no more, I presume, to an American, than, that this principle is a fundamental one, in all the constitutions of our own states; there is not one of them but what is either founded on a declaration or bill of rights, or has certain express reservation of rights interwoven in the body of them. From this it appears, that at a time when the pults of liberty beat high and when an appeal was made to the people to form constitutions for the government of themselves, it was their universal sense, that such declarations should make a part of their frames of government. It is therefore the more astonishing, that this grand security, to the rights of the people, is not to be found in this constitution.

It has been said, in answer to this objection, that such declaration of rights, however requisite they might be in the constitutions of the states, are not necessary in the general constitution, because, "in the former case, every thing which is not reserved is given, but in the latter the reverse of the proposition prevails, and every thing which is not given is reserved."[5] It requires but little attention to discover, that this mode of reasoning is rather specious than solid. The powers, rights, and authority, granted to the general government by this constitution, are as complete, with respect to every object to which they extend, as that of any state government—It reaches to every thing which concerns human happiness—Life, liberty, and property, are under its controul. There is the same reason, therefore, that the exercise of power, in this case, should be restrained within proper limits, as in that of the state governments. To set this matter in a clear light, permit me to instance some of the articles of the bills of rights of the individual states, and apply them to the case in question.

For the security of life, in criminal prosecutions, the bills of rights of most of the states have declared, that no man shall be held to answer for a crime until he is made fully acquainted with the charge brought against him; he shall not be compelled to accuse, or furnish evidence against himself—The witnesses against him shall be brought face to face, and he shall be fully heard by himself or counsel. That it is essential to the security of life and liberty, that trial of facts be in the vicinity where they happen. Are not provisions of this kind as necessary in the general government, as in that of a particular state? The powers vested in the new Congress extend in many cases to life; they are authorised to provide for the punishment of a variety of capital crimes, and no restraint is laid upon them in its exercise, save only, that "the trial of all crimes, except in cases of impeachment, shall be by jury; and such trial shall be in the state where the said crimes shall have been committed." No man is secure of a trial in the county where he is charged to have committed a crime; he may be brought from Niagara to New-York, or carried from Kentucky to Richmond for trial for an offence, supposed to be committed. What security is there, that a man shall be furnished with a full and plain description of the charges against him? That he shall be allowed to produce all proof he can in his favor? That he shall see the witnesses against him face to face, or that he shall be fully heard in his own defence by himself or counsel?

For the security of liberty it has been declared, "that excessive bail should not be required, nor excessive fines imposed, nor cruel or unusual

_____

[5] Quoting from James Wilson's speech of October 6, 1787.

punishments inflicted—That all warrants, without oath or affirmation, to search suspected places, or seize any person, his papers or property, are grievous and oppressive."

These provisions are as necessary under the general government as under that of the individual states; for the power of the former is as complete to the purpose of requiring bail, imposing fines, inflicting punishments, granting search warrants, and seizing persons, papers, or property, in certain cases, as the other.

For the purpose of securing the property of the citizens, it is declared by all the states, "that in all controversies at law, respecting property, the ancient mode of trial by jury is one of the best securities of the rights of the people, and ought to remain sacred and inviolable."

Does not the same necessity exist of reserving this right, under this national compact, as in that of this state? Yet nothing is said respecting it. In the bills of rights of the states it is declared, that a well regulated militia is the proper and natural defence of a free government—That as standing armies in time of peace are dangerous, they are not to be kept up, and that the military should be kept under strict subordination to, and controuled by the civil power.

The same security is as necessary in this constitution, and much more so; for the general government will have the sole power to raise and to pay armies, and are under no controul in the exercise of it; yet nothing of this is to be found in this new system.

I might proceed to instance a number of other rights, which were as necessary to be reserved, such as, that elections should be free, that the liberty of the press should be held sacred; but the instances adduced, are sufficient to prove, that this argument is without foundation.—Besides, it is evident, that the reason here assigned was not the true one, why the framers of this constitution omitted a bill of rights; if it had been, they would not have made certain reservations, while they totally omitted others of more importance. We find they have, in the 9th section of the 1st article, declared, that the writ of habeas corpus shall not be suspended, unless in cases of rebellion—that no bill of attainder, or expost facto law, shall be passed—that no title of nobility shall be granted by the United States, &c. If every thing which is not given is reserved, what propriety is there in these exceptions? Does this constitution any where grant the power of suspending the habeas corpus, to make expost facto laws, pass bills of attainder, or grant titles of nobility? It certainly does not in express terms. The only answer that can be given is, that these are implied in the general powers granted. With equal truth it may be said, that all the powers, which the bills of right, guard against the abuse of, are contained or implied in the general ones granted by this constitution.

So far it is from being true, that a bill of rights is less necessary in the general constitution than in those of the states, the contrary is evidently the fact.—This system, if it is possible for the people of America to accede to it, will be an original compact; and being the last, will, in the nature of things, vacate every former agreement inconsistent with it. For it being a plan of government received and ratified by the whole people, all other forms, which are in existence at the time of its adoption, must yield to it. This is expressed in positive and unequivocal terms, in the 6th article, "That this constitution and the laws of the United States, which shall be made in pursuance thereof, and all treaties made, or which shall be made, under the authority of the United States, shall be the supreme law of the land; and the judges in every state shall be bound thereby, any thing in the *constitution, or laws of any state, to the contrary* notwithstanding.

"The senators and representatives before-mentioned, and the members of the several state legislatures, and all executive and judicial officers, both of the United States, and of the several states, shall be bound, by oath or affirmation, to support this constitution."

It is therefore not only necessarily implied thereby, but positively expressed, that the different state constitutions are repealed and entirely done away, so far as they are inconsistent with this, with the laws which shall be made in pursuance thereof, or with treaties made, or which shall be made, under the authority of the United States; of what avail will the constitutions of the respective states be to preserve the rights of its citizens? should they be plead, the answer would be, the constitution of the United States, and the laws made in pursuance thereof, is the supreme law, and all legislatures and judicial officers, whether of the general or state governments, are bound by oath to support it. No priviledge, reserved by the bills of rights, or secured by the state government, can limit the power granted by this, or restrain any laws made in pursuance of it. It stands therefore on its own bottom, and must receive a construction by itself without any reference to any other—And hence it was of the highest importance, that the most precise and express declarations and reservations of rights should have been made.

This will appear the more necessary, when it is considered, that not only the constitution and laws made in pursuance thereof, but all treaties made, or which shall be made, under the authority of the United States, are the supreme law of the land, and supersede the constitutions of all the states. The power to make treaties, is vested in the president, by and with the advice and consent of two thirds of the senate. I do not find any limitation, or restriction, to the exercise of this power. The most important article in any constitution may therefore be repealed, even without a legislative act. Ought not a government, vested with such extensive and indefinite authority, to have been restricted by a declaration of rights? It certainly ought.

So clear a point is this, that I cannot help suspecting, that persons who attempt to persuade people, that such reservations were less necessary under this constitution than under those of the states, are wilfully endeavouring to deceive, and to lead you into an absolute state of vassalage.

RIGHTS AND THE EDUCATION OF CITIZENS

Some Anti-Federalists regarded a bill of rights as a set of commands issued to government itself—in effect, a list of fundamental rules for legislators, officials, and jurists. But other Anti-Federalists thought that bills of rights were addressed to a different audience: the people themselves. Without a bill of rights, the people would never know when the government had exceeded its just powers; they would therefore find themselves unable to resist its pretensions, because they would have no fixed standard against which to measure its acts. If a bill of rights was a command to anyone, then, it was directed to the citizens themselves, *not* their government. It was meant to remind them of the rights and liberties that they had to preserve, as they vigilantly monitored the acts of their governors. Properly understood, bills of rights were not so much legal documents as statements of principle needed to educate the citizenry. Without a bill of rights, some Anti-Federalists worried, the people would literally forget what their rights were.

Few Anti-Federalist essays voiced this notion more astutely than *The Letters from the Federal Farmer,* the short title of one of the most influential pamphlets opposing the Constitution.[6] In five original letters pub-

---

[6]Its author was long believed to be Richard Henry Lee, but that identification has now been largely discredited. Current scholarship favors Melancton Smith, a moderate Anti-Federalist from New York who was sitting in Congress when Lee proposed his amendments to the Constitution. Smith later played a decisive role in the ratification convention in New York, where he carried enough Anti-Federalists with him to prevent the state's act of ratification from being made legally contingent upon the future adoption of amendments. See Robert H. Webking, "Melancton Smith and the *Letters from the Federal Farmer,*" *William and Mary Quarterly,* 3d ser., 44 (1987), 510–28; Gordon Wood, "The Authorship of the *Letters from the Federal Farmer,*" ibid., 31 (1974), 299–308; and Robin Brooks, "Alexander Hamilton, Melancton Smith, and the Ratification of the Constitution in New York," *ibid.,* 24 (1967), 339–58.

lished in the early fall of 1787 and thirteen additional letters written the following winter, the "Federal Farmer" avoided the strident tone so many Anti-Federalists favored, and instead offered a measured assessment of the potential benefits and drawbacks of the Constitution. When he discussed the role of representation and trial by jury in maintaining republican government, the "Federal Farmer" stressed the way in which these institutions would foster the civic attachments of ordinary citizens.[7] A similar concern underlay the insightful discussion of bills of rights in his sixteenth letter, originally published January 20, 1788.

[7]See, for example, the fourth essay of the "Federal Farmer," in John Kaminski and Gaspare Saladino, eds., *The Documentary History of the Ratification of the Constitution* (Madison: State Historical Society of Wisconsin, 1976–), XIV, 46–7.

16

FEDERAL FARMER

Letter XVI

January 20, 1788

JANUARY 20, 1788.

DEAR SIR,

Having gone through with the organization of the government, I shall now proceed to examine more particularly those clauses which respect its powers. I shall begin with those articles and stipulations which are necessary for accurately ascertaining the extent of powers, and what is given, and for guarding, limiting, and restraining them in their exercise. We often find, these articles and stipulations placed in bills of rights; but they may as well be incorporated in the body of the constitution, as selected and placed by themselves. The constitution, or whole social compact, is

An Additional Number of Letters from the Federal Farmer to the Republican; Leading to a Fair Examination of the System of Government, Proposed by the Late Convention; to Several Essential and Necessary Alterations in it; and Calculated to Illustrate and Support the Principles and Positions Laid Down in the Preceding Letters (New York, 1788), from Houghton Library, Harvard University, AAS copy, microfiche W2571, Readex Early American Imprints 21197, pp. [2], [43]–181.

but one instrument, no more or less, than a certain number of articles or stipulations agreed to by the people, whether it consists of articles, sections, chapters, bills of rights, or parts of any other denomination, cannot be material. Many needless observations, and idle distinctions, in my opinion, have been made respecting a bill of rights. On the one hand, it seems to be considered as a necessary distinct limb of the constitution, and as containing a certain number of very valuable articles, which are applicable to all societies: and, on the other, as useless, especially in a federal government, possessing only enumerated power—nay, dangerous, as individual rights are numerous, and not easy to be enumerated in a bill of rights, and from articles, or stipulations, securing some of them, it may be inferred, that others not mentioned are surrendered. There appears to me to be general indefinite propositions without much meaning—and the man who first advanced those of the latter description, in the present case, signed the federal constitution, which directly contradicts him.[8] The supreme power is undoubtedly in the people, and it is a principle well established in my mind, that they reserve all powers not expressly delegated by them to those who govern; this is as true in forming a state as in forming a federal government. There is no possible distinction but this founded merely in the different modes of proceeding which take place in some cases. In forming a state constitution, under which to manage not only the great but the little concerns of a community: the powers to be possessed by the government are often too numerous to be enumerated; the people to adopt the shortest way often give general powers, indeed all powers, to the government, in some general words, and then, by a particular enumeration, take back, or rather say they however reserve certain rights as sacred, and which no laws shall be made to violate: hence the idea that all powers are given which are not reserved: but in forming a federal constitution, which *ex vi termine*,[9] supposes state governments existing, and which is only to manage a few great national concerns, we often find it easier to enumerate particularly the powers to be delegated to the federal head, than to enumerate particularly the individual rights to be reserved; and the principle will operate in its full force, when we carefully adhere to it. When we particularly enumerate the powers given, we ought either carefully to enumerate the rights reserved, or be totally silent about them; we must either particularly enumerate both, or else suppose the particular enumeration of the powers given adequately draws the line between them and the rights

[8]James Wilson.
[9]From the force of its end (or purposes).

reserved, particularly to enumerate the former and not the latter, I think most advisable: however, as men appear generally to have their doubts about these silent reservations, we might advantageously enumerate the powers given, and then in general words, according to the mode adopted in the 2d art. of the confederation, declare all powers, rights and privileges, are reserved, which are not explicitly and expressly given up. People, and very wisely too, like to be express and explicit about their essential rights, and not to be forced to claim them on the precarious and unascertained tenure of inferences and general principles, knowing that in any controversy between them and their rulers, concerning those rights, disputes may be endless, and nothing certain: — But admitting, on the general principle, that all rights are reserved of course, which are not expressly surrendered, the people could with sufficient certainty assert their rights on all occasions, and establish them with ease, still there are infinite advantages in particularly enumerating many of the most essential rights reserved in all cases; and as to the less important ones, we may declare in general terms, that all not expressly surrendered are reserved. We do not by declarations change the nature of things, or create new truths, but we give existence, or at least establish in the minds of the people truths and principles which they might never otherwise have thought of, or soon forgot. If a nation means its systems, religious or political, shall have duration, it ought to recognize the leading principles of them in the front page of every family book. What is the usefulness of a truth in theory, unless it exists constantly in the minds of the people, and has their assent: — we discern certain rights, as the freedom of the press, and the trial by jury, &c. which the people of England and of America of course believe to be sacred, and essential to their political happiness, and this belief in them is the result of ideas at first suggested to them by a few able men, and of subsequent experience; while the people of some other countries hear these rights mentioned with the utmost indifference; they think the privilege of existing at the will of a despot much preferable to them. Why this difference amongst beings every way formed alike. The reason of the difference is obvious — it is the effect of education, a series of notions impressed upon the minds of the people by examples, precepts and declarations. When the people of England got together, at the time they formed Magna Charta, they did not consider it sufficient, that they were indisputably entitled to certain natural and unalienable rights, not depending on silent titles, they, by a declaratory act, expressly recognized them, and explicitly declared to all the world, that they were entitled to enjoy those rights; they made an instrument in writing, and enumerated those they then thought essential, or in danger, and this wise men saw was not sufficient: and therefore, that the people might not forget these rights, and gradually become prepared for arbitrary government, their discerning and honest leaders caused this instrument to be confirmed near forty times, and to be read twice a year in public places, not that it would lose its validity without such confirmations, but to fix the contents of it in the minds of the people, as they successively come upon the stage.—Men, in some countries do not remain free, merely because they are entitled to natural and unalienable rights; men in all countries are entitled to them, not because their ancestors once got together and enumerated them on paper, but because, by repeated negociations and declarations, all parties are brought to realize them, and of course to believe them to be sacred. Were it necessary, I might shew the wisdom of our past conduct, as a people in not merely comforting ourselves that we were entitled to freedom, but in constantly keeping in view, in addresses, bills of rights, in news-papers, &c. the particular principles on which our freedom must always depend.

It is not merely in this point of view, that I urge the engrafting in the constitution additional declaratory articles. The distinction, in itself just, that all powers not given are reserved, is in effect destroyed by this very constitution, as I shall particularly demonstrate—and even independent of this, the people, by adopting the constitution, give many general undefined powers to congress, in the constitutional exercise of which, the rights in question may be effected. Gentlemen who oppose a federal bill of rights, or further declaratory articles, seem to view the subject in a very narrow imperfect manner. These have for their objects, not only the enumeration of the rights reserved, but principally to explain the general powers delegated in certain material points, and to restrain those who exercise them by fixed known boundaries. Many explanations and restrictions necessary and useful, would be much less so, were the people at large all well and fully acquainted with the principles and affairs of government. There appears to be in the constitution, a studied brevity, and it may also be probable, that several explanatory articles were omitted from a circumstance very common. What we have long and early understood ourselves in the common concerns of the community, we are apt to suppose is understood by others, and need not be expressed; and it is not unnatural or uncommon for the ablest men most frequently to make this mistake. To make declaratory articles unnecessary in an instrument of government, two circumstances must exist; the rights reserved must be indisputably so, and in their nature defined; the powers delegated to the government, must be precisely defined by the words that convey them, and clearly be of such extent and nature as that, by no reasonable construction, they can be made to invade the rights and prerogatives intended to be left in the people.

The first point urged, is, that all power is reserved not expressly given, that particular enumerated powers only are given, that all others are not given, but reserved, and that it is needless to attempt to restrain congress in the exercise of powers they possess not. This reasoning is logical, but of very little importance in the common affairs of men; but the constitution does not appear to respect it even in any view. To prove this, I might cite several clauses in it. I shall only remark on two or three. By article 1, section 9, "No title of nobility shall be granted by congress." Was this clause omitted, what power would congress have to make titles of nobility? in what part of the constitution would they find it? The answer must be, that congress would have no such power—that the people, by adopting the constitution, will not part with it. Why then by a negative clause, restrain congress from doing what it would have no power to do? This clause, then, must have no meaning, or imply, that were it omitted, congress would have the power in question, either upon the principle that some general words in the constitution may be so construed as to give it, or on the principle that congress possess the powers not expressly reserved. But this clause was in the confederation, and is said to be introduced into the constitution from very great caution. Even a cautionary provision implies a doubt, at least, that it is necessary; and if so in this case, clearly it is also alike necessary in all similar ones. The fact appears to be, that the people in forming the confederation, and the convention, in this instance, acted, naturally, they did not leave the point to be settled by general principles and logical inferences; but they settle the point in a few words, and all who read them at once understand them.

The trial by jury in criminal as well as in civil causes, has long been considered as one of our fundamental rights, and has been repeatedly recognized and confirmed by most of the state conventions. But the constitution expressly establishes this trial in criminal, and wholly omits it in civil causes. The jury trial in criminal causes, and the benefit of the writ of habeas corpus, are already as effectually established as any of the fundamental or essential rights of the people in the United States. This being the case, why in adopting a federal constitution do we now establish these, and omit all others, or all others, at least, with a few exceptions, such as again agreeing there shall be no ex post facto laws, no titles of nobility, &c. We must consider this constitution when adopted as the supreme act of the people, and in construing it hereafter, we and our posterity must strictly adhere to the letter and spirit of it, and in no instance depart from them: in construing the federal constitution, it will be not only impracticable, but improper to refer to the state constitutions. They are entirely distinct instruments and inferior acts: besides, by the people's now establishing certain fundamental rights, it is strongly implied, that they are of opinion, that they would not otherwise be secured as a part of the federal system, or be regarded in the federal administration as fundamental. Further, these same rights, being established by the state constitutions, and secured to the people, our recognizing them now, implies, that the people thought them insecure by the state establishments, and extinguished or put afloat by the new arrangement of the social system, unless re-established. — Further, the people, thus establishing some few rights, and remaining totally silent about others similarly circumstanced, the implication indubitably is, that they mean to relinquish the latter, or at least feel indifferent about them. Rights, therefore, inferred from general principles of reason, being precarious and hardly ascertainable in the common affairs of society, and the people, in forming a federal constitution, explicitly shewing they conceive these rights to be thus circumstanced, and accordingly proceed to enumerate and establish some of them, the conclusion will be, that they have established all which they esteem valuable and sacred. On every principle, then, the people especially having began, ought to go through enumerating, and establish particularly all the rights of individuals, which can by any possibility come in question in making and executing federal laws. I have already observed upon the excellency and importance of the jury trial in civil as well as in criminal causes, instead of establishing it in criminal causes only; we ought to establish it generally; — instead of the clause of forty or fifty words relative to this subject, why not use the language that has always been used in this country, and say, "the people of the United States shall always be entitled to the trial by jury." This would shew the people still hold the right sacred, and enjoin it upon congress substantially to preserve the jury trial in all cases, according to the usage and custom of the country. I have observed before, that it is *the jury trial* we want; the little different appendages and modifications tacked to it in the different states, are no more than a drop in the ocean: the jury trial is a solid uniform feature in a free government; it is the substance we would save, not the little articles of form.

Security against expost facto laws, the trial by jury, and the benefits of the writ of habeas corpus, are but a part of those inestimable rights the people of the United States are entitled to, even in judicial proceedings, by the course of the common law. These may be secured in general words, as in New-York, the Western Territory, &c. by declaring the people of the United States shall always be entitled to judicial proceedings according to the course of the common law, as used and established in the said states.[10] Perhaps it would be better to enumerate the particular essential rights the people are entitled to in these proceedings, as has been done in many of the states, and as has been done in England. In this case, the people may proceed to declare, that no man shall be held to answer to any offence, till the same be fully described to him; nor to furnish evidence against himself: that, except in the government of the army and navy, no person shall be tried for any offence, whereby he may incur loss of life, or an infamous punishment, until he be first indicted by a grand jury: that every person shall have a right to produce all proofs that may be favourable to him, and to meet the witnesses against him face to face: that every person shall be entitled to obtain right and justice freely and without delay: that all persons shall have a right to be secure from all unreasonable searches and seizures of their persons, houses, papers, or possessions; and that all warrants shall be deemed contrary to this right, if the foundation of them be not previously supported by oath, and there be not in them a special designation of persons or objects of search, arrest, or seizure: and that no person shall be exiled or molested in his person or effects, otherwise than by the judgment of his peers, or according to the law of the land. A celebrated writer observes upon this last article, that in itself it may be said to comprehend the whole end of political society.[11] These rights are not necessarily reserved, they are established, or enjoyed but in few countries: they are stipulated rights, almost peculiar to British and American laws. In the execution of those laws, individuals, by long custom, by magna charta, bills of rights &c. have become entitled to them. A man, at first, by act of parliament, became entitled to the benefits of the writ of habeas corpus—men are entitled to these rights and benefits in the judicial proceedings of our state courts generally: but it will by no means follow, that they will be entitled to them in the federal courts, and have a right to assert them, unless secured and established by the constitution or federal laws. We certainly, in federal processes, might as well claim the benefits of the writ of habeas corpus, as to claim trial by a jury—the right to have council—to have witnesses face to face—to be secure against unreasonable search warrants, &c. was the constitution silent as to the whole of them:—but the establishment of the former, will evince that we could not claim them without it; and the

---

[10]Such provisions could be found in Article XXXV of the New York constitution of 1777 and in Article II of the "compact" section of the Northwest Ordinance of 1787.

[11]The quotation is from William Blackstone, *Commentaries on the Laws of England* (London, 1765), III, 379.

omission of the latter, implies they are relinquished, or deemed of no importance. These are rights and benefits individuals acquire by compact; they must claim them under compacts, or immemorial usage—it is doubtful, at least, whether they can be claimed under immemorial usage in this country; and it is, therefore, we generally claim them under compacts, as charters and constitutions.

The people by adopting the federal constitution, give congress general powers to institute a distinct and new judiciary, new courts, and to regulate all proceedings in them, under the eight limitations mentioned in a former letter; and the further one, that the benefits of the habeas corpus act shall be enjoyed by individuals. Thus general powers being given to institute courts, and regulate their proceedings, with no provision for securing the rights principally in question, may not congress so exercise those powers, and constitutionally too, as to destroy those rights? clearly, in my opinion, they are not in any degree secured. But, admitting the case is only doubtful, would it not be prudent and wise to secure them and remove all doubts, since all agree the people ought to enjoy these valuable rights, a very few men excepted, who seem to be rather of opinion that there is little or nothing in them? Were it necessary I might add many observations to shew their value and political importance.

The constitution will give congress general powers to raise and support armies. General powers carry with them incidental ones, and the means necessary to the end. In the exercise of these powers, is there any provision in the constitution to prevent the quartering of soldiers on the inhabitants? you will answer, there is not. This may sometimes be deemed a necessary measure in the support of armies; on what principle can the people claim the right to be exempt from this burden? they will urge, perhaps, the practice of the country, and the provisions made in some of the state constitutions—they will be answered, that their claim thus to be exempt, is not founded in nature, but only in custom and opinion, or at best, in stipulations in some of the state constitutions, which are local, and inferior in their operation, and can have no controul over the general government—that they had adopted a federal constitution—had noticed several rights, but had been totally silent about this exemption—that they had given general powers relative to the subject, which, in their operation, regularly destroyed the claim. Though it is not to be presumed, that we are in any immediate danger from this quarter, yet it is fit and proper to establish, beyond dispute, those rights which are particularly valuable to individuals, and essential to the permanency and duration of free government. An excellent writer observes, that the English, always in possession of their freedom, are frequently unmindful of the value of it: we, at this period, do not seem to be so well off, having, in some instances abused ours; many of us are quite disposed to barter it away for what we call energy, coercion, and some other terms we use as vaguely as that of liberty — There is often as great a rage for change and novelty in politics, as in amusements and fashions.

All parties apparently agree, that the freedom of the press is a fundamental right, and ought not to be restrained by any taxes, duties, or in any manner whatever. Why should not the people, in adopting a federal constitution, declare this, even if there are only doubts about it. But, say the advocates, all powers not given are reserved. — true; but the great question is, are not powers given, in the exercise of which this right may be destroyed? The people's or the printers claim to a free press, is founded on the fundamental laws, that is, compacts, and state constitutions, made by the people. The people, who can annihilate or alter those constitutions, can annihilate or limit this right. This may be done by giving general powers, as well as by using particular words. No right claimed under a state constitution, will avail against a law of the union, made in pursuance of the federal constitution: therefore the question is, what laws will congress have a right to make by the constitution of the union, and particularly touching the press? By art. 1. sect. 8. congress will have power to lay and collect taxes, duties, imposts and excise. By this congress will clearly have power to lay and collect all kind of taxes whatever — taxes on houses, lands, polls, industry, merchandize, &c. — taxes on deeds, bonds, and all written instruments — on writs, pleas, and all judicial proceedings, on licences, naval officers papers, &c. on newspapers, advertisements, &c. and to require bonds of the naval officers, clerks, printers, &c. to account for the taxes that may become due on papers that go through their hands. Printing, like all other business, must cease when taxed beyond its profits; and it appears to me, that a power to tax the press at discretion, is a power to destroy or restrain the freedom of it. There may be other powers given, in the exercise of which this freedom may be effected; and certainly it is of too much importance to be left thus liable to be taxed, and constantly to constructions and inferences. A free press is the channel of communication as to mercantile and public affairs; by means of it the people in large countries ascertain each others sentiments: are enabled to unite, and become formidable to those rulers who adopt improper measures. Newspapers may sometimes be the vehicles of abuse, and of many things not true; but these are but small inconveniences, in my mind, among many advantages. A celebrated writer, I have several times quoted, speaking in high terms of the English liberties, says, "lastly the key stone was put to the arch, by the final establishment of the freedom of the press."[12] I shall not dwell longer upon the fundamental rights, to some of which I have attended in this letter, for the same reasons that these I have mentioned, ought to be expressly secured, lest in the exercise of general powers given they may be invaded: it is pretty clear, that some other of less importance, or less in danger, might with propriety also be secured.

I shall now proceed to examine briefly the powers proposed to be vested in the several branches of the government, and especially the mode of laying and collecting internal taxes.

---

[12]The source is Jean Louis De Lolme, *The Constitution of England . . .* (originally published in Paris, 1771, and frequently reprinted in English), book I, chapter 3.

11
The Federalist Position

While Federalists repeated the essential case against a federal bill of rights that James Wilson had advanced in October 1787, they also developed further reasons to resist the Anti-Federalist clamor for amendments. Above all, Federalists knew that their Anti-Federalist opponents had other ends in mind. The adoption of a bill of rights would do little good, most Anti-Federalists thought, if other changes in the structure of the Constitution could not be attained. If they could have had their way, the Anti-Federalists would have forced the new government to rely for its revenues on the old system of requisitions used by the Continental Congress, in which the state legislatures were expected to levy the taxes needed for national expenses. They would have imposed further restrictions on the ability of the national government to maintain a "standing army." They would also have doubled or more the size of the House of Representatives, shortened the terms of senators and made them subject to recall, and reduced the formal powers of the Senate, which most Anti-Federalists regarded as a nursery of a dangerous aristocracy. And rather than rest content with Wilson's assurance that the new government would possess only limited, delegated powers, Anti-Federalists repeatedly called for the adoption of something like Article 2 of the Confederation, which explicitly recognized the sovereignty of the states.

Federalists found all these proposals objectionable for three complementary sets of reasons. First and foremost, the changes Anti-Federalists sought would transform the Constitution itself in radical and potentially harmful ways, making the new national government into a slightly improved model of the old. Second, a willingness to accede to any scheme of amendments while the Constitution remained unratified—as Anti-Federalists insisted it should—would create a procedural nightmare. Who would propose such amendments, or agree upon a definitive list of changes, and how would they then be approved? The most plausible scenario would be to assemble a second convention to revise the Constitution. But that suggestion exposed a third dilemma. Would not the delegates attending such a convention come bound by so many different instructions, each reflecting the particular interests of their individual states, as to make agreement on a second constitution utterly unlikely? The Convention of 1787, after all, had benefited from the relative absence of formal instructions, which had enabled the framers to reason and bargain on their own authority. The members of a second convention would have much less leeway, however; a second convention would be a formula not for consensus but for impasse.[1]

All of these considerations suggest that the Federalist aversion to a bill of rights cannot be separated from their other reasons for opposing all amendments until the Constitution was unconditionally ratified. In a sense, they viewed the call for a bill of rights as a Trojan horse. Open the gates to let it in, and a host of evils might issue forth to destroy the Constitution itself.

But Federalists had other reasons to question the need for a bill of rights.

CAN WE ENUMERATE ALL OUR RIGHTS?

Anti-Federalists thought that drafting a bill of rights was a relatively simple matter. When the issue had been discussed at the Federal Convention, Mason had said it would take only a few hours to whip one up, taking the state declarations as a model. Had the framers been so inclined, they probably could have proved Mason right. Even if they avoided the rhetorical flourishes found in many articles in the state declarations, a compendium of basic civil liberties and such crucial rights as freedom of conscience and of the press would not have been hard to cobble together.

But after the Constitution was published, Federalists did have cause to question whether compiling a list of rights was truly a good idea. The issue was not whether enumerating rights was difficult in itself. It was rather that a positive enumeration of some rights could be read as a negative relegation of other omitted rights to an inferior, less-than-constitutional status. Were Anti-Federalists not implying, after all, that the security of rights would henceforth depend on their being formally incorporated in the written text of a constitution—for if rights went unmentioned, their authority would henceforth be suspect. If that premise were conceded—and this was a big if—it followed that an incomplete enumeration would leave other rights subject to violation. And what about rights whose existence was not yet known or whose extent had not yet

---

[1] Jack N. Rakove, *Original Meanings: Politics and Ideas in the Making of the Constitution* (New York: Alfred Knopf, 1996), 112.

been adequately measured? Would such rights acquire their due authority only if they were added to the Constitution via the amendment process? If these concerns were taken seriously, one would have to be very sure that the list of rights to be enumerated now was correct because future generations would pay the cost of omission.

One of the most succinct statements of this concern was delivered by James Iredell, the leader of the beleaguered Federalist minority in the first North Carolina ratifying convention, who would soon sit on the first Supreme Court of the United States. In a speech that tried to imagine how future generations would read a bill of rights, Iredell warned of the dangers of an incomplete enumeration.

17

JAMES IREDELL

Speech in the North Carolina Ratification Convention

July 28, 1788

With regard to a bill of rights, this is a notion originating in England, where no written Constitution is to be found, and the authority of their government is derived from the most remote antiquity. Magna Charta itself is no Constitution, but a solemn instrument ascertaining certain rights of individuals, by the Legislature for the time being, and every article of which the Legislature may at any time alter. This, and a bill of rights also, the invention of later times, were occasioned by great usurpations of the crown, contrary, as was conceived, to the principles of their government, about which there was a variety of opinions. But neither that instrument or any other instrument ever attempted to abridge the authority of Parliament, which is supposed to be without any limitation whatever. Had their Constitution been fixed and certain, a bill of rights would

James Iredell, Speech in the North Carolina Ratification Convention, *Proceedings and Debates of the Convention of North Carolina, July 28, 1788* (North Carolina: Edenton, Hodge & Wills, 1789), from Houghton Library, Harvard University, AAS copy, microfiche W2571, Readex Early American Imprints 22037, p. 280.

have been useless, for the Constitution would have shewn plainly the extent of that authority which they were disputing about. Of what use therefore can a bill of rights be in this Constitution, where the people expressly declare how much power they do give, and consequently retain all they do not? It is a declaration of particular powers by the people to their Representatives for particular purposes. It may be considered as a great power of attorney, under which no power can be exercised but what is expressly given. Did any man ever hear before that at the end of a power of attorney it was said, that the Attorney should not exercise more power than was there given him? Suppose for instance a man had lands in the counties of Anson and Caswell, and he should give another a power of attorney to sell his lands in Anson; would the other have any authority to sell the lands in Caswell? or could he without absurdity say, " 'Tis true you have not expressly authorized me to sell the lands in Caswell, but as you had lands there, and did not say I should not, I thought I might as well sell those lands as the other." A bill of rights, as I conceive, would not only be incongruous, but dangerous. No man, let his ingenuity be what it will, could enumerate all the individual rights not relinquished by this Constitution. Suppose therefore an enumeration of a great many, but an omission of some, and that long after all traces of our present disputes were at an end, any of the omitted rights should be invaded, and the invasion be complained of; what would be the plausible answer of the government to such a complaint? Would they not naturally say, "We live at a great distance from the time when this Constitution was established. We can judge of it much better by the ideas of it entertained at the time, than by any ideas of our own. The bill of rights passed at that time, shewed that the people did not think every power retained which was not given, else this bill of rights was not only useless, but absurd. But we are not at liberty to charge an absurdity upon our ancestors, who have given such strong proofs of their good sense, as well as their attachment to liberty. So long as the rights enumerated in the bill of rights remain unviolated, you have no reason to complain. This is not one of them." Thus a bill of rights might operate as a snare, rather than a protection. If we had formed a General Legislature, with undefined powers, a bill of rights would not only have been proper, but necessary; and it would have then operated as an exception to the legislative authority in such particulars. It has this effect in respect to some of the American Constitutions, where the powers of legislation are general. But where they are powers of a particular nature, and expressly defined, as in the case of the Constitution before us, I think, for the reasons I have given, a bill of rights is not only unnecessary, but would be absurd and dangerous.

12

Madison and Jefferson: The Classic Exchange

Among all the letters, essays, columns, and speeches that were written about the question of a bill of rights in 1787–89, the documents that command the greatest attention are the letters that James Madison and Thomas Jefferson exchanged on this subject. There are several reasons this attention is well deserved.

The first has to do with the crucial roles that the two men played in the politics of amending the Constitution. Even from his distant vantage point in Paris, where he was serving as American minister to France, Jefferson's public endorsement of a bill of rights counted heavily in the court of public opinion. For his part, Madison converted his own grudging decision to support the addition of a bill of rights into a personal commitment that he felt duty bound to execute when the new Congress convened in 1789. Had he not felt this commitment so deeply, it is entirely possible that Congress would have left this issue untouched.[1]

Second, the Madison-Jefferson exchanges offer a remarkable insight into the complementary yet distinct ways in which these two allies reasoned about fundamental questions of politics. The two men had first met in 1776; they had developed something of a working friendship when they both held executive office in Virginia in 1778–79; and then, in the 1780s, their attachment had flourished through their correspondence. While the absent Jefferson pondered the manifest inequalities he observed in the decaying *ancien régime* of France, Madison fretted about the danger that potential inequalities of wealth might soon pose to the American republic. From these divergent perspectives, they drew divergent lessons about the questions of rights. Yet their differences of opinion, though real, only deepened the foundation of the political alliance

---

[1] The most balanced assessment of the influence that Jefferson exerted on Madison's reconsideration of this question is Paul Finkelman, "James Madison and the Bill of Rights: A Reluctant Paternity," *Supreme Court Review* (1990), 301–47.

that would carry them into opposition to Alexander Hamilton and his policies in the 1790s.[2]

Third, and most important, the different opinions they expressed about bills of rights illuminated the great dilemma with which this book is concerned. By insisting that any bill of rights, however incomplete, was better than none, Jefferson expressed a common sense that American history has largely vindicated. In the final analysis, it is hard to deny that the existence of a federal Bill of Rights did become a powerful engine for the protection of individual liberties and minority rights against the abuse of coercive power by the state. Yet the Bill gained that authority only after it languished, largely forgotten, for the better part of a century and a half, so that clearly other changes had to occur in American politics and law for a national bill of rights to gain its force. Madison's persisting doubts about the value of bills of rights thus demonstrate an equal and perhaps greater wisdom. Of all the participants in the constitutional debates of 1787–89, Madison was the one who grasped the crucial point that the real threats to rights in a republic lay not in the arbitrary acts of a government misruling its people but in the more disturbing possibility that popular majorities, acting *through* government, would willfully trample on the rights of individuals and minorities. And Madison was also the one founder of the republic who best understood that the states, rather than the national government, were the arena within which rights-endangering acts were most likely to occur.

DEFENDING THE VETO

In a letter written eleven days before the Federal Convention adjourned, Madison warned Jefferson that even should the Constitution "be adopted [it] will neither effectually answer its national object nor prevent the local mischiefs which every where excite disgusts ag[ain]st the state government. The grounds of this opinion will be the subject of a future letter."[3] When he found time to draft this letter seven weeks later, Madison devoted the heart of its seventeen pages to a prolonged defense of his

---

[2]The complete literary history of this friendship can be followed in James Morton Smith, ed., *The Republic of Letters: The Correspondence between Thomas Jefferson and James Madison, 1776–1826*, 3 vols. (New York: W. W. Norton, 1995); and for further discussion, see Adrienne Koch, *Jefferson and Madison: The Great Collaboration* (New York, 1950), and Lance Banning, *Jefferson and Madison: Three Conversations from the Founding* (Madison: Madison House, 1995).

[3]Madison to Jefferson, September 6, 1787, in Robert Rutland et al., eds., *The Papers of James Madison* (Chicago: University of Chicago Press, 1977), X: 163–64.

proposed scheme for an unlimited national veto on all state laws. Madison would not have spent so much time defending a rejected proposal as an academic lark; his letter reveals how much he still regretted its defeat.

After first explaining why this drastic weapon was needed to enable the national government to defend itself against the interference of the states, Madison turned to the equally valuable role it would play in the protection of rights. His argument on this point not only repeated the position he had fashioned on the eve of the Convention and several times repeated during its deliberations; it also directly foretold the public statement of his ideas that he finally presented a month later in *Federalist* 10. In this essay, as in his earlier memoranda, speeches, and letters, Madison restated his theory of the popular sources of factious politics and the danger they posed to rights and liberties.

But there was one crucial difference between the public and private versions of Madison's theory. In *Federalist* 10, Madison had no reason to discuss the idea of a negative on state laws, since it was not part of the Constitution he was now defending. Here all he had to do was to explain why an extended national republic was less likely to violate rights than were the states. In private, though, Madison could voice his concern that individual rights would remain subject to infringement within the states, and that without a national government empowered to intervene within states' affairs, these rights would indeed be violated. And if the negative on state laws offered the best solution to the problem of protecting rights, as Madison still believed, then the adoption of a national bill of rights would be simply irrelevant.

18

JAMES MADISON

Letter to Thomas Jefferson

October 24, 1787

---

2. A constitutional negative on the laws of the States seems equally necessary to secure individuals agst. encroachments on their rights. The mutability of the laws of the States is found to be a serious evil. The injustice of them has been so frequent and so flagrant as to alarm the most stedfast friends of Republicanism. I am persuaded I do not err in saying that the evils issuing from these sources contributed more to that uneasiness which produced the Convention, and prepared the public mind for a general reform, than those which accrued to our national character and interest from the inadequacy of the Confederation to its immediate objects. A reform therefore which does not make provision for private rights, must be materially defective. The restraints agst. paper emissions, and violations of contracts are not sufficient.[4] Supposing them to be effectual as far as they go, they are short of the mark. Injustice may be effected by such an infinitude of legislative expedients, that where the disposition exists it can only be controuled by some provision which reaches all cases whatsoever. The partial provision made, supposes the disposition which will evade it. It may be asked how private rights will be more secure under the Guardianship of the General Government than under the State Governments, since they are both founded on the republican principle which refers the ultimate decision to the will of the majority, and are distinguished rather by the extent within which they will operate, than by any material difference in their structure. A full discussion of this question would, if I mistake not, unfold the true principles of Republican Government, and prove in contradiction to the concurrent opinions of theoretical writers, that this form of Government, in order to effect its purposes, must operate not within a small but an extensive sphere. I will state some of the ideas which have occurred to me on this subject. Those who contend for a simple Democracy, or a pure republic, actuated by the sense of the majority, and operating within narrow limits, assume or suppose a case which is altogether fictitious. They

[4]Cf. Article I, Section 10 of the Constitution.

Madison to Jefferson, October 24, 1787, Jefferson Papers, Library of Congress. From Rutland et al., eds., *Papers of Madison,* X: 212–14.

found their reasoning on the idea, that the people composing the Society, enjoy not only an equality of political rights; but that they have all precisely the same interests, and the same feelings in every respect. Were this in reality the case, their reasoning would be conclusive. The interest of the majority would be that of the minority also; the decisions could only turn on mere opinion concerning the good of the whole, of which the major voice would be the safest criterion; and within a small sphere, this voice could be most easily collected, and the public affairs most accurately managed. We know however that no Society ever did or can consist of so homogeneous a mass of Citizens. In the savage State indeed, an approach is made towards it; but in that State little or no Government is necessary. In all civilized Societies, distinctions are various and unavoidable. A distinction of property results from that very protection which a free Government gives to unequal faculties of acquiring it. There will be rich and poor; creditors and debtors; a landed interest, a monied interest, a mercantile interest, a manufacturing interest. These classes may again be subdivided according to the different productions of different situations & soils, & according to different branches of commerce, and of manufacturers. In addition to these natural distinctions, artificial ones will be founded, on accidental differences in political, religious or other opinions, or an attachment to the persons of leading individuals. However erroneous or ridiculous these grounds of dissention and faction, may appear to the enlightened Statesman, or the benevolent philosopher, the bulk of mankind who are neither Statesmen nor Philosophers, will continue to view them in a different light. It remains then to be enquired whether a majority having any common interest, or feeling any common passion, will find sufficient motives to restrain them from oppressing the minority. An individual is never allowed to be a judge or even a witness in his own cause. If two individuals are under the biass of interest or enmity agst. a third, the rights of the latter could never be safely referred to the majority of the three. Will two thousand individuals be less apt to oppress one thousand, or two hundred thousand, one hundred thousand? Three motives only can restrain in such cases. 1. a prudent regard to private or partial good, as essentially involved in the general and permanent good of the whole. This ought no doubt to be sufficient of itself. Experience however shews that it has little effect on individuals, and perhaps still less on a collection of individuals, and least of all on a majority with the public authority in their hands. If the former are ready to forget that honesty is the best policy; the last do more. They often proceed on the converse of the maxim: that whatever is politic is honest. 2. respect for character. This motive is not found sufficient to restrain individuals from injustice, and loses its efficacy in proportion to the number which is to divide the praise or the blame. Besides as it has reference to public opinion, which is that of the majority, the Standard is fixed by those whose conduct is to be measured by it. 3. Religion. The inefficacy of this restraint on individuals is well known. The conduct of every popular Assembly, acting on oath, the strongest of religious ties, shews that individuals join without remorse in acts agst. which their consciences would revolt, if proposed to them separately in their closets. When Indeed Religion is kindled into enthusiasm, its force like that of other passions is increased by the sympathy of a multitude. But enthusiasm is only a temporary state of Religion, and whilst it lasts will hardly be seen with pleasure at the helm. Even in its coolest state, it has been much oftener a motive to oppression than a restraint from it. If then there must be different interests and parties in Society; and a majority when united by a common interest or passion can not be restrained from oppressing the minority, what remedy can be found in a republican Government, where the majority must ultimately decide, but that of giving such an extent to its sphere, that no common interest or passion will be likely to unite a majority of the whole number in an unjust pursuit. In a large Society, the people are broken into so many interests and parties, that a common sentiment is less likely to be felt, and the requisite concert less likely to be formed, by a majority of the whole. The same security seems requisite for the civil as for the religious rights of individuals. If the same sect form a majority and have the power, other sects will be sure to be depressed. Divide et impera,[5] the reprobated axiom of tyranny, is under certain qualifications, the only policy, by which a republic can be administered on just principles. It must be observed however that this doctrine can only hold within a sphere of a mean extent. As in too small a sphere oppressive combinations may be too easily formed agst. the weaker party; so in too extensive a one, a defensive concert may be rendered too difficult against the oppression of those entrusted with the administration. The great desideratum[6] in Government is, so to modify the sovereignty as that it may be sufficiently neutral between different parts of the Society to controul one part from invading the rights of another, and at the same time sufficiently controuled itself, from setting up an interest adverse to that of the entire Society. In absolute monarchies, the Prince may be tolerably neutral towards different classes of his sub-

---

[5]Divide and rule.
[6]Necessity.

jects, but may sacrifice the happiness of all to his personal ambition or avarice. In small republics, the sovereign will is controuled from such a sacrifice of the entire Society, but is not sufficiently neutral towards the parts composing it. In the extended Republic of the United States, The General Government would hold a pretty even balance between the parties of particular States,[7] and be at the same time sufficiently restrained by its dependence on the community, from betraying its general interests.

THE VIEW FROM PARIS

In his diplomatic position in Paris, Jefferson was never out of touch with events at home—but he viewed them with less alarm than Madison. When Madison worried that Shays' Rebellion—an uprising of debtor farmers in Massachusetts in 1786–87—was a portent of anarchy, Jefferson reflected that "a little rebellion now and then is a good thing, & as necessary in the political world as storms in the physical."[8] Next to the gross disparities of wealth and power that he observed in France, which was just on the brink of its own revolution, Jefferson thought that the situation of America remained fundamentally sound. He agreed that reform of the Confederation was essential, but he balanced his early praise of the proposed Constitution with regret that it did not contain a bill of rights.

Jefferson conveyed his ideas about the contents and uses of a bill of rights in the two letters that follow, the first written after he received Madison's defense of the national negative, the second after eleven states had ratified the Constitution. Had Jefferson expressed his sentiments only in private, Madison would not have been much troubled. But Jefferson also gave a copy of the first letter to one Uriah Forrest, and when Forrest returned to America early in 1788, Jefferson's criticism of James Wilson's argument and his own endorsement of a bill of rights became public knowledge. "Can this possibly be Jefferson?" one anguished framer, Daniel Carroll, soon asked Madison.[9] Alas it was, Madison knew. Rather than hew to the united Federalist front, the absent Jefferson had inadvertently become an implicit Anti-Federalist ally.

---

[7] I.e., the federal government would use its negative on state laws to mediate conflicts between majority and minority factions within individual states.

[8] Jefferson to Madison, January 30, 1787, in Rutland et al., eds., *Papers of Madison,* IX: 248.

[9] Carroll to Madison, May 28, 1788, in Rutland et al., eds., *Papers of Madison*(Charlottesville: University Press of Virginia, 1977), XI: 64–65; and see Jefferson to Uriah Forrest, December 31, 1787, in Julian P. Boyd, ed., *The Papers of Thomas Jefferson* (Princeton: Princeton University Press, 1950–), XII: 475–79, enclosing a copy of Jefferson's letter to Madison of December 20.

Jefferson's two letters nevertheless diverged in tone and substance from the common Anti-Federalist position. He did not go so far as to suggest that the omission of a bill of rights would fatally imperil American liberties. Yet Jefferson did imply that bills of rights were vital safeguards against all governments, and he briskly challenged the standard Federalist line about the potential danger of enumerating some rights and omitting others. Protecting rights was so essential, Jefferson reasoned, that it was always better to err on their side, rather than to allow silence to spur on improper action of government.

19

THOMAS JEFFERSON

Letter to James Madison

December 20, 1787

The season admitting only of operations in the Cabinet,[10] and these being in a great measure secret, I have little to fill a letter. I will therefore make up the deficiency by adding a few words on the Constitution proposed by our Convention. I like much the general idea of framing a government which should go on of itself peaceably, without needing continual recurrence to the state legislatures. I like the organization of the government into Legislative, Judiciary & Executive. I like the power given the Legislature to levy taxes, and for that reason solely approve of the greater house being chosen by the people directly. For tho' I think a house chosen by them will be very illy qualified to legislate for the Union, for foreign nations &c. yet this evil does not weigh against the good of preserving inviolate the fundamental principle that the people are not to be taxed but by representatives chosen immediately by themselves. I am captivated by the compromise of the opposite claims of the great & little states, of the latter to equal, and the former to proportional influence. I am much pleased too with the substitution of the method of voting by persons,[11]

[10]King Louis XVI and his ministers.
[11]In Congress.

Thomas Jefferson to James Madison, December 20, 1787, Madison Papers, Library of Congress. From Rutland et al., eds., *Papers of Madison,* X: 336–37.

Perhaps the best known and most appealing portrait of Thomas Jefferson is this painting by Charles Willson Peale, completed in 1791 when Jefferson was secretary of state. Of all the members of his generation, Jefferson was the most complicated: connoisseur of fine objects and fine wines, master architect, diplomat, political philosopher, celebrant of yeoman farmers and democracy, apostle of religious liberty, and slaveholder.

instead of that of voting by states: and I like the negative given to the Executive with a third of either house, though I should have liked it better had the Judiciary been associated for that purpose, or invested with a similar and separate power. There are other good things of less moment. I will now add what I do not like. First the omission of a bill of rights providing clearly & without the aid of sophisms for freedom of religion, freedom of the press, protection against standing armies, restriction against monopolies, the eternal & unremitting force of the habeas corpus laws, and trials by jury in all matters of fact triable by the laws of the land & not by the law of Nations. To say, as mr. Wilson does, that a bill of rights was not necessary because all is reserved in the case of the general government which is not given, while in the particular ones all is given which is not reserved, might do for the Audience to whom it was addressed, but is surely a gratis dictum,[12] opposed by strong inferences from the body of the instrument, as well as from the omission of the clause of our present confederation which had declared that in express terms.[13] It was a hard conclusion to say because there has been no uniformity among the states as to the cases triable by jury, because some have been so incautious as to abandon this mode of trial, therefore the more prudent states shall be reduced to the same level of calamity. It would have been much more just & wise to have concluded the other way that as most of the states had judiciously preserved this palladium, those who had wandered should be brought back to it, and to have established general right instead of general wrong. Let me add that a bill of rights is what the people are entitled to against every government on earth, general or particular, & what no just government should refuse or rest on inference. . . .

---

[12]This could be loosely translated, "gratuitous observation."

[13]Article 2 of the Confederation affirmed that the states retained all sovereign powers not expressly delegated to the Union.

20

THOMAS JEFFERSON

Letter to James Madison

July 31, 1788

I sincerely rejoice at the acceptance of our new constitution by nine states. It is a good canvas, on which some strokes only want retouching. What these are, I think are sufficiently manifested by the general voice from North to South, which calls for a bill of rights. It seems pretty generally understood that this should go to Juries, Habeas corpus, Standing armies, Printing, Religion & Monopolies. I conceive there may be difficulty in finding general modifications of these suited to the habits of all the states. But if such cannot be found then it is better to establish trials by Jury, the right of Habeas corpus, freedom of the press & freedom of religion in all cases, and to abolish standing armies in time of peace, and Monopolies, in all cases, than not to do it in any. The few cases wherein these things may do evil, cannot be weighed against the multitude wherein the want of them will do evil. In disputes between a foreigner & a native, a trial by jury may be improper. But if this exception cannot be agreed to, the remedy will be to model the jury by giving the medietas linguae[14] in civil as well as criminal cases. Why suspend the Hab. corp. in insurrections & rebellions? The parties who may be arrested may be charged instantly with a well defined crime. Of course the judge will remand them. If the publick safety requires that the government should have a man imprisoned on less probable testimony in those than in other emergencies; let him be taken & tried, retaken & retried, while the necessity continues, only giving him redress against the government for damages. Examine the history of England: see how few of the cases of the suspension of the Habeas corpus law have been worthy of that suspension. They have been either real treasons wherein the parties might as well have been charged at once, or sham-plots where it was shameful they should ever have been suspected. Yet for the few cases wherein the suspension of the hab. corp. has done real good, that operation is now become habitual, & the minds of the nation almost prepared to live under it's

[14]The mediating tongue (or, more loosely, voice).

Thomas Jefferson to James Madison, July 31, 1788, Madison Papers, Library of Congress. From Rutland et al., eds., *Papers of Madison,* XI: 212–13.

constant suspension. A declaration that the federal government will never restrain the presses from printing any thing they please, will not take away the liability of the printers for false facts printed. The declaration that religious faith shall be unpunished, does not give impunity to criminal acts dictated by religious error. The saying there shall be no monopolies lessens the incitements to ingenuity, which is spurred on by the hope of a monopoly for a limited time, as of 14. years; but the benefit even of limited monopolies is too doubtful to be opposed to that of their general suppression. If no check can be found to keep the number of standing troops within safe bounds, while they are tolerated as far as necessary, abandon them altogether, discipline well the militia, & guard the magazines with them. More than magazine-guards will be useless if few, & dangerous if many. No European nation can ever send against us such a regular army as we need fear, & it is hard if our militia are not equal to those of Canada or Florida. My idea then is, that tho' proper exceptions to these general rules are desireable & probably practicable, yet if the exceptions cannot be agreed on, the establishment of the rules in all cases will do ill in very few. I hope therefore a bill of rights will be formed to guard the people against the federal government, as they are already guarded against their state governments in most instances.

MADISON'S RESPONSE

Like other Federalists, Madison did not think that the absence of a bill of rights marred the Constitution; like them, too, he suspected that what the Anti-Federalists really wanted was to secure sweeping changes in the Constitution itself. Yet as the Constitution met stiffer opposition in Massachusetts, New Hampshire, Virginia, and New York, Federalist leaders realized that some gesture of accommodation was required to conciliate moderate Anti-Federalists and secure the majorities needed for ratification. In practice, this meant acceding to some list of amendments, including but not limited to statements of rights, which these states would *recommend* to the consideration of the new Congress. Federalists struggled, with some difficulty but successfully, to prevent these amendments from being proposed as *conditions* of ratification. They insisted, that is, that amendments could be seriously considered only *after* the Constitution took effect.

At the June 1788 convention held in Richmond, Madison initially resisted the call for recommendatory amendments. But in the closing days of debate, he and his leading allies concluded that the even balance of strength between the two parties made some concession necessary. "The plan mediated by the friends [of] the Constitution," he wrote to Hamilton on June 22,

> is to preface the ratification with some plain & general truths that can not affect the validity of the Act: & to subjoin a recommendation which may hold up amendments as objects to be pursued in the constitutional mode. These expedients are rendered prudent by the nice balance of numbers, and the scruples entertained by some who are in general well affected.[15]

This strategy worked, making Virginia the tenth state to approve the Constitution, days after New Hampshire's approval provided the decisive ninth vote needed for ratification. Though Madison thought that many of the amendments recommended by Virginia were "highly objectionable," the crucial point had been gained.[16]

But Madison's commitment to the cause of amendments probably owed more to the aftermath of the ratification struggle. He knew that a substantial segment of the public remained nervous about the character of the Constitution. This opinion was confirmed when Madison found himself engaged in a tough campaign against his friend James Monroe for election to the first House of Representatives. In the course of this campaign, Madison issued public letters, affirming his support for adding amendments protective of rights to the Constitution, and promising that, if elected, he would take responsibility for carrying these articles through Congress.[17]

This conversion notwithstanding, Madison still doubted that adoption of a bill of rights would remedy a crucial defect in the Constitution. Its passage was necessary not to make rights more secure but rather to reconcile well-meaning citizens who were fearful of the Constitution. Thus, when he finally answered Jefferson's letters with a considered response of his own, his analysis conceded little if anything to either his friend's concerns or the fears of the people at large. Like his defense of the veto on state laws a year earlier, Madison's letter of October 17, 1788, restated his profound concern with the dangers of popular politics in republican government. Would a bill of rights, by itself, provide any check on the passions and interests of the popular majorities who were the true sovereigns in a republican government, Madison pointedly asked.

On this key point, Madison remained skeptical. He distilled one of his

---

[15]Madison to Hamilton, June 22, 1788, in Rutland et al., eds., *Papers of Madison*, XI: 166.
[16]Madison to Hamilton, June 27, 1788, in Rutland et al., eds., *Papers of Madison*, XI: 181.
[17]Madison to George Eve, January 2, 1789; to Thomas Mann Randolph, January 13, 1789; and printed extract of a letter addressed "To a Resident of Spotsylvania County," [January 27, 1789]; in Rutland et al., eds., *Papers of Madison*, XI: 404–405, 415–17, 428–29.

most important observations into a single sentence. A republican bill of rights might prove useful for this reason: "The political truths declared in that solemn manner acquire by degrees the character of fundamental maxims of free Government, and as they become incorporated with the national sentiment, counteract the impulses of interest and passion." Bills of rights would work best not by codifying particular legal rights that individuals could ask the courts to enforce (as we might expect); rather, they would achieve their true end if the citizens at large absorbed and, in a sense, internalized the deeper principles of political morality that they embodied. Bills of rights were thus as much educational treatises as legal documents.

Read in this way, Madison's letter can be said to combine modern and traditional elements of the theory of rights. On the one hand, he defined rights in essentially modern terms, as a problem of protecting individuals and minorities against the tyranny of the majority—and not of protecting the people as a whole against an arbitrary government. In this sense, Madison's theory of rights was liberal, in the same way that John Stuart Mill's classic essay *On Liberty* (1859) epitomized nineteenth-century liberalism. Yet Madison's emphasis on the way in which bills of rights should encourage citizens to act with restraint tied his theory to the traditional concept that linked rights with duties and mutual obligations.

21

JAMES MADISON

Letter to Thomas Jefferson

October 17, 1788

The little pamphlet herewith inclosed will give you a collective view of the alterations which have been proposed for the new Constitution. Various and numerous as they appear they certainly omit many of the true grounds of opposition. The articles relating to Treaties—to paper money, and to contracts, created more enemies than all the errors in the System positive & negative put together. It is true nevertheless that not a few, particularly in Virginia have contended for the proposed alter-

---

James Madison to Thomas Jefferson, October 17, 1788, Madison Papers, Library of Congress. From Rutland et al., eds., *Papers of Madison,* XI: 297–300.

ations from the most honorable & patriotic motives; and that among the advocates for the Constitution, there are some who wish for further guards to public liberty & individual rights. As far as these may consist of a constitutional declaration of the most essential rights, it is probable they will be added; though there are many who think such addition unnecessary, and not a few who think it misplaced in such a Constitution. There is scarce any point on which the party in opposition is so much divided as to its importance and its propriety. My own opinion has always been in favor of a bill of rights; provided it be so framed as not to imply powers not meant to be included in the enumeration. At the same time I have never thought the omission a material defect, nor been anxious to supply it even by *subsequent* amendment, for any other reason than that it is anxiously desired by others. I have favored it because I supposed it might be of use, and if properly executed could not be of disservice. I have not viewed it in an important light 1. because I conceive that in a certain degree, though not in the extent argued by Mr. Wilson, the rights in question are reserved by the manner in which the federal powers are granted. 2 because there is great reason to fear that a positive declaration of some of the most essential rights could not be obtained in the requisite latitude. I am sure that the rights of Conscience in particular, if submitted to public definition would be narrowed much more than they are likely ever to be by an assumed power. One of the objections in New England was that the Constitution by prohibiting religious tests opened a door for Jews Turks & infidels. 3. because the limited powers of the federal Government and the jealousy of the subordinate Governments, afford a security which has not existed in the case of the State Governments, and exists in no other. 4 because experience proves the inefficacy of a bill of rights on those occasions when its controul is most needed. Repeated violations of these parchment barriers have been committed by overbearing majorities in every State. In Virginia I have seen the bill of rights violated in every instance where it has been opposed to a popular current. Notwithstanding the explicit provision contained in that instrument for the rights of Conscience it is well known that a religious establishment wd. have taken place in that State, if the legislative majority had found as they expected, a majority of the people in favor of the measure; and I am persuaded that if a majority of the people were now of one sect, the measure would still take place and on narrower ground than was then proposed, notwithstanding the additional obstacle which the law has since created. Wherever the real power in a Government lies, there is the danger of oppression. In our Governments the real power lies in the majority of the Community, and the invasion of private rights is *cheifly* to be apprehended, not from acts of Government contrary to the sense of its constituents, but from acts in which the Government is the mere instrument of the major number of the constituents. This is a truth of great importance, but not yet sufficiently attended to: and is probably more strongly impressed on my mind by facts, and reflections suggested by them, than on yours which has contemplated abuses of power issuing from a very different quarter. Wherever there is an interest and power to do wrong, wrong will generally be done, and not less readily by a powerful & interested party than by a powerful and interested prince. The difference, so far as it relates to the superiority of republics over monarchies, lies in the less degree of probability that interest may prompt abuses of power in the former than in the latter; and in the security in the former agst. oppression of more than the smaller part of the society, whereas in the former it may be extended in a manner to the whole. The difference so far as it relates to the point in question — the efficacy of a bill of rights in controuling abuses of power — lies in this, that in a monarchy the latent force of the nation is superior to that of the sovereign, and a solemn charter of popular rights must have a great effect, as a standard for trying the validity of public acts, and a signal for rousing & uniting the superior force of the community; whereas in a popular Government, the political and physical power may be considered as vested in the same hands, that is in a majority of the people, and consequently the tyrannical will of the sovereign is not [to] be controuled by the dread of an appeal to any other force within the community. What use then it may be asked can a bill of rights serve in popular Governments? I answer the two following which though less essential than in other Governments, sufficiently recommend the precaution. 1. The political truths declared in that solemn manner acquire by degrees the character of fundamental maxims of free Government, and as they become incorporated with the national sentiment, counteract the impulses of interest and passion. 2. Altho' it be generally true as above stated that the danger of oppression lies in the interested majorities of the people rather than in usurped acts of the Government, yet there may be occasions on which the evil may spring from the latter sources; and on such, a bill of rights will be a good ground for an appeal to the sense of the community. Perhaps too there may be a certain degree of danger, that a succession of artful and ambitious rulers, may by gradual & well-timed advances, finally erect an independent[18] Government on the subversion of liberty. Should this danger exist at

---

[18]That is, independent of the people.

all, it is prudent to guard agst. it, especially when the precaution can do no injury. At the same time I must own that I see no tendency in our governments to danger on that side. It has been remarked that there is a tendency in all Governments to an augmentation of power at the expence of liberty. But the remark as usually understood does not appear to me well founded. Power when it has attained a certain degree of energy and independence goes on generally to further degrees. But when below that degree, the direct tendency is to further degrees of relaxation, until the abuses of liberty beget a sudden transition to an undue degree of power. With this explanation the remark may be true; and in the latter sense only is it in my opinion applicable to the Governments in America. It is a melancholy reflection that liberty should be equally exposed to danger whether the Government have too much or too little power, and that the line which divides these extremes should be so inaccurately defined by experience.

Supposing a bill of rights to be proper the articles which ought to compose it, admit of much discussion. I am inclined to think that *absolute* restrictions in cases that are doubtful, or where emergencies may overrule them, ought to be avoided. The restrictions however strongly marked on paper will never be regarded when opposed to the decided sense of the public; and after repeated violations in extraordinary cases, they will lose even their ordinary efficacy. Should a Rebellion or insurrection alarm the people as well as the Government, and a suspension of the Hab. Corp. be dictated by the alarm, no written prohibitions on earth would prevent the measure. Should an army in time of peace be gradually established in our neighbourhood by Britn: or Spain, declarations on paper would have as little effect in preventing a standing force for the public safety. The best security agst. these evils is to remove the pretext for them. With regard to monopolies they are justly classed among the greatest nusances in Government. But is it clear that as encouragements to literary works and ingenious discoveries, they are not too valuable to be wholly renounced? Would it not suffice to reserve in all cases a right to the Public to abolish the privilege at a price to be specified in the grant of it? Is there not also infinitely less danger of this abuse in our Governments, than in most others? Monopolies are sacrifices of the many to the few. Where the power is in the few it is natural for them to sacrifice the many to their own partialities and corruptions. Where the power, as with us, is in the many not in the few, the danger can not be very great that the few will be thus favored. It is much more to be dreaded that the few will be unnecessarily sacrificed to the many.

JEFFERSON'S COMMON SENSE

Five months passed before Jefferson answered this letter. By then Madison was already in New York, anxiously waiting for the new Congress to muster a quorum and get to work. In his difficult congressional race against James Monroe, word had spread not only that Madison opposed a bill of rights but even that he had "ceased to be a friend to the rights of Conscience"—the one issue to which in fact he had been most ardently committed since his boyhood. Madison responded with a public letter affirming his support for adding a statement of rights to the Constitution. This concession to electoral politics may have made Madison more sensitive to the importance "of satisfying the minds of well meaning opponents" of the Constitution—even as he remained convinced that diehard Anti-Federalists should not be allowed to pursue wholesale changes or even the project of a second general convention.[19]

Jefferson opened his response by noting that Madison had omitted an important consideration: that a bill of rights might strengthen the hands of the judiciary as an independent protector of rights. To modern readers, it may seem surprising both that Madison overlooked this point and that Jefferson needed to call it to his attention. We are used to thinking of an independent judiciary as the branch of government preeminently committed to the defense of individual rights. Yet in the late eighteenth century, this seemingly self-evident proposition was a matter of some dispute. Judges were historically regarded not as independent arbiters of justice but as agents (even lackeys) of the executive branch of government. Juries, not judges, were expected to protect rights. To say that a bill of rights might be specially addressed to the judiciary as an independent department thus anticipated the new enlarged role that this third branch of government would now come to play. It was in fact a prediction of the course that American constitutionalism would take, not a description of its initial status.

But Jefferson's letter is notable for another reason. As was often the case in their long correspondence, Jefferson answered Madison's carefully drawn distinctions with a few clear truths of his own. Even if a bill of rights were liable to the flaws and defects Madison claimed, Jefferson asked, were societies not better off with them than without them? Even if some rights were omitted or stated in weak terms, "Half a loaf is better than no bread. If we cannot secure all our rights, let us secure what we can."

[19]Madison to George Eve, January 2, 1789, in Rutland et al., eds., *Papers of Madison,* XI: 404.

22

THOMAS JEFFERSON

Letter to James Madison

March 15, 1789

Your thoughts on the subject of the Declaration of rights in the letter of
Oct. 17. I have weighed with great satisfaction. Some of them had not
occurred to me before, but were acknoleged just in the moment they were
presented to my mind. In the arguments in favor of a declaration of rights,
you omit one which has great weight with me, the legal check which it
puts into the hands of the judiciary. This is a body, which if rendered independent, & kept strictly to their own department merits great confidence
for their learning & integrity. In fact what degree of confidence would be
too much for a body composed of such men as Wythe, Blair & Pendleton? On characters like these the 'civium ardor prava jubentium'[20] would
make no impression. I am happy to find that on the whole you are a friend
to this amendment. The Declaration of rights is like all other human blessings alloyed with some inconveniences, and not accomplishing fully it's
object. But the good in this instance vastly overweighs the evil. I cannot
refrain from making short answers to the objections which your letter
states to have been raised. 1. That the rights in question are reserved
by the manner in which the federal powers are granted. Answer. A constitutive act may certainly be so formed as to need no declaration of
rights. The act itself has the force of a declaration as far as it goes: and if
it goes to all material points nothing more is wanting. In the draught of
a constitution which I had once a thought of proposing in Virginia, &
printed afterwards, I endeavored to reach all the great objects of public
liberty, and did not mean to add a declaration of rights.[21] Probably the
object was imperfectly executed: but the deficiencies would have been
supplied by others in the course of discussion. But in a constitutive act
which leaves some precious articles unnoticed, and raises implications
against others, a declaration of rights becomes necessary by way of sup-

---

[20]With such right-minded Virginians as George Wythe, John Blair, and Edmund Pendleton on the bench, Jefferson is saying that "the frenzy of [their] fellow-citizens bidding what
is wrong" would prove unavailing.

[21]Jefferson here means the constitution he drafted in 1783, not the earlier one he had
prepared in 1776.

Jefferson to Madison, March 15, 1789, Madison Papers, Library of Congress. From Rutland et al., eds., *Papers of Madison*, XII: 13–15.

plement. This is the case of our new federal constitution. This instrument forms us into one state as to certain objects, and gives us a legislative & executive body for these objects. It should therefore guard us against their abuses of power within the feild submitted to them. 2. A positive declaration of some essential rights could not be obtained in the requisite latitude. Answer. Half a loaf is better than no bread. If we cannot secure all our rights, let us secure what we can. 3. The limited powers of the federal government & jealousy of the subordinate governments afford a security which exists in no other instance. Answer. The first member of this seems resolvable into the 1st. objection before stated. The jealousy of the subordinate governments is a precious reliance. But observe that those governments are only agents. They must have principles furnished them whereon to found their opposition. The declaration of rights will be the text whereby they will try all the acts of the federal government. In this view it is necessary to the federal government also: as by the same text they may try the opposition of the subordinate governments. 4. Experience proves the inefficacy of a bill of rights. True. But tho it is not absolutely efficacious under all circumstances, it is of great potency always, and rarely inefficacious. A brace the more will often keep up the building which would have fallen with that brace the less. There is a remarkeable difference between the characters of the Inconveniencies which attend a Declaration of rights, & those which attend the want of it. The inconveniences of the Declaration are that it may cramp government in it's useful exertions. But the evil of this is shortlived, moderate, & reparable. The inconveniencies of the want of a Declaration are permanent, afflicting & irreparable: they are in constant progression from bad to worse. The executive in our governments is not the sole, it is scarcely the principal object of my jealousy. The tyranny of the legislatures is the most formidable dread at present, and will be for long years. That of the executive will come in it's turn, but it will be at a remote period. I know there are some among us who would now establish a monarchy. But they are inconsiderable in number and weight of character. The rising race are all republicans. We were educated in royalism: no wonder if some of us retain that idolatry still. Our young people are educated in republicanism. An apostacy from that to royalism is unprecedented & impossible. I am much pleased with the prospect that a declaration of rights will be added: and hope it will be done in that way which will not endanger the whole frame of the government, or any essential part of it.

13
Framing the Bill of Rights

By the time the new Congress mustered a quorum—a month late—in early April 1789, the political situation had shifted yet again. Though a few Anti-Federalists had been elected to Congress, Federalists controlled both houses—and thus the amendment process that Madison urged his colleagues to support.[1] By contrast, Anti-Federalist congressmen like Elbridge Gerry and Richard Henry Lee showed little enthusiasm for the project of a bill of rights because they knew that the structural changes they sought had no chance of passage. So, too, most Federalists thought Congress had more important tasks to complete: organizing executive departments, enacting revenue laws, and dealing with the deteriorating state of Indian relations along the frontier. The promise of amendments extracted from Federalists the previous summer had lost much of its force. Madison had to work hard to force his colleagues to pursue what he privately called "the nauseous project of amendments."[2]

The passage through Congress of the amendments that we now know as the Bill of Rights was thus a more complicated story than many textbook accounts suggest. From our vantage point, the proposal of these amendments seems a fitting capstone and culmination to the deliberations of the preceding two years, and the most noteworthy legacy of the First Federal Congress. But at the time, many congressmen and observers "out-of-doors" had good reason to adopt a more modest view. They regarded Madison's campaign more as an appendix or postscript to the campaign for ratification, likely to have neither immediate nor lasting importance to the operations of government. The proposals under

---

[1]Most of the extant evidence for these elections has been collected in Merrill Jensen, Robert A. Becker, and Gordon DenBoer, eds., *The Documentary History of the First Federal Elections, 1788–1790*, 4 vols. (Madison: University of Wisconsin Press, 1976–89); for a short survey, see Robert A. Becker, *The Politics of Opposition: Antifederalists and the Acceptance of the Constitution* (Millwood, N.Y.: KTO Press, 1979).

[2]Madison to Richard Peters, August 19, 1789, Robert Rutland et al., eds., *The Papers of James Madison* (Charlottesville: University Press of Virginia, 1979), XII: 346–47.

consideration, one Anti-Federalist congressman complained, "are not those solid and substantial amendments which the people expect; they are little better than whip-syllabub, frothy and full of wind, formed only to please the palate, or they are like a tub thrown out to a whale, to secure the freight of the ship and its peaceable voyage."[3] This perception may well explain why the amendments, supposedly so eagerly sought, were largely ignored in the press, or why the Virginia assembly, now dominated by Anti-Federalists, delayed their ratification for nearly two years.

MADISON'S STATESMANSHIP

Madison was used to dealing with recalcitrant legislators. Not for the first time in his career, he took personal responsibility for drafting the proposals his colleagues would consider—in part because he knew he had to take the initiative but also because he understood the advantage of shaping the agenda. From the more than two hundred amendments (many repetitive) that the state conventions had recommended,[4] Madison culled nineteen substantive proposals, which he presented to the House of Representatives in a lengthy speech on June 8, 1789. His great task after this speech was less to justify his particular proposals than to persuade his colleagues that the topic of amendments was worth discussing at all.

Madison's speech deserves careful reading for a number of reasons. Unlike the Continental Congress (and the new Senate), which met behind closed doors, the House of Representatives had opened its doors to the public and the press, and excerpts of its debates were already being widely printed in American newspapers. In preparing his speech, then, Madison addressed a dual audience: his colleagues whom he had to per-

---

[3] Aedanus Burke, speech of August 19, 1789, in Helen E. Veit, Kenneth R. Bowling, and Charlene Bangs Bickford, eds., *Creating the Bill of Rights: The Documentary Record from the First Federal Congress* (Baltimore and London: The Johns Hopkins University Press, 1991), 175. A syllabub is a wine-flavored, whipped cream and gelatin dessert; a "tub . . . to a whale" refers to seamen's practice of tossing empty barrels into the sea to divert whales from battering a ship.

[4] These amendments had been conveniently printed in a pamphlet entitled *The Ratifications of the New Fœderal Constitution, Together with the Amendments, Proposed by the Several States* (Richmond, 1788). The amendments officially recommended by the ratification conventions of Massachusetts, South Carolina, New Hampshire, Virginia, and New York are reprinted in Veit et al., eds., *Creating the Bill of Rights,* 14–28. Federalist majorities in Pennsylvania and Maryland blocked Anti-Federalist efforts to recommend amendments; there the dissenting minority members separately published the proposals that they wished to make.

suade to take this subject seriously, and a public whose misgivings about the Constitution he hoped to ease. Yet far from pandering to either Congress or the public, Madison sought to restate his underlying concerns about the protection of rights. Not only did he acknowledge his own political motives in proposing amendments; he also reiterated his basic concerns about where the greatest dangers to rights lay. No one hearing or reading his speech would have recognized Madison as an enthusiast for amendments in general, much less for a bill of rights in particular.

Consistent with those concerns, Madison thought that his amendments should *not* take the same form as the state bills of rights. Except for three statements of principle that he proposed to be "prefixed" to the Constitution, his other amendments were all meant to be interwoven into the body of the text. Framed in that way, they would operate not as vague statements of principle of uncertain legal effect but instead as explicit commands or restrictions addressed to specific branches of government. If articles of rights remained freestanding declarations, Madison argued, their authority and import would remain ambiguous and problematic. Interpreters would have to go back and forth between the Constitution and its amendments; and in that case, Madison told the House on August 13, "it will be difficult to ascertain to what parts of the instrument the amendments particularly refer."[5] In fact, Madison proposed to insert most of his rights-protecting amendments in that section of Article I that already contained a number of prohibitions on the authority of Congress. This placement would indicate that rights were most vulnerable to violation by the legislative branch of government, representing as it would the popular passions and interests that Madison most feared. As Madison had argued at the Convention and in *The Federalist,* it was against the "impetuous vortex" of the legislature that the friends of republican liberty had to direct their greatest vigilance.[6]

---

[5]Veit et al., eds., *Creating the Bill of Rights,* 118. In an important and challenging essay, the legal scholar Akhil Amar has argued that these structural features of Madison's original amendments carry important clues to the relation between the amendments and the larger design of the Constitution. See Amar, "The Bill of Rights as a Constitution," *Yale Law Journal* 100 (1991): 1131–1210.

[6]Madison, speech of July 21, 1787; and *Federalist* 48, in Rutland et al., eds., *Papers of Madison* (Chicago: University of Chicago Press, 1977), X: 109, 456.

23

JAMES MADISON

Speech to the House of Representatives

June 8, 1789

I am sorry to be accessary to the loss of a single moment of time by the house. If I had been indulged in my motion, and we had gone into a committee of the whole, I think we might have rose, and resumed the consideration of other business before this time; that is, so far as it depended on what I proposed to bring forward. As that mode seems not to give satisfaction, I will withdraw the motion, and move you, sir, that a select committee be appointed to consider and report such amendments as are proper for Congress to propose to the legislatures of the several States, conformably to the 5th article of the constitution. I will state my reasons why I think it proper to propose amendments; and state the amendments themselves, so far as I think they ought to be proposed. If I thought I could fulfil the duty which I owe to myself and my constituents, to let the subject pass over in silence, I most certainly should not trespass upon the indulgence of this house. But I cannot do this; and am therefore compelled to beg a patient hearing to what I have to lay before you. And I do most sincerely believe that if congress will devote but one day to this subject, so far as to satisfy the public that we do not disregard their wishes, it will have a salutary influence on the public councils, and prepare the way for a favorable reception of our future measures. It appears to me that this house is bound by every motive of prudence, not to let the first session pass over without proposing to the state legislatures some things to be incorporated into the constitution, as will render it as acceptable to the whole people of the United States, as it has been found acceptable to a majority of them. I wish, among other reasons why something should be done, that those who have been friendly to the adoption of this constitution, may have the opportunity of proving to those who were opposed to it, that they were as sincerely devoted to liberty and a republican government, as those who charged them with wishing the adoption of this constitution

James Madison, Speech of June 8, 1789 to the House of Representatives, *The Congressional Register or History of the Proceedings and Debates of the First House of Representatives of the United States of America,* vol. 1 (New York: Harrison and Purdy, 1789), from Houghton Library, Harvard University, AAS copy, microfiche W2571, Readex Early American Imprints 22203, 614, [2] pp.

in order to lay the foundation of an aristocracy or despotism. It will be a desirable thing to extinguish from the bosom of every member of the community any apprehensions, that there are those among his countrymen who wish to deprive them of the liberty for which they valiantly fought and honorably bled. And if there are amendments desired, of such a nature as will not injure the constitution, and they can be ingrafted so as to give satisfaction to the doubting part of our fellow citizens; the friends of the federal government will evince that spirit of deference and concession for which they have hitherto been distinguished.

It cannot be a secret to the gentlemen in this house, that, notwithstanding the ratification of this system of government by eleven of the thirteen United States, in some cases unanimously, in others by large majorities; yet still there is a great number of our constituents who are dissatisfied with it; among whom are many respectable for their talents, their patriotism, and respectable for the jealousy they have for their liberty, which, though mistaken in its object, is laudable in its motive. There is a great body of the people falling under this description, who at present feel much inclined to join their support to the cause of federalism, if they were satisfied in this one point: We ought not to disregard their inclination, but, on principles of amity and moderation, conform to their wishes, and expressly declare the great rights of mankind secured under this constitution. The acquiescence which our fellow citizens shew under the government, calls upon us for a like return of moderation. But perhaps there is a stronger motive than this for our going into a consideration of the subject; it is to provide those securities for liberty which are required by a part of the community. I allude in a particular manner to those two states who have not thought fit to throw themselves into the bosom of the confederacy: it is a desirable thing, on our part as well as theirs, that a re-union should take place as soon as possible. I have no doubt, if we proceed to take those steps which would be prudent and requisite at this juncture, that in a short time we should see that disposition prevailing in those states that are not come in, that we have seen prevailing [in] those states which are.

But I will candidly acknowledge, that, over and above all these considerations, I do conceive that the constitution may be amended; that is to say, if all power is subject to abuse, that then it is possible the abuse of the powers of the general government may be guarded against in a more secure manner than is now done, while no one advantage, arising from the exercise of that power, shall be damaged or endangered by it.

We have in this way something to gain, and, if we proceed with caution, nothing to lose; and in this case it is necessary to proceed with caution; for while we feel all these inducements to go into a revisal of the constitution, we must feel for the constitution itself, and make that revisal a moderate one. I should be unwilling to see a door opened for a re-consideration of the whole structure of the government, for a re-consideration of the principles and the substance of the powers given; because I doubt, if such a door was opened, if we should be very likely to stop at that point which would be safe to the government itself: But I do wish to see a door opened to consider, so far as to incorporate those provisions for the security of rights, against which I believe no serious objection has been made by any class of our constituents, such as would be likely to meet with the concurrence of two-thirds of both houses, and the approbation of three-fourths of the state legislatures. I will not propose a single alteration which I do not wish to see take place, as intrinsically proper in itself, or proper because it is wished for by a respectable number of my fellow citizens; and therefore I shall not propose a single alteration but is likely to meet the concurrence required by the constitution.

There have been objections of various kinds made against the constitution: Some were levelled against its structure, because the president was without a council; because the senate, which is a legislative body, had judicial powers in trials on impeachments; and because the powers of that body were compounded in other respects, in a manner that did not correspond with a particular theory; because it grants more power than is supposed to be necessary for every good purpose; and controuls the ordinary powers of the state governments. I know some respectable characters who opposed this government on these grounds; but I believe that the great mass of the people who opposed it, disliked it because it did not contain effectual provision against encroachments on particular rights, and those safeguards which they have been long accustomed to have interposed between them and the magistrate who exercised the sovereign power: nor ought we to consider them safe, while a great number of our fellow citizens think these securities necessary.

It has been a fortunate thing that the objection to the government has been made on the ground I stated; because it will be practicable on that ground to obviate the objection, so far as to satisfy the public mind that their liberties will be perpetual, and this without endangering any part of the constitution, which is considered as essential to the existence of the government by those who promoted its adoption.

The amendments which have occurred to me, proper to be recommended by congress to the state legislatures, are these:

First. That there be prefixed to the constitution a declaration — That all power is originally vested in, and consequently derived from the people.

That government is instituted, and ought to be exercised for the benefit of the people; which consists in the enjoyment of life and liberty, with the right of acquiring and using property, and generally of pursuing and obtaining happiness and safety.

That the people have an indubitable, unalienable, and indefeasible right to reform or change their government, whenever it be found adverse or inadequate to the purposes of its institution.

Secondly. That in article 1st. section 2, clause 3, these words be struck out, to wit, "The number of representatives shall not exceed one for every thirty thousand, but each state shall have at least one representative, and until such enumeration shall be made." And that in place thereof be inserted these words, to wit, "After the first actual enumeration, there shall be one representative for every thirty thousand, until the number amount to   after which the proportion shall be so regulated by congress, that the number shall never be less than   nor more than   but each state shall after the first enumeration, have at least two representatives; and prior thereto."

Thirdly. That in article 1st, section 6, clause 1, there be added to the end of the first sentence, these words, to wit, "But no law varying the compensation last ascertained shall operate before the next ensuing election of representatives."

Fourthly. That in article 1st, section 9, between clauses 3 and 4, be inserted these clauses, to wit, The civil rights of none shall be abridged on account of religious belief or worship, nor shall any national religion be established, nor shall the full and equal rights of conscience be in any manner, or on any pretext infringed.

The people shall not be deprived or abridged of their right to speak, to write, or to publish their sentiments; and the freedom of the press, as one of the great bulwarks of liberty, shall be inviolable.

The people shall not be restrained from peaceably assembling and consulting for their common good; nor from applying to the legislature by petitions, or remonstrances for redress of their grievances.

The right of the people to keep and bear arms shall not be infringed; a well armed, and well regulated militia being the best security of a free country: but no person religiously scrupulous of bearing arms, shall be compelled to render military service in person.

No soldier shall in time of peace be quartered in any house without the consent of the owner; nor at any time, but in a manner warranted by law.

No person shall be subject, except in cases of impeachment, to more than one punishment, or one trial for the same offence; nor shall be compelled to be a witness against himself; nor be deprived of life, liberty, or property without due process of law; nor be obliged to relinquish his property, where it may be necessary for public use, without a just compensation.

Excessive bail shall not be required, nor excessive fines imposed, nor cruel and unusual punishments inflicted.

The rights of the people to be secured in their persons, their houses, their papers, and their other property from all unreasonable searches and seizures, shall not be violated by warrants issued without probable cause, supported by oath or affirmation, or not particularly describing the places to be searched, or the persons or things to be seized.

In all criminal prosecutions, the accused shall enjoy the right to a speedy and public trial, to be informed of the cause and nature of the accusation, to be confronted with his accusers, and the witnesses against him; to have a compulsory process for obtaining witnesses in his favor; and to have the assistance of counsel for his defence.

The exceptions here or elsewhere in the constitution, made in favor of particular rights, shall not be so construed as to diminish the just importance of other rights retained by the people; or as to enlarge the powers delegated by the constitution; but either as actual limitations of such powers, or as inserted merely for greater caution.

Fifthly. That in article 1st, section 10, between clauses 1 and 2, be inserted this clause, to wit:

No state shall violate the equal rights of conscience, or the freedom of the press, or the trial by jury in criminal cases.

Sixthly. That article 3d, section 2, be annexed to the end of clause 2d, these words to wit: but no appeal to such court shall be allowed where the value in controversy shall not amount to   dollars: nor shall any fact triable by jury, according to the course of common law, be otherwise re-examinable than may consist with the principles of common law.

Seventhly. That in article 3d, section 2, the third clause be struck out, and in its place be inserted the clauses following, to wit:

The trial of all crimes (except in cases of impeachments, and cases arising in the land or naval forces, or the militia when on actual service in time of war or public danger) shall be by an impartial jury of freeholders of the vicinage, with the requisite of unanimity for conviction, of the right of challenge, and other accustomed requisites; and in all crimes punishable with loss of life or member, presentment or indictment by a grand jury, shall be an essential preliminary, provided that in cases of crimes committed within any county which may be in possession of an enemy, or in which a general insurrection may prevail, the trial may by law be authorised in some other county of the same state, as near as may be to the seat of the offence.

In cases of crimes committed not within any county, the trial may by law be in such county as the laws shall have prescribed. In suits at common law, between man and man, the trial by jury, as one of the best securities to the rights of the people, ought to remain inviolate.

Eighthly. That immediately after article 6th, be inserted, as article 7th, the clauses following, to wit:

The powers delegated by this constitution, are appropriated to the departments to which they are respectively distributed: so that the legislative department shall never exercise the powers vested in the executive or judicial; nor the executive exercise the powers vested in the legislative or judicial; nor the judicial exercise the powers vested in the legislative or executive departments.

The powers not delegated by this constitution, nor prohibited by it to the states, are reserved to the States respectively.

Ninthly. That article 7th, be numbered as article 8th.

The first of these amendments, relates to what may be called a bill of rights; I will own that I never considered this provision so essential to the federal constitution, as to make it improper to ratify it, until such an amendment was added; at the same time, I always conceived, that in a certain form and to a certain extent, such a provision was neither improper nor altogether useless. I am aware, that a great number of the most respectable friends to the government and champions for republican liberty, have thought such a provision, not only unnecessary, but even improper, nay, I believe some have gone so far as to think it even dangerous. Some policy has been made use of perhaps by gentlemen on both sides of the question: I acknowledge the ingenuity of those arguments which were drawn against the constitution, by a comparison with the policy of Great Britain, in establishing a declaration of rights; but there is too great a difference in the case to warrant the comparison: therefore the arguments drawn from that source, were in a great measure inapplicable. In the declaration of rights which that country has established, the truth is, they have gone no farther, than to raise a barrier against the power of the crown; the power of the legislature is left altogether indefinite. Altho' I know whenever the great rights, the trial by jury, freedom of the press, or liberty of conscience, came in question in that body, the invasion of them is resisted by able advocates, yet their Magna Charta does not contain any one provision for the security of those rights, respecting which, the people of America are most alarmed. The freedom of the press and rights of conscience, those choicest privileges of the people, are unguarded in the British constitution.

But altho' the case may be widely different, and it may not be thought necessary to provide limits for the legislative power in that country, yet a different opinion prevails in the United States. The people of many states, have thought it necessary to raise barriers against power in all forms and departments of government, and I am inclined to believe, if once bills of rights are established in all the states as well as the federal constitution, we shall find that altho' some of them are rather unimportant, yet, upon the whole, they will have a salutary tendency.

It may be said, in some instances they do no more than state the perfect equality of mankind; this to be sure is an absolute truth, yet it is not absolutely necessary to be inserted at the head of a constitution.

In some instances they assert those rights which are exercised by the people in forming and establishing a plan of government. In other instances, they specify those rights which are retained when particular powers are given up to be exercised by the legislature. In other instances, they specify positive rights, which may seem to result from the nature of the compact. Trial by jury cannot be considered as a natural right, but a right resulting from the social compact which regulates the action of the community, but is as essential to secure the liberty of the people as any one of the pre-existent rights of nature. In other instances they lay down dogmatic maxims with respect to the construction of the government; declaring, that the legislative, executive, and judicial branches shall be kept separate and distinct: Perhaps the best way of securing this in practice is to provide such checks, as will prevent the encroachment of the one upon the other.

But whatever may be form which the several states have adopted in making declarations in favor of particular rights, the great object in view is to limit and qualify the powers of government, by excepting out of the grant of power those cases in which the government ought not to act, or to act only in a particular mode. They point these exceptions sometimes against the abuse of the executive power, sometimes against the legislative, and, in some cases, against the community itself; or, in other words, against the majority in favor of the minority.

In our government it is, perhaps, less necessary to guard against the abuse in the executive department than any other; because it is not the stronger branch of the system, but the weaker: It therefore must be levelled against the legislative, for it is the most powerful, and most likely to be abused, because it is under the least controul; hence, so far as a declaration of rights can tend to prevent the exercise of undue power, it cannot be doubted but such declaration is proper. But I confess that I do conceive, that in a government modified like this of the United States, the great danger lies rather in the abuse of the community than in the legislative body. The prescriptions in favor of liberty, ought to be levelled against that quarter where the greatest danger lies, namely, that which possesses the highest prerogative of power: But this [is] not found in either the executive or legislative departments of government, but in the body of the people, operating by the majority against the minority.

It may be thought all paper barriers against the power of the community, are too weak to be worthy of attention. I am sensible they are not so strong as to satisfy gentlemen of every description who have seen and examined thoroughly the texture of such a defence; yet, as they have a tendency to impress some degree of respect for them, to establish the public opinion in their favor, and rouse the attention of the whole community, it may be one mean to controul the majority from those acts to which they might be otherwise inclined.

It has been said by way of objection to a bill of rights, by many respectable gentlemen out of doors, and I find opposition on the same principles likely to be made by gentlemen on this floor, that they are unnecessary articles of a republican government, upon the presumption that the people have those rights in their own hands, and that is the proper place for them to rest. It would be a sufficient answer to say that this objection lies against such provisions under the state governments as well as under the general government; and there are, I believe, but few gentlemen who are inclined to push their theory so far as to say that a declaration of rights in those cases is either ineffectual or improper. It has been said that in the federal government they are unnecessary, because the powers are enumerated, and it follows that all that are not granted by the constitution are retained: that the constitution is a bill of powers, the great residuum being the rights of the people; and therefore a bill of rights cannot be so necessary as if the residuum was thrown into the hands of the government. I admit that these arguments are not entirely without foundation; but they are not conclusive to the extent which has been supposed. It is true the powers of the general government are circumscribed; they are directed to particular objects; but even if government keeps within those limits, it has certain discretionary powers with respect to the means, which may admit of abuse to a certain extent, in the same manner as the powers of the state governments under their constitutions may to an indefinite extent; because in the constitution of the United States there is a clause granting to Congress the power to make all laws which shall be necessary and proper for carrying into execution all the powers vested in the government of the United States, or in any department or officer thereof; this enables them to fulfil every purpose for which the government was established. Now, may not laws be considered necessary and proper by Congress, for it is them who are to judge of the necessity and propriety to accomplish those special purposes which they may have in contemplation, which laws in themselves are neither necessary or proper; as well as improper laws could be enacted by the state legislatures, for fulfilling the more extended objects of those governments. I will state an instance which I think in point, and proves that this might be the case. The general government has a right to pass all laws which shall be necessary to collect its revenue; the means for enforcing the collection are within the direction of the legislature: may not general warrants be considered necessary for this purpose, as well as for some purposes which it was supposed at the framing of their constitutions the state governments had in view. If there was reason for restraining the state governments from exercising this power, there is like reason for restraining the federal government.

It may be said, because it has been said, that a bill of rights is not necessary, because the establishment of this government has not repealed those declarations of rights which are added to the several state constitutions: that those rights of the people, which had been established by the most solemn act, could not be annihilated by a subsequent act of that people, who meant, and declared at the head of the instrument, that they ordained and established a new system, for the express purpose of securing to themselves and posterity the liberties they had gained by an arduous conflict.

I admit the force of this observation, but I do not look upon it to be conclusive. In the first place, it is too uncertain ground to leave this provision upon, if a provision is at all necessary to secure rights so important as many of those I have mentioned are conceived to be, by the public in general, as well as those in particular who opposed the adoption of this constitution. Beside some states have no bills of rights, there are others provided with very defective ones, and there are others whose bills of rights are not only defective, but absolutely improper; instead of securing some in the full extent which republican principles would require, they limit them too much to agree with the common ideas of liberty.

It has been objected also against a bill of rights, that, by enumerating particular exceptions to the grant of power, it would disparage those rights which were not placed in that enumeration, and it might follow by implication, that those rights which were not singled out, were intended to be assigned into the hands of the general government, and were consequently insecure. This is one of the most plausible arguments I have ever heard urged against the admission of a bill of rights into this system; but, I conceive, that may be guarded against. I have attempted it, as gentlemen may see by turning to the last clause of the 4th resolution.

It has been said, that it is unnecessary to load the constitution with this provision, because it was not found effectual in the constitution of the particular states. It is true, there are a few particular states in which some of the most valuable articles have not, at one time or other, been violated; but does it not follow but they may have, to a certain degree, a salutary effect against the abuse of power. If they are incorporated into the constitution, independent tribunals of justice will consider themselves in a peculiar manner the guardians of those rights; they will be an impenetrable bulwark against every assumption of power in the legislative or executive; they will be naturally led to resist every encroachment upon rights expressly stipulated for in the constitution by the declaration of rights. Beside this security, there is a great probability that such a declaration in the federal system would be inforced; because the state legislatures will jealously and closely watch the operations of this government, and be able to resist with more effect every assumption of power than any other power on earth can do; and the greatest opponents to a federal government admit the state legislates to be sure guardians of the people's liberty. I conclude from this view of the subject, that it will be proper in itself, and highly politic, for the tranquility of the public mind, and the stability of the government, that we should offer something, in the form I have proposed, to be incorporated in the system of government, as a declaration of the rights of the people.

In the next place I wish to see that part of the constitution revised which declares, that the number of representatives shall not exceed the proportion of one for every thirty thousand persons, and allows one representative to every state which rates below that proportion. If we attend to the discussion of this subject, which has taken place in the state conventions, and even in the opinion of the friends to the constitution, an alteration here is proper. It is the sense of the people of America, that the number of representatives ought to be encreased, but particularly that it should not be left in the discretion of the government to diminish them, below that proportion which certainly is in the power of the legislature as the constitution now stands; and they may, as the population of the country encreases, increase the house of representatives to a very unwieldy degree. I confess I always thought this part of the constitution defective, though not dangerous; and that it ought to be particularly attended to whenever congress should go into the consideration of amendments.

There are several lesser cases enumerated in my proposition, in which I wish also to see some alteration take place. That article which leaves it in the power of the legislature to ascertain its own emolument is one to which I allude. I do not believe this is a power which, in the ordinary course of government, is likely to be abused, perhaps of all the powers granted, it is least likely to abuse; but there is a seeming impropriety in leaving any set of men without controul to put their hand into the public coffers, to take out money to put in their pockets; there is a seeming indecorum in such power, which leads me to propose a change. We have a guide to this alteration in several of the amendments which the different conventions have proposed. I have gone therefore so far as to fix it, that no law, varying the compensation, shall operate until there is a change in the legislature; in which case it cannot be for the particular benefit of those who are concerned in determining the value of the service.

I wish also, in revising the constitution, we may throw into that section, which interdicts the abuse of certain powers in the state legislatures, some other provisions of equal if not greater importance than those already made. The words, "No state shall pass any bill of attainder, ex post facto law, &c." were wise and proper restrictions in the constitution. I think there is more danger of those powers being abused by the state governments than by the government of the United States. The same may be said of other powers which they possess, if not controuled by the general principle, that laws are unconstitutional which infringe the rights of the community. I should therefore wish to extend this interdiction, and add, as I have stated in the 5th resolution, that no state shall violate the equal right of conscience, freedom of the press, or trial by jury in criminal cases; because it is proper that every government should be disarmed of powers which trench upon those particular rights. I know in some of the state constitutions the power of the government is controuled by such a declaration, but others are not. I cannot see any reason against obtaining even a double security on those points; and nothing can give a more sincere proof of the attachment of those who opposed this constitution to these great and important rights, than to see them join in obtaining the security I have now proposed; because it must be admitted, on all hands, that the state governments are as liable to attack these invaluable privileges as the general government is, and therefore ought to be as cautiously guarded against.

I think it will be proper, with respect to the judiciary powers, to satisfy the public mind on those points which I have mentioned. Great inconvenience has been apprehended to suitors from the distance they would be dragged to obtain justice in the supreme court of the United States, upon an appeal on an action for a small debt. To remedy this, declare, that no appeal shall be made unless the matter in controversy amounts to a particular sum: This, with the regulations respecting jury trials in criminal cases, and suits at common law, it is to be hoped will quiet and reconcile the minds of the people to that part of the constitution.

I find, from looking into the amendments proposed by the state conventions, that several are particularly anxious that it should be declared in the constitution, that the powers not therein delegated, should be reserved to the several states. Perhaps words which may define this more precisely, than the whole of the instrument now does, may be considered as superfluous. I admit they may be deemed unnecessary; but there can be no harm in making such a declaration, if gentlemen will allow that the fact is as stated. I am sure I understand it so, and do therefore propose it.

These are the points on which I wish to see a revision of the constitution take place. How far they will accord with the sense of this body, I cannot take upon me absolutely to determine; but I believe every gentleman will readily admit that nothing is in contemplation, so far as I have mentioned, that can endanger the beauty of the government in any one important feature, even in the eyes of its most sanguine admirers. I have proposed nothing that does not appear to me as proper in itself, or eligible as patronised by a respectable number of our fellow citizens; and if we can make the constitution better in the opinion of those who are opposed to it, without weakening its frame, or abridging its usefulness, in the judgment of those who are attached to it, we act the part of wise and liberal men to make such alterations as shall produce that effect.

Having done what I conceived was my duty, in bringing before this house the subject of amendments, and also stated such as I wish for and approve, and offered the reasons which occurred to me in their support; I shall content myself for the present with moving, that a committee be appointed to consider of and report such amendments as ought to be proposed by congress to the legislatures of the states, to become, if ratified by three-fourths thereof, part of the constitution of the United States. By agreeing to this motion, the subject may be going on in the committee, while other important business is proceeding to a conclusion in the house. I should advocate greater dispatch in the business of amendments, if I was not convinced of the absolute necessity there is of pursuing the organization of the government; because I think we should obtain the confidence of our fellow citizens, in proportion as we fortify the rights of the people against the encroachments of the government.

UNWEAVING THE AMENDMENTS

Madison's appeal did not fall on deaf ears, but the House remained reluctant to abandon its agenda. Six weeks passed before it assigned Madison's proposals to a select committee of one member from each state. The committee modified Madison's amendments only slightly and then delivered its report in late July. Another fortnight passed before the House took up the committee's report.

The principal change the House then made was to reject Madison's scheme to interweave the amendments with the original text. On this point, Madison's chief critic was Roger Sherman of Connecticut, a veteran politician who has the distinction of being a member of the Stamp Act Congress of 1765 and a signer of the Declaration of Independence, the Articles of Confederation, the Constitution, and (in effect) the Bill of Rights. As a member of the House committee, Sherman had drafted his own set of amendments, which resembled the models of the state declarations far more than Madison's.[7] The committee had set Sherman's proposals aside, but that did not stop him from pursuing his ends by other means. In his rather legalistic view, Congress lacked the right and authority to tamper with the original form of the Constitution, which was an act of the sovereign people, while the amendments, if adopted, would rest on the lesser majesty of the state legislatures. Twice the House rebuffed Sherman and his supporters in their efforts to present the amendments as "a distinct supplementary act." But that did not stop this dogged parliamentarian from trying a third time and finally gaining his point on August 19.[8] On the same day, the House eliminated Madison's proposed preamble to the preamble. From this point on, the amendments were des-

---

[7]Sherman's draft, recently discovered by James Hutson, is printed in Veit et al., eds., *Creating the Bill of Rights*, 266–68.

[8]The debate can be followed in Veit et al., eds., *Creating the Bill of Rights,* 105–12, 117–28, 197–98.

tined to take the form of separate, additional articles, not interwoven modifications to an existing text.

24

U.S. HOUSE OF REPRESENTATIVES

Constitutional Amendments
Proposed to the Senate
August 24, 1789

**Congress of the United States
In the House of Representatives,**

Monday, 24th August, 1789,

RESOLVED, BY THE SENATE AND HOUSE OF REPRESENTATIVES OF THE UNITED STATES OF AMERICA IN CONGRESS ASSEMBLED, two thirds of both Houses deeming it necessary, That the following Articles be proposed to the Legislatures of the several States, as Amendments to the Constitution of the United States, all or any of which Articles, when ratified by three fourths of the said Legislatures, to be valid to all intents and purposes as part of the said Constitution — Viz.

ARTICLES in addition to, and amendment of, the Constitution of the United States of America, proposed by Congress, and ratified by the Legislatures of the several States, pursuant to the fifth Article of the original Constitution.

ARTICLE THE FIRST

After the first enumeration, required by the first Article of the Constitution, there shall be one Representative for every thirty thousand, until the number shall amount to one hundred, after which the proportion shall be so regulated by Congress, that there shall be not less than one hundred Representatives, nor less than one Representative for every forty

Helen E. Veit, Kenneth R. Bowling, and Charlene Bangs Bickford, eds., *Creating the Bill of Rights: The Documentary Record from the First Federal Congress* (Baltimore: The Johns Hopkins University Press, 1991), 37–41.

thousand persons, until the number of Representatives shall amount to two hundred, after which the proportion shall be so regulated by Congress, that there shall not be less than two hundred Representatives, nor less than one Representative for every fifty thousand persons.

ARTICLE THE SECOND

No law varying the compensation to the members of Congress, shall take effect, until an election of Representatives shall have intervened.

ARTICLE THE THIRD

Congress shall make no law establishing religion or prohibiting the free exercise thereof, nor shall the rights of Conscience be infringed.

ARTICLE THE FOURTH

The Freedom of Speech, and of the Press, and the right of the People peaceably to assemble, and consult for their common good, and to apply to the Government for a redress of grievances, shall not be infringed.

ARTICLE THE FIFTH

A well regulated militia, composed of the body of the People, being the best security of a free State, the right of the People to keep and bear arms, shall not be infringed, but no one religiously scrupulous of bearing arms, shall be compelled to render military service in person.

ARTICLE THE SIXTH

No soldier shall, in time of peace, be quartered in any house without the consent of the owner, nor in time of war, but in a manner to be prescribed by law.

ARTICLE THE SEVENTH

The right of the People to be secure in their persons, houses, papers and effects, against unreasonable searches and seizures, shall not be violated, and no warrants shall issue, but upon probable cause supported by oath or affirmation, and particularly describing the place to be searched, and the persons or things to be seized.

ARTICLE THE EIGHTH

No person shall be subject, except in case of impeachment, to more than one trial, or one punishment for the same offense, nor shall be compelled in any criminal case, to be a witness against himself, nor be deprived of life, liberty or property, without due process of law; nor shall private property be taken for public use without just compensation.

ARTICLE THE NINTH

In all criminal prosecutions, the accused shall enjoy the right to a speedy and public trial, to be informed of the nature and cause of the accusation, to be confronted with the witnesses against him, to have compulsory process for obtaining witnesses in his favor, and to have the assistance of counsel for his defence.

ARTICLE THE TENTH

The trial of all crimes (except in cases of impeachment, and in cases arising in the land or naval forces, or in the militia when in actual service in time of War or public danger) shall be by an impartial Jury of the Vicinage, with the requisite of unanimity for conviction, the right of challenge, and other accostomed requisites; and no person shall be held to answer for a capital, or otherways infamous crime, unless on a presentment or indictment by a Grand Jury; but if a crime be committed in a place in the possession of an enemy, or in which an insurrection may prevail, the indictment and trial may by law be authorised in some other place within the same State.

ARTICLE THE ELEVENTH

No appeal to the Supreme Court of the United States, shall be allowed, where the value in controversy shall not amount to one thousand dollars, nor shall any fact, triable by a Jury according to the course of the common law, be otherwise re-examinable, than according to the rules of common law.

ARTICLE THE TWELFTH

In suits at common law, the right of trial by Jury shall be preserved.

ARTICLE THE THIRTEENTH

Excessive bail shall not be required, nor excessive fines imposed, nor cruel and unusual punishments inflicted.

ARTICLE THE FOURTEENTH

No State shall infringe the right of trial by Jury in criminal cases, nor the rights of conscience, nor the freedom of speech, or of the press.

ARTICLE THE FIFTEENTH

The enumeration in the Constitution of certain rights, shall not be construed to deny or disparage others retained by the people.

ARTICLE THE SIXTEENTH

The powers delegated by the Constitution to the government of the United States, shall be exercised as therein appropriated, so that the Legislative shall never exercise the powers vested in the Executive or Judicial; nor the Executive the powers vested in the Legislative or Judicial; nor the Judicial the powers vested in the Legislative or Executive.

ARTICLE THE SEVENTEENTH

The powers not delegated by the Constitution, nor prohibited by it, to the States, are reserved to the States respectively.

Teste,
JOHN BECKLEY, CLERK
In SENATE, *August* 25, 1789
Read and ordered to be printed for the consideration of the Senate.
Attest, SAMUEL A. OTIS, Secretary
NEW-YORK, PRINTED BY T. GREENLEAF, near the COFFEE-HOUSE.

EDITORIAL CHANGES

Little is known about the substance of the Senate debates. Unlike the House, the Senate met behind closed doors until 1794; and when the amendments were taken up, William Maclay, the one senator who kept extensive notes of debates during this period, was incapacitated with a severely inflamed knee and other assorted aches and pains. But the revised amendments the Senate returned to the House are noteworthy in at least three respects.

First, the Senate consolidated the multiple articles the House had recommended into the more compact form with which we are now familiar. By grouping related articles together in this way, its editorial labor may have encouraged later interpreters to search for the deeper principles that informed the framers' conceptions of rights.[9] If, for example, we find the right to the "free exercise of religion" (or freedom of conscience) linked

[9] One can also speculate whether the grouping of multiple clauses in one article was designed to make ratification of particular provisions more likely than would have been the case had they gone forward as separate articles. On this point, see Amar, "The Bill of Rights as a Constitution," 1181; and the comments by Sanford Levinson in his introductory chapter, "Imperfection and Amendability," in Levinson, ed., *Responding to Imperfection: The Theory and Practice of Constitutional Amendment* (Princeton: Princeton University Press, 1995), 3–36 and esp. 25n.40.

to freedom of speech and the press and the right to petition for redress of grievances, we can ask whether the First Amendment rests upon deeper presumptions about the nature of the human intellect and the diverse forms in which it expresses itself—in religion, in culture, in politics, in daily life. (The symbolic importance we attach to these freedoms has also benefited from the rejection by the states of the amendments relating to the apportionment of the House and congressional pay raises, for what is now the First Amendment was originally the third proposed.)

Second, the Senate proposed a specific change in the wording of the religion clause of the (eventual) First Amendment that in turn sparked a sharp reaction from the House and especially, historians have supposed, from Madison. The religion clause, as it came from the Senate, read: "Congress shall make no laws establishing articles of faith, or a mode of worship, or prohibiting the free exercise of religion." Read narrowly, the first two members of this clause suggested that Congress was barred only from enacting laws supporting particular points of doctrine (for example, belief in the Holy Trinity or the divinity of Jesus or the reality of transubstantiation) or requiring certain forms of worship. Legislation supporting (or establishing) religion in other ways would presumably be acceptable.

In the earlier debate in the House, Madison had spoken as if his principal goal was to prevent Congress from making either a particular religion (Christianity) or a particular denomination (Episcopalians or Presbyterians or Congregationalists, for example) from being anointed as an official national church, on the model of the Church of England.[10] Given that Madison believed that the sectarian divisions and antiestablishment bias of the existing Protestant denominations made such an event extremely unlikely, he might not have cared all that deeply about the vagueness of his own original proposal. But the language preferred by the Senate narrowed the import of this clause far too much, because it could be read to imply that Congress was prohibited from legislating in religious matters only in these specified ways. Accordingly, in the conference committee to which he was appointed to resolve the differences between the Senate and House texts, Madison succeeded in restating the principle in broader terms that flatly commanded Congress to "make no

[10]In the debates of August 15, Madison explained the clause this way: "He apprehended the meaning of the words to be, that congress shall not establish a religion, and enforce the legal observation of it by law, nor compel men to worship God in any manner contrary to their conscience." Madison then declined to state whether "the words were necessary or not," indicating, as on other occasions, that the clause was needed to reassure the public, not to rectify a potential danger. Veit et al., eds., *Creating the Bill of Rights*, 157–58.

law respecting an establishment of religion." Given both the choices available at the time and the ample evidence of Madison's early and profound opposition to any connection between church and state, the most plausible explanation of this change suggests that Madison—in reaction to the narrow language used by the Senate—was now looking to state the core principle of separation of church and state as broadly as possible. The conference committee, and later Congress, could have preserved either the language used by the Senate or Madison's own original prohibitions on laws establishing "a national religion." Instead, the amendment was cast in the broader language that became so fruitful a source of controversy (precisely because it is so broad) in the twentieth century.[11]

The third substantial change the Senate made in the House proposals was to eliminate the article prohibiting the states from "infring[ing] the right to trial by jury in criminal cases, nor the rights of conscience, nor the freedom of speech, or of the press." In the House, Madison had boldly described this clause "as the most valuable amendment on the whole list"—and so he certainly thought it was, because it was the one amendment directed against the states, where he believed rights would still be most endangered. But in deleting this provision, the Senate was acting consistently with its own constitutional duty. As a body elected by the state legislatures, senators might suppose that they should resist these infringements on the authority of their constituents. However, as far as Madison was concerned, this omission was most disturbing. Not until the ratification of the Civil War Amendments would the national government acquire a general constitutional basis for protecting the rights of individuals and minorities against the injustice of state lawmaking that so alarmed Madison in the 1780s. (Madison was less concerned, however, that the Senate had rejected his formulaic article restating the principle of separation of powers; privately he probably doubted that this clause was worth the quill with which he had drafted it.)

---

[11]The literature on the modern interpretation of the religion clauses is enormous. Two good places to begin are Leonard W. Levy, *The Establishment Clause: Religion and the First Amendment* (New York: Macmillan, 1986); Michael McConnell, "The Origins and Historical Understanding of Free Exercise of Religion," *Harvard Law Review* 103 (1989–90): 1409–1517.

25

U.S. CONGRESS

Constitutional Amendments
Proposed to the States

September 28, 1789

The Conventions of a number of the States, having at the time of their adopting the Constitution, expressed a desire, in order to prevent misconstruction or abuse of its powers, that further declaratory and restrictive clauses should be added: And as extending the ground of public confidence in the Government, will best ensure the benificent ends of its institution

RESOLVED by the Senate and House of Representatives of the United States of America, in Congress assembled, two thirds of both Houses concurring, that the following Articles be proposed to the Legislatures of the several States, as amendments to the Constitution of the United States, all or any of which Articles, when ratified by three fourths of the said Legislatures, to be valid to all intents and purposes, as part of the said Constitution; vizt.

ARTICLES in addition to, and amendment of the Constitution of the United States of America, proposed by Congress, and ratified by the Legislatures of the several States, pursuant to the fifth Article of the original Constitution.

ARTICLE THE FIRST

After the first enumeration required by the first Article of the Constitution, there shall be one Representative for every thirty thousand, until the number shall amount to one hundred, after which, the proportion shall be so regulated by Congress, that there shall be not less than one hundred Representatives, nor less than one Representative for every forty thousand persons, until the number of Representatives shall amount to two hundred, after which the proportion shall be so regulated by Congress, that there shall not be less than two hundred Representatives, nor more than one Representative for every fifty thousand persons.

From Veit et al., eds., *Creating the Bill of Rights*, 3–5.

ARTICLE THE SECOND

No law, varying the compensation for the services of the Senators and Representatives, shall take effect, until an election of Representatives shall have intervened.

ARTICLE THE THIRD

Congress shall make no law respecting an establishment of religion, or prohibiting the free exercise thereof; or abridging the freedom of speech, or of the press, or the right of the people peaceably to assemble, and to petition the Government for a redress of grievances.

ARTICLE THE FOURTH

A well regulated militia, being necessary to the security of a free State, the right of the people to keep and bear arms, shall not be infringed.

ARTICLE THE FIFTH

No Soldier shall, in time of peace be quartered in any House, without the consent of the owner, nor in time of war, but in a manner to be prescribed by law.

ARTICLE THE SIXTH

The right of the people to be secure in their persons, houses, papers, and effects, against unreasonable searches and seizures, shall not be violated, and no warrants shall issue, but upon probable cause, supported by oath or affirmation, and particularly describing the place to be searched and the persons or things to be seized.

ARTICLE THE SEVENTH

No person shall be held to answer for a capital, or otherwise infamous crime, unless on a presentment or indictment of [a] Grand Jury, except in cases arising in the land or naval forces, or in the militia, when in actual service in time of war or public danger; nor shall any person be subject for the same offence to be twice put in jeopardy of life or limb; nor shall be compelled in any criminal case to be a witness against himself, nor be deprived of life, liberty, or property, without due process of law; nor shall private property be taken for public use, without just compensation.

ARTICLE THE EIGHTH

In all criminal prosecutions, the accused shall enjoy the right to a speedy and public trial, by an impartial jury of the State and district wherein the crime shall have been committed; which district shall have been previously ascertained by law, and to be informed of the nature and cause of the accusation; to be confronted with the witnesses against him; to have compulsory process for obtaining witnesses in his favor, and to have the assistance of counsel for his defence.

ARTICLE THE NINTH

In suits at common law, where the value in controversy shall exceed twenty dollars, the right of trial by jury shall be preserved, and no fact tried by a jury, shall be otherwise re-examined in any Court of the United States, than according to the rules of the common law.

ARTICLE THE TENTH

Excessive bail shall not be required, nor excessive fines imposed, nor cruel and unusual punishments inflicted.

ARTICLE THE ELEVENTH

The enumeration in the Constitution, of certain rights, shall not be construed to deny or disparage others retained by the people.

ARTICLE THE TWELFTH

The powers not delegated to the United States by the Constitution, nor prohibited by it to the States, are reserved to the States respectively, or to the people.

FREDERICK AUGUSTUS MUHLENBERG
Speaker of the House of Representatives

JOHN ADAMS
Vice-President of the United States, and
President of the Senate

ATTEST,
JOHN BECKLEY, Clerk of the House of Representatives
SAM. A. OTIS, Secretary of the Senate

RESIDUAL AMBIGUITIES

Strictly speaking, the twelve articles that Congress sent to the states were not a bill of rights in the usual sense. The first two proposed amendments were not statements of rights at all but regulations relating to the apportionment of the House of Representatives and the approval of changes in congressional salaries. Neither amendment was approved by the states (at least at first, for in 1992 the latter article did join the Constitution as the Twenty-seventh Amendment).[12] Once those two proposals fell by the wayside, however, the surviving amendments could come to be regarded as a bill of rights—but one that departed, in notable ways, from its venerable antecedents, even as many of its clauses echoed their language.

Was the Bill of Rights an act of negotiation between the people and their governors? At first glance, the idea that it was a concession to the Anti-Federalist opposition, voicing a deep popular mistrust of the political elite who had framed the Constitution, seems to fit that historical image. But on closer examination, that interpretation is hard to square with the political circumstances of 1789—either with Federalist cynicism about the real value of a bill of rights or with Anti-Federalist indifference to the substance of Madison's proposals.

By comparison with the rhetorical flourishes of the state bills of rights, moreover, the amendments of 1789 struck a less eloquent chord. Gone were the appeals to natural rights and first principles. In their place lay a set of spare commands presupposing that the people already knew what the moral purposes and ultimate sources of their rights were. Only the Second Amendment, protecting "the right of the people to keep and bear arms," came encumbered with a preamble stating its purpose. Ironically, its most zealous modern adherents prefer to dismiss its reference to the benefits of a "well-regulated militia" as so much persiflage— because to take that purpose seriously might imply that individuals have no constitutional right to keep tanks and howitzers in their garages or to bear machine guns to the shopping mall.

Nor is it completely clear to which parts of government the commands of the Bill of Rights were addressed. The First Amendment, it is true, explicitly bars Congress from enacting whole categories of law infringing fundamental rights of belief and expression. Then why were the next seven amendments, which make no reference to Congress, not regarded as binding both the Union and the states? A plain-text reading could sug-

---

[12]Herein lies a tale. In 1981 a young Texas college student named Gregory Watson learned of these two failed amendments, and soon began a ten-year campaign to revive the second one and secure the additional states needed for ratification. Ignoring the scoffing of scholars, who thought that there was something absurd about the idea of approving a proposal that had circulated in constitutional limbo for two centuries, Watson pursued his campaign. When Michigan, New Jersey, and Illinois ratified in a rush in May 1992, Madison's original proposal was brought safely to harbor after a voyage of 203 years. Watson's heroic efforts are discussed in Richard Bernstein, with Jerome Agel, *Amending America: If We Love the Constitution So Much, Why Do We Keep Trying to Change It?* (New York: Times Books, 1993), 243–48.

gest that these rights, reinforced with the authority of the supremacy clause, might have been applied against the states without needing the later authority of the Fourteenth Amendment and the incorporation doctrine. Yet until these later extensions of constitutional theory and judicial doctrine took shape, Americans implicitly understood that the Bill of Rights affected only the national government and not the states.

The final two amendments seem more mysterious still—or simply pointless. The Ninth Amendment was long regarded as a constitutional nullity—neither identifying other rights left unenumerated, nor providing an independent source of authority for the discovery or invention of new rights. And the favorite description of the Tenth Amendment treats it as a "truism" devoid of useful meaning—a vacuous statement that simply requires us to look to the original text of the Constitution to determine what powers have in fact been delegated to the Union. In fact, a good case can be made that both amendments recapitulate essential Federalist reasons for questioning whether a bill of rights was either necessary or proper. The Ninth Amendment, after all, is consistent with the idea that it is dangerous to enumerate rights because something essential might be omitted or not foreseen or inadequately stated. And the Tenth Amendment, as James Hutson observes, can be read as an "anti-bill of rights, a repetition of the argument used by the Federalists to repudiate a bill of rights during the ratification controversy," because it only affirmed James Wilson's argument that powers not delegated to the national government were inherently reserved.[13]

The amendments originally attracted relatively little interest in either the press or the states. Scholars who try to look for additional evidence of how Americans originally understood the meaning of the amendments once they were proposed invariably come away disappointed. The amendments made their way through the state assemblies almost by stealth, with little recorded discussion or public commentary. By December 1791, final action by Virginia produced the approval of the tenth state required to ratify the ten amendments that we now call the Bill of Rights.

[13]James H. Hutson, "The Bill of Rights and the American Revolutionary Experience," in Michael Lacey and Knud Haakonssen, eds., *A Culture of Rights: The Bill of Rights in Philosophy, Politics, and Law: 1791 and 1991* (New York: Cambridge University Press, 1991), 95.

Epilogue: After Two Centuries

For the better part of a century and a half, the Bill of Rights had little apparent effect on the course of American law and politics. An early test of its potential use came in 1798, when a Federalist[1] Congress adopted the Sedition Act to enable the administration of President John Adams to punish those who wrote too critically about its foreign and domestic policies. Neither the free speech nor free press clauses of the First Amendment, nor the Tenth Amendment's affirmation that the national government could exercise only delegated powers, proved effective restraints against the abuse of this power. Nor did they have much effect in succeeding decades (though it is noteworthy that the Republican administrations of Jefferson, Madison, and Monroe insisted upon Sunday delivery of the mail, on the grounds that not delivering the mail would constitute an establishment of religion by virtue of recognizing the Christian Sabbath as a day of rest). In a notable opinion of 1833, Chief Justice John Marshall held (in *Barron v. The Mayor of Baltimore*[2]) that the Bill of Rights restrained the national government only, not the states; and since the national government played only a minimal role in the daily lives of most Americans (except those in frontier territories), the original amendments were, for all intents and purposes, little more than a dusty testament to the political anxieties of the late 1780s. It was the Declaration of Independence that spoke most powerfully to nineteenth-century Americans, not least because its statement of equality was a beacon to all those groups whose rights and liberties were valued less highly than those of free white male property holders.

Perhaps this early history confirms that Madison had not been so wrong to dismiss bills of rights as parchment barriers — nice to read, perhaps, but not especially useful. Even today, most Americans — though not

---

[1]Federalist, as used here, no longer identifies the advocates of ratification of the Constitution, but rather the supporters of the policies pursued by the administrations of George Washington and John Adams, as well as the adherents of Alexander Hamilton, who was in many ways the party's true leader.

[2]*Barron v. Baltimore,* 7 Peters 243 (1833).

(of course) the readers of this book—probably never read the Bill of Rights, or if they do read it, they quickly forget its contents. Public opinion polls reveal dismaying ignorance about its contents, and when citizens are asked whether they agree with its provisions, if read to them separately, they tend to demur.[3]

Yet history has a cunning and irony of its own. Slowly, after the First World War, the Supreme Court began to apply specific provisions of the Bill of Rights against the states, under the sheltering power of the Fourteenth Amendment.[4] Once that foundation was laid—initially in the realm of freedom of speech, where the Court began to recognize the rights of political dissenters — a legal foundation was laid for other groups to seek judicial protection for fundamental rights; this in turn gave the Bill of Rights (again, linked to the Fourteenth Amendment) an authority and immediacy it previously lacked. In the second half of the twentieth century, the meaning, extent, and application of the Bill of Rights posed the most important questions about the interpretation of the Constitution.[5]

In this transformation, five groups of claimants deserve special notice. First, and arguably most important, was the legal attack on the edifice of racial segregation launched by the National Association for the Advancement of Colored People (NAACP) in the 1940s. The NAACP's great culminating victory in *Brown v. Board of Education of Topeka*[6] set both a legal precedent and a moral example of the first magnitude. Second, attorneys for urban voters whose communities had been denied their proportional weight in the malapportioned legislative chambers of the states and the federal House of Representatives secured a series of judicial decisions making the principle of one person, one vote the sole acceptable rule for apportioning representation.[7] Third, a series of landmark decisions in the

---

[3]For a brief discussion, see Michael Kammen, *A Machine That Would Go of Itself: The Constitution in American Culture* (New York: Alfred Knopf, 1987), 336–56.

[4]For an overview, see Richard C. Cortner, *The Supreme Court and the Second Bill of Rights: The Fourteenth Amendment and the Nationalization of Civil Liberties* (Madison: University of Wisconsin Press, 1981).

[5]For historically grounded overviews of these developments, see the essays collected in David J. Bodenhamer and James W. Ely, Jr., eds., *The Bill of Rights in Modern America: After 200 Years* (Bloomington and Indianapolis: Indiana University Press, 1993).

[6]*Brown v. Board of Education of Topeka,* 349 U.S. 294 (1954). Mark Tushnet, *The NAACP's Legal Strategy Against Segregated Education* (Chapel Hill: University of North Carolina Press, 1987) demonstrates how the National Association for the Advancement of Colored People, long the leading civil rights organization in the African-American community, pursued a course of litigation designed to make the overturning of segregation possible.

[7]See, in general, Richard Cortner, *The Apportionment Cases* (Knoxville: University of Tennessee Press, 1970). The leading cases include *Baker v. Carr,* 369 U.S. 186 (1962), and *Reynolds v. Sims,* 377 U.S. 533 (1964).

1960s and 1970s produced an elaborate and still controversial body of judicial doctrine requiring police, courts, and prisons to extend to those accused and convicted of crimes the protection of the Fourth, Fifth, Sixth, and Eighth Amendments in new and far-reaching ways.[8] Fourth, in the *Griswold v. Connecticut* decision of 1965 (striking down a Connecticut law prohibiting the sale of contraceptives) and the *Roe v. Wade* decision of 1973 (striking down a Texas law limiting a woman's right to obtain an abortion), the Supreme Court moved beyond the explicit language of the Constitution to argue that its general presumptions of personal autonomy could be extended to fundamental aspects of reproduction and sexuality.[9] Finally, whole phalanxes of political, religious, and cultural dissenters have generated a host of disputes about the contemporary meaning of the freedoms of speech, religion, press, and expression covered by the First Amendment, plunging government agencies and courts at every level of society into a seemingly unending forest of controversies from which we seem to glimpse no path of escape.[10]

Taken together, these decisions, and the reactions they have provoked, have converted the original Bill of Rights and the Fourteenth Amendment into the most significant and controversial elements of the Constitution. They have generated an enormous scholarly literature that alternately defends and impugns the legal and moral principles on which this rights-based jurisprudence has been grounded. These controversies, in turn, have brought renewed interest in the historical origins of the Bill of Rights.[11] In part this interest exists because we want to know whether contemporary interpretations of its clauses can be squared with the original intentions and understandings of its adopters. In part, too, it may reflect anxiety about allowing the judiciary, the least politically accountable branch of government, to make decisions overturning those of elected officials.

[8]Leading cases include *Mapp v. Ohio,* 367 U.S. 643 (1961), applying federal rules for the exclusion of improperly attained evidence to state criminal proceedings; *Gideon v. Wainwright,* 372 U.S. 335 (1963), extending the right to counsel in criminal trials; and *Miranda v. Arizona* (1966), 377 U.S. 201, voiding confessions obtained from suspects who had not been advised of their right to remain silent or to receive the assistance of legal counsel (since made familiar to Americans through the wonders of television and countless police dramas).

[9]*Griswold v. Connecticut,* 381 U.S. 479 (1965); *Roe v. Wade,* 410 U.S. 113 (1973).

[10]For an introduction to many but by no means all of the leading issues, see Rodney A. Smolla, *Free Speech in an Open Society* (New York: Alfred Knopf, 1992).

[11]For a representative statement of mostly (though not exclusively) conservative attacks on modern rights-expanding jurisprudence, grounded in "originalist" methodology, see Eugene W. Hickok, Jr., ed., *The Bill of Rights: Original Meaning and Current Understanding* (Charlottesville: University Press of Virginia, 1991).

But perhaps most important, our concern about the historical origins and meaning of the Bill of Rights may reflect the dilemma that Federalists and Anti-Federalists pondered. Clearly the very existence and security of our rights do not depend on text alone. Any constitutional text is a dead letter, unless citizens and officials are imbued with the principles and norms that a constitution expresses and promotes. This means both that citizens must have the confidence and often the courage to assert the rights they believe are deservedly theirs, and that courts and legislatures must be receptive to their concerns. Yet in staking and affirming these claims, it has clearly mattered a great deal that the Bill of Rights and the Fourteenth Amendment operate as a powerful beacon and bright banner. They remind citizens and officials alike that the Republic has at one time or another forged a constitutional commitment not simply to rules of deliberation and governance, but also to fundamental principles designed to protect citizens against the abuse of power.

Thus even if Madison's original ambition for the Bill of Rights was modest, and even if the first ten amendments had little import before the mid-twentieth century, their presence in the Constitution now looms large in American law and politics. Yet we have not entirely escaped the dilemma with which the framers and ratifiers of the Constitution originally grappled. No comprehensive theory of the freedom of expression can be distilled from the spare language of the First Amendment. Its affirmation of freedom of speech and press and the right to assemble cannot by fiat explain whether public censorship of the Internet is constitutionally permissible, or whether neo-Nazis have a right to parade through Skokie (a Chicago suburb whose population includes a number of Holocaust survivors), or what distance antiabortion protesters must keep from the offices of reproductive health care clinics. Interpreters can only start with the language of the First Amendment; they still must balance a range of concerns and conditions to apply its general principle to the modern world.

So, too, efforts to state a right explicitly may prove constraining in a different way, much as Madison feared. Consider the ongoing debate about the right to bear arms guaranteed by the Second Amendment. One might think that thousands of deaths caused annually by firearms and the casual use of automatic weapons by gangs might lead us to regard the language of the Second Amendment as a relic of another age, of little value in trying to determine how civilian gun use might best be regulated. But Americans seem to be locked in an unending if fruitless debate about whether or not the Second Amendment vests an absolute right of ownership in individual citizens, or a more limited right tied to the existence of "a well-regulated militia."[12] Supporting evidence can be found to affirm either of two mutually inconsistent propositions: that the Second Amendment was conceived largely to reassure the states that their militias would continue to exist, and thereby to deter the national government from using its "standing army" as an agency of tyranny; or that it was designed to protect a private right of ownership, in the belief that an armed citizenry would itself provide a further deterrent against the same specter. Given the relative lack of recorded attention paid to the actual wording of the amendment when it was framed and adopted, it may seem rather silly to invest each syllable of the Second Amendment with scriptural meaning. Nevertheless, for better or worse, that is the language we have to work with.

Or consider, finally, the ongoing debate about whether or not a woman's right to terminate a pregnancy by abortion should or should not enjoy constitutional status, so that its regulation by the state (or states) must have some limits. If one holds that all such rights should rest on an explicit foundation in the text of the Constitution, then the case for the validity of *Roe v. Wade* obviously becomes suspect. But if one holds that the decision to bear children is an essential element of individual autonomy and liberty, then the issue of whether reproductive rights need an explicit anchor in the Constitution becomes more problematic—though here the unenumerated rights of the Ninth Amendment might indeed provide some authority. Is not the decision to conceive and bear a child one of those natural rights that individuals would never yield to the state, and thus potentially a right "retained by the people"?

So we wrestle still with the dilemma of 1787–89. Rights can indeed become more secure when they are incorporated in the text of a written constitution. But so, too, our conceptions of rights have sources and foundations other than the Constitution itself. Here as elsewhere, knowledge of history—even the distant past of the eighteenth century—is essential to understanding the sources of our contemporary concerns. Yet, if knowledge of the past is a foundation of our understanding, it cannot absolve us of the duty to exercise the independent judgment that republican government expects of its citizens, as a matter of right.

---

[12]For an introduction to this vexed issue, see Joyce Malcolm, *To Keep and Bear Arms: The Origins of an Anglo-American Right* (Cambridge: Harvard University Press, 1994); Sanford Levinson, "The Embarrassing Second Amendment," *Yale Law Journal* 99 (1989): 637–59; and the important review article by Garry Wills, "To Keep and Bear Arms," *New York Review of Books* 42 (1995): 62–73, which argues on historical grounds that the right stated in the Second Amendment pertains only to the state militia, not to individual citizens in a private capacity.

A Constitutional Chronology

(1603–1791)

1603: Death of Queen Elizabeth I and accession of King James VI of Scotland as King James I of England.

1607: Establishment of settlement at Jamestown, Virginia.

1619: First representative assembly in mainland English colonies meets in Virginia.

1621: House of Commons presents James I with Protestation asserting its right to free discussion.

1625: Death of James I and accession of his son, Charles I.

1628: Parliament adopts Petition of Right.

1630: Settlement of Massachusetts Bay colony.

1641: General Court of Massachusetts Bay enacts a statement of rights under the title of "The Body of Liberties of the Massachusetts Colonie in New England."

1642: English Civil War begins.

1647: Levellers present first draft of an Agreement of the People as model of a written constitution for England.

1649: Execution of Charles I, abolition of monarchy and House of Lords, and beginning of Commonwealth period.

1651: Thomas Hobbes publishes *Leviathan.*

1653: Oliver Cromwell becomes Lord Protector.

1658: Death of Cromwell.

1660: Restoration of King Charles II.

1678–81: Exclusion Crisis as Parliament seeks to bar James, Catholic younger brother of Charles II, from succession to the throne.

c. 1680: John Locke begins drafting his *Two Treatises of Government.*

1683: New York assembly adopts Charter of Libertyes and Priviledges (abrogated by James II in 1685).

1685: Death of Charles II, accession of James II.

1688: Glorious Revolution: Prince William of Orange invades England; James II abandons his throne and flees the country; Convention Parliament offers throne to William and Mary (Protestant daughter of James).

1688, February 12 o.s.:   Convention Parliament presents Declaration of Rights to William and Mary.

1689, October: First publication of Locke's *Two Treatises of Government.*

1701:   William Penn grants Charter of Privileges to Pennsylvania.

1714:   Death of Queen Anne, and accession of George I, first of the Hanoverian kings.

1720:   John Trenchard and Thomas Gordon begin publishing *Cato's Letters.*

1735:   In a landmark libel case, New York printer John Peter Zenger is acquitted on a charge of slandering royal officials.

1748:   Montesquieu publishes *De L'esprit des Lois* (translated into English in 1750).

1756:   Seven Years' War begins, after several years of skirmishing along northern frontier.

1760:   French surrender Montreal to British forces.

1763:   Treaty of Paris confirms British possession of Canada.

1765:   Parliament adopts Stamp Act, provoking colonial resistance and calling of Stamp Act Congress.

1766:   Parliament repeals Stamp Act but enacts Declaratory Act affirming its jurisdiction over the American colonies "in all cases whatsoever."

1767:   Parliament enacts Townshend duties imposing "external taxes" (duties) on the colonies.

1770:   Mounting colonial resistance compels Parliament to repeal Townshend duties, save that on tea.

1772–73:   Renewed constitutional controversy erupts in Massachusetts between Governor Thomas Hutchinson and the General Court.

1773:   Parliament enacts the Tea Act, granting East India Company a tea monopoly in America and lowering the duty; colonial resistance culminates in the Boston Tea Party.

1774:   Parliament enacts Coercive Acts (Boston Port Act, Massachusetts Government Act, Administration of Justice Act, Quartering Act), punishing Massachusetts for its defiance; twelve colonies send deputies to First Continental Congress in Philadelphia.

1775, April: War begins in Massachusetts.

1776:   With permission of Second Continental Congress, new constitutions of government are written in New Hampshire, Georgia, South Carolina, Virginia, Delaware, Maryland, Pennsylvania, North Carolina, and

New Jersey; of these states, New Hampshire, Georgia, Virginia, Delaware, Maryland, Pennsylvania, and North Carolina also adopt distinct declarations of rights.

1776, July: Congress declares Independence and begins debating Articles of Confederation.

1776, October: Concord, Mass., protests authority of Massachusetts General Court to promulgate a constitution.

1777: New York adopts a constitution without a separate declaration of rights; in November, Congress sends Articles of Confederation to the states.

1778: Massachusetts towns reject constitution framed by the General Court.

1779: Thomas Jefferson introduces Bill for Religious Freedom in Virginia assembly.

1780: Massachusetts towns approve a constitution written in the fall of 1779 by a specially elected convention.

1781: Maryland becomes the last state to ratify Articles of Confederation; surrender of British army at Yorktown signals end of war.

1783: Treaty of Paris signed recognizing American independence.

1785: James Madison leads campaign to defeat General Assessment bill providing public assistance for all Christian ministers.

1786: Passage of Virginia Statute for Religious Freedom; commissioners from five states assemble at Annapolis in September and issue call for a general convention to meet at Philadelphia in May.

1787, April: Madison completes his preparations for the Federal Convention, concluding that national legislature should be given a negative "in all cases whatsoever" over state laws.

1787, May: Federal Convention slowly assembles.

1787, September 17: Convention adjourns, transmitting proposed Constitution to Congress.

1788, February: Massachusetts becomes sixth state to ratify the Constitution and the first to propose amendments.

1788, June 21: New Hampshire becomes the ninth state to ratify, assuring that the Constitution will take effect.

1788, June 25–27: Virginia ratifies but proposes a lengthy list of amendments to the consideration of Congress.

1788, July 26: New York becomes eleventh state to ratify while also proposing a lengthy list of amendments and calling for a second constitutional convention.

1789, January: Madison publicly affirms his support for amendments.

1789, June 8:   Madison introduces his amendments in the House of Representatives.

1789, August 24:   House completes action on Bill of Rights.

1789, September 9–25:   Senate reports its revisions, and conference committee produces final text of amendments.

1791, December: Ratification by Virginia permits amendments III–XII, as proposed by Congress, to become Amendments I–X to the Constitution.

Questions for Consideration

1. How did the English and American peoples define the concept of a constitution of government in the seventeenth and eighteenth centuries? How did this concept change and evolve after 1776?

2. What are the different forms that a declaration or bill of rights might take? Who are the different audiences or objects to which they might be addressed? How might the form and content of a declaration of rights reflect the political circumstances under which it was adopted?

3. Compare the Virginia, Pennsylvania, and Massachusetts bills of rights with the federal Bill of Rights of 1789. What are the principal differences between the early state declarations and the later national one? Why do these documents vary in tone and scope?

4. How does the Virginia Statute for Religious Freedom illustrate the problem of grounding a particular right on a firm constitutional foundation?

5. In the constitutional debates of 1787–88, Federalists warned that the addition of a bill of rights to the Constitution might actually prove dangerous, while Anti-Federalists replied that a Constitution without a Bill of Rights would be far more threatening. On what theoretical foundation did each side rest its arguments? In your view, who had the better case? Why?

6. Even though James Madison was the principal author and mover of the federal Bill of Rights, he seems to have remained skeptical that the amendments he sought would actually do much good. What was the basis for his skepticism? Conversely, if Madison could have had his own way, what proposals would he have favored to secure individual and minority rights on the firmest ground possible? How did Madison think that a bill of rights would work? Why did he think a national negative on all state laws would provide the best security for rights?

7. Today we read the various protections of the Bill of Rights as legally enforceable commands that courts are obliged to recognize and execute. Is that how the framers and adopters of these amendments would have thought of them? Why or why not?

Selected Bibliography

PRIMARY SOURCES

Numerous editions of the political literature of the seventeenth and eighteenth centuries are available. The most important documents illustrating the disputes between the Stuart Crown and its opponents in Parliament can be found in J. P. Kenyon, ed., *The Stuart Constitution, 1603–1688: Documents and Commentary*, 2d ed. (New York: Cambridge University Press, 1986). Two major collections of Anglo-American sources relevant to the evolution of ideas about particular rights are Bernard Schwartz, *The Bill of Rights: A Documentary History*, 2 volumes (New York: Chelsea House, 1971); and Philip Kurland and Ralph Lerner, eds., *The Founders' Constitution* (Chicago: University of Chicago Press, 1987), especially volumes 1 and 5.

When it is completed, the definitive source for the public debates surrounding the ratification of the Constitution will be Merrill Jensen, John P. Kaminski, and Gaspare Saladino, eds., *The Documentary History of the Ratification of the Constitution* (Madison, Wis.: State Historical Society of Wisconsin, 1976–). Somewhat less cumbersome to use, but still quite ample, is Bernard Bailyn, ed., *The Debate on the Constitution*, 2 volumes (New York: Library of America, 1993). The progress of the amendments through the First Federal Congress can be traced in Helen E. Veit, Kenneth R. Bowling, and Charlene Bangs Bickford, eds., *Creating the Bill of Rights: The Documentary Record from the First Federal Congress* (Baltimore and London: The Johns Hopkins University Press, 1991). For special subjects, see Leonard W. Levy, ed., *Freedom of the Press from Zenger to Jefferson* (Indianapolis: Bobbs Merrill, 1966); and Robert S. Alley, ed., *James Madison on Religious Liberty* (Buffalo: Prometheus Books, 1985).

SECONDARY SOURCES

The scholarly literature on Anglo-American constitutionalism is enormous. Few if any centuries in the history of any society have been studied more intensively than that of seventeenth-century England, which must be the starting point for any understanding of the legacy that eighteenth-century Americans both inherited and transformed. This bibliography only scratches the surface of this literature. Readers interested in a far more comprehensive survey should consult Gaspare Saladino, "The Bill of Rights: A Bibliographic Essay," in Patrick T. Conley and John P. Kaminski, eds., *The Bill of Rights and the States: The Colonial and Revolutionary Origins of American Liberties* (Madison, Wis.: Madison House, 1992), 460–514.

The best short introduction to the origins of early modern ideas about rights is Richard Tuck, *Natural Rights Theories: Their Origin and Development* (Cambridge, Eng.: Cambridge University Press, 1979). The political-constitutional disputes of the Stuart era that allowed the language of rights to acquire new meanings have been the subject of numerous works. The classic study of the intellectual debate about the nature of the English constitution is J. G. A. Pocock, *The Ancient Constitution and the Feudal Law* (Cambridge, Eng.: Cambridge University Press, 1957). The essays collected in J. H. Hexter, ed., *Parliament and Liberty: From the Reign of Elizabeth to the English Civil War* (Stanford: Stanford University Press, 1992) survey the major issues in dispute. For two model monographs, reflecting somewhat different perspectives, see Conrad Russell, *Parliaments and English Politics, 1621–1629* (Oxford: Oxford University Press, 1979); and Lois G. Schwoerer, *The Declaration of Rights, 1689* (Baltimore and London: The Johns Hopkins University Press, 1981). A second monograph by Schwoerer, *No Standing Armies! The Antiarmy Ideology in Seventeenth-Century England* (Baltimore and London: The Johns Hopkins University Press, 1974), examines an issue that continued to resonate deeply in the American colonies. More recently, Joyce Malcolm, *To Keep and Bear Arms: The Origins of an Anglo-American Right* (Cambridge: Harvard University Press, 1994) pursues an issue that looms far larger today than it did when the Constitution was adopted.

Though a good case can be made for the importance of Thomas Hobbes as a theorist of individual rights, American scholars tend to pay greater attention to John Locke, whose emphasis on resistance and rights of conscience seems more congenial to us. Richard Ashcraft, *Revolutionary Politics & Locke's Two Treatises of Government* (Princeton: Princeton University Press, 1986) is the definitive study of the composition of Locke's best-known political work. For other recent studies, see Kirstie M. McClure, *Judging Rights: Lockean Politics and the Limits of Consent* (Ithaca: Cornell University Press, 1996); A. John Simmons, *The Lockean Theory of Rights* (Princeton: Princeton University Press, 1992); and Michael Zuckert, *Natural Rights and the New Republicanism* (Princeton: Princeton University Press, 1994), which takes issue with recent historical scholarship questioning Locke's influence.

Two eminent senior scholars have recently written books that make the connections between the seventeenth-century English disputes and the innovations of American constitutionalism explicit: Samuel H. Beer, *To Make a Nation: The Rediscovery of American Federalism* (Cambridge: Harvard University Press, 1993); and Edmund S. Morgan, *Inventing the People: The Rise of Popular Sovereignty in England and America* (New York: W. W. Norton, 1988). Jack P. Greene, *Peripheries and Center: Constitutional Development in the Extended Polities of the British Empire and the United States, 1607–1788* (Athens, Ga.: University of Georgia Press, 1986) views this connection from a slightly different vantage point, emphasizing continuities between problems of imperial governance and those of federalism.

A work worthy of special mention is John Phillip Reid's four-volume *Constitutional History of the American Revolution* (Madison, Wis.: University of Wisconsin Press, 1986–1995), especially volume I, *The Authority of Rights*; an abridged summary of the larger work is also available. Also see Reid, *The Concept of Liberty in the Age of the American Revolution* (Chicago: University of Chicago Press, 1988). In all these books, Reid examines, in great detail, the dramatic divergences between English and American understandings of their common legal and constitutional vocabulary.

The modern reinterpretation of the constitutional origins of the American Revolution was driven by two pathbreaking works. Edmund S. Morgan and Helen M. Morgan, *The Stamp Act Crisis: Prologue to Revolution* (New York: Collier Books, 1963 [orig. pub. 1953]) emphasized the sincerity and consistency of colonial claims; while Bernard Bailyn, *The Ideological Origins of the American Revolution* (enlarged edition, Cambridge: Harvard University Press, 1992) traced the special influence that political dissenters like John Trenchard and Thomas Gordon exerted over the colonists. It fell to one of Bailyn's students, however, to demonstrate just how deeply this revolutionary ideology shaped the constitutional experiments that began with the crisis of independence: Gordon S. Wood, *The Creation of the American Republic, 1776–1787* (Chapel Hill: University of North Carolina Press, 1969). Among other works examining the state constitutions, two stand out: Willi Paul Adams, *The First American Constitutions: Republican Ideology and the Making of the State Constitutions in the Revolutionary Era,* trans. Rita and Robert Kimber (Chapel Hill: University of North Carolina Press, 1980); and Donald S. Lutz, *Popular Consent and Popular Control: Whig Political Theory in the Early State Constitutions* (Baton Rouge: Louisiana State University Press, 1980). For the important role that Massachusetts played in the evolution of American ideas, there remains no source superior to Oscar Handlin and Mary F. Handlin, eds., *The Popular Sources of Political Authority: Documents on the Massachusetts Constitution of 1780* (Cambridge: Harvard University Press, 1966).

Forrest McDonald, *Novus Ordo Seclorum: The Intellectual Origins of the Constitution* (Lawrence, Kans.: University Press of Kansas, 1985) contains a concise survey of the rights that Americans held dear. For the politics of the Federal Convention, see Jack N. Rakove, *Original Meanings: Politics and Ideas in the Making of the Constitution* (New York: Alfred Knopf, 1996), which has a decidedly Madisonian twist. Madison's constitutional concerns and his ideas of rights are also closely examined in Lance Banning, *The Sacred Fire of Liberty: James Madison and the Founding of the American Republic* (Ithaca: Cornell University Press, 1995); Paul Finkelman, "James Madison and the

Bill of Rights: A Reluctant Paternity," *Supreme Court Review* (1990), 301–47; and Jennifer Nedelsky, *Private Property and the Limits of American Constitutionalism: The Madisonian Framework and Its Legacy* (Chicago: University of Chicago Press, 1990).
For an overview of the ratification campaign and the adoption of the Bill of Rights, two works by Robert A. Rutland remain the standard narratives: *The Ordeal of the Constitution: The Antifederalists and the Ratification Struggle of 1787–1788* (Norman: University of Oklahoma Press, 1966); and *The Birth of the Bill of Rights, 1776–1791* (Chapel Hill: University of North Carolina Press, 1955); and see Robert A. Goldwin, *From Parchment to Power: How James Madison Used the Bill of Rights to Save the Constitution* (Washington: American Enterprise Institute, 1997). The role that each state played in the ratification and amendment of the Constitution is examined in the essays collected in two volumes edited by Patrick T. Conley and John P. Kaminski: *The Constitution and the States: The Role of the Original Thirteen States in the Framing and Ratification of the Constitution* (Madison, Wis.: Madison House, 1988); and *The Bill of Rights and the States: The Colonial and Revolutionary Origins of American Liberties* (Madison, Wis.: Madison House, 1992). See also Michael A. Gillespie and Michael Lienesch, eds., *Ratifying the Constitution* (Lawrence: University Press of Kansas, 1989); and Jon Kukla, ed., *The Bill of Rights: A Lively Heritage* (Richmond: Virginia State Library, 1987). A particularly intriguing interpretation of the origins of the first amendments is offered in Akhil Amar, "The Bill of Rights as a Constitution," *Yale Law Journal*, 100 (1991), 1131–1210. Neil H. Cogan, ed., *The Complete Bill of Rights: The Drafts, Debates, Sources, and Origins* (New York: Oxford University Press, 1997) appears to provide the most comprehensive collection of primary sources relating to the origins of the Bill of Rights.
Many studies of the origins of the Bill of Rights pursue a monographic approach of asking how each of the provisions encoded in the final amendments evolved from Anglo-American legal doctrine and practice. The great pioneer of this approach is Leonard W. Levy. Many of his findings about particular rights are distilled in Levy, *Original Intent and the Framers' Constitution* (New York: Macmillan, 1988). But for the full flavor of the Levy approach, see two other works: *The Emergence of a Free Press* (New York: Oxford University Press, 1985); and *Origins of the Fifth Amendment: The Right Against Self-Incrimination* (New York: Oxford University Press, 1968). For other leading studies of particular rights and clauses, see James H. Kettner, *The Development of American Citizenship, 1608–1760* (Chapel Hill: University of North Carolina Press, 1978); Thomas J. Curry, *The First Freedoms: Church and State in America to the Passage of the First Amendment* (New York: Oxford University Press, 1986); Michael McConnell, "The Origins and Historical Understanding of Free Exercise of Religion," *Harvard Law Review*, 103 (1989–90), 1409–1517. Questions of freedom of conscience remain among the most sensitive questions of

rights; here the essays collected in Merrill D. Peterson and Robert C. Vaughan, eds., *The Virginia Statute for Religious Freedom: Its Evolution and Consequences in American History* (Cambridge, Eng.: Cambridge University Press, 1988) shed important light on the background to the First Amendment.

Finally, three collections of essays help to bridge the gap between historical origins and contemporary understandings: Michael Lacey and Knud Haakonssen, eds., *A Culture of Rights: The Bill of Rights in Philosophy, Politics, and Law: 1791 and 1991* (New York: Cambridge University Press, 1991); David J. Bodenhamer and James W. Ely, Jr., eds., *The Bill of Rights in Modern America: After 200 Years* (Bloomington and Indianapolis: Indiana University Press, 1993); and Eugene W. Hickok, Jr., eds., *The Bill of Rights: Original Meaning and Current Understanding* (Charlottesville: University Press of Virginia, 1991).

(Continued from p. iv)

James Wilson, Statehouse Speech. Courtesy, State Historical Society of Wisconsin.

Letter from Thomas Jefferson to James Madison, July 31, 1788. Reprinted with permission from the University Press of Virginia.

Letter from James Madison to Thomas Jefferson, October 17, 1788. Reprinted with permission from the University Press of Virginia.

Letter from Thomas Jefferson to James Madison, March 15, 1789. Reprinted with permission from the University Press of Virginia.

Constitutional Amendments Proposed to the Senate. Helen E. Veit, Kenneth R. Bowling, and Charlene Bangs Bickford, eds., *Creating the Bill of Rights: The Documentary Record from the First Federal Congress,* pp. 37–41. © 1991. The Johns Hopkins University.

Constitutional Amendments Proposed to the States. Helen E. Veit, Kenneth R. Bowling, and Charlene Bangs Bickford, eds., *Creating the Bill of Rights: The Documentary Record from the First Federal Congress,* pp. 3–5. © 1991. The Johns Hopkins University.

PORTRAITS

James Madison by Charles Willson Peale. Courtesy Thomas Gilcrease Institute of American History and Art, Tulsa, Oklahoma.

George Mason by John Toole. The Library of Virginia.

Thomas Jefferson by Charles Willson Peale. Independence National Historical Park.

John Adams by Benjamin Blyth. Massachusetts Historical Society, Boston, Massachusetts.

Index